This book provides a complete course for the beginner in
Serbo-Croat, the principal language of Yugoslavia. Divided
into twenty-five carefully graded lessons, it explains the pronunciation and grammar of the language and introduces a
basic, everyday vocabulary. Each lesson contains exercises and
translation pieces, keys to which are given in the Appendix
along with useful verb lists and a general vocabulary.

TEACH YOURSELF BOOKS

It is undoubtedly the best work of its kind to have appeared in this country and will certainly be welcomed by the increasing numbers of British travellers and students who desire to learn the principal language of Yugoslavia.

*Slavonic and East European Review*

This is the book we have all been waiting for as it supplies a long felt need—a direct, compact, up-to-date and reliable text-book of Serbo-Croat.

*Novine (British-Yugoslav Society)*

# SERBO-CROAT

## Vera Javarek
B.A., Ph.D.(London)

*Formerly Lecturer in Serbo-Croatian Language and
Literature in the University of London*

## and

## Miroslava Sudjić
*Graduate of the University of Belgrade,
Lecturer in Serbo-Croat at the Holborn College of Law,
Languages and Commerce, London*

TEACH YOURSELF BOOKS
Hodder and Stoughton

*First printed 1963*
*Second edition 1972*
*Second impression 1973*
*Third impression 1978*
*Fourth impression 1978*

This book is published in the U.S.A. by David McKay Company Inc., 750 Third Avenue, New York, N.Y. 10017.

ISBN 0 340 16553 7

*Printed and bound in Great Britain for*
*Hodder and Stoughton Paperbacks,*
*a division of Hodder and Stoughton Ltd*
*Mill Road, Dunton Green, Sevenoaks, Kent*
*(Editorial Office: 47 Bedford Square, London WC1 3DP)*
*by Richard Clay (The Chaucer Press), Ltd., Bungay, Suffolk*

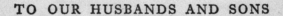

TO OUR HUSBANDS AND SONS

# PREFACE

Serbo-Croat is considered one of the easiest of European languages for English-speaking people to pronounce, and as it is pronounced exactly as it is written, what is often one of the major difficulties in teaching oneself a foreign language does not exist here. Nevertheless it is obvious that however conscientiously you study and observe the explanation of the pronunciation given in Lesson I, the sooner you can hear the language spoken by a native (if only on the wireless or on a gramophone record) the better.

Although you will, of course, try to memorise each new word as you come across it, you are strongly advised to compile your own English–Serbo-Croatian vocabulary from the beginning, writing it as far as possible in alphabetical order, and including in it not only words mentioned in the Lessons but those given in the individual Vocabularies in each Lesson. In this way you will supply yourself with a source of easy reference for all the words you will need for translation into Serbo-Croat as the lessons proceed. The general Serbo-Croatian–English Vocabulary will be found at the end of the book. The Key on page 156 gives you the translation of the English sentences and passages at the end of each Lesson, but not of the shorter exercises occurring in the Lessons.

For additional practice in translation into Serbo-Croat we recommend you to write English translations of the Serbo-Croatian sentences and passages, to translate these back into Serbo-Croat a little later, and to check your translation from the original version.

Rules for punctuation have not been given, as you will learn these from observation of the Serbo-Croatian passages in the Lessons and Key.

We have not devoted a Lesson to an account of the uses of the prepositions; the commonest of these are introduced gradually, and experience has shown us that students find most helpful a complete list for reference such as we have given in the Appendix.

We understand the difficulties of students teaching themselves a language in which the grammatical structure and vocabulary are so different from those of their own language. Our advice to you is to study at least a little every day, consolidating, as you go, what you have already learned. In any case, however rapid or however slow your progress, of one thing you may be confident : that as a student of Serbo-Croat you will receive the warmest welcome and every help when you visit Yugoslavia.

Vera Javarek
Miroslava Sudjić

## ACKNOWLEDGMENTS

Kind permission was received from the Director of the Department of Literature of the Yugoslav Authors' Agency, Belgrade, for the inclusion of the extracts from works of Serbian and Croatian writers. We should like to record our thanks to him, as well as to Yugoslav authorities in Belgrade and Zagreb for helpful interest in this Grammar, and particularly to our colleague in London, Dr. Oton Grozdić, who gave his advice most generously whenever another opinion was of value.

## NOTE TO THE SECOND EDITION

In response to general demand, a key to the sentences and passages for translation into English has been added to the Appendix for this new edition.

# CONTENTS

# INTRODUCTION

## THE YUGOSLAV LANGUAGES, DIALECTS AND ALPHABETS [1]

The language which is usually called in English 'Serbo-Croat' [2] is spoken over the greater part of Yugoslavia. It differs considerably from the language of Slovenia, in the north-west, and to a less extent from that of Macedonia, in the south-east.

Serbo-Croat has three dialects, named after the word for 'what' in each of them. Two of these, the *kaj* and *ča* dialects, are spoken over relatively small areas : the *kaj*-dialect (which somewhat resembles Slovene) in a region to the west of Zagreb, and the *ča*-dialect in parts of northern Dalmatia and the islands. Elsewhere the *što*-dialect is spoken, and is nearly always used in literature. You will therefore be studying the *što*-dialect of Serbo-Croat.

This *što*-dialect as spoken by the Serbs of Serbia and the north-eastern regions of Yugoslavia is slightly different from that spoken by the Croats and inhabitants of other western regions. The subdivision of the *što*-dialect spoken by the former is known as the *e*-dialect, and that spoken by the latter as the *ije*-dialect. The principal difference between these two dialects is in certain words containing the vowel *e* in the *e*-dialect. Some words containing a long *e* in the *e*-dialect have *ije* in the *ije*-dialect, e.g. *reka*, *rijeka* (river) ; and some words containing a short *e* in the *e*-dialect have *je* in the

---

[1] You are recommended to read this Introduction again after you have studied the alphabets and pronunciation.

[2] We generally use the form 'Serbo-Croatian' as an adjective : e.g. 'A Serbo-Croatian Grammar' ; but 'Teach yourself Serbo-Croat'.

*ije*-dialect, e.g. *pesma, pjesma* (song, poem); but sometimes the vowel *e* is the same in both dialects, e.g. *selo* (village). There are also a few regional variations in vocabulary.

Some reading passages in the *ije*-dialect of Serbo-Croat are given in this book, and differences in the forms of words are noted in the General Vocabulary thus : r(ij)eka ; p(j)esma ; but otherwise the simpler *e*-dialect as spoken in Belgrade is used. The student who becomes familiar with this dialect will have no difficulty at all in understanding the *ije*-dialect, and may, from the beginning, use either a Serbian-English dictionary (*srpsko-engleski rečnik*) or a Croatian-English dictionary (*hrvatsko-engleski rječnik*). In Yugoslavia the language is called either *srpskohrvatski* or *hrvatskosrpski* ; in the English form of the name ' Serbo ' is placed first for the sake of euphony.

The Cyrillic alphabet was adopted by Yugoslavs belonging to the Orthodox church ; and the Latin alphabet—supplemented by ' diacritic signs ' placed over certain letters—by the Roman Catholics. Hence the Serbs of Belgrade use the *e*-dialect and the Cyrillic alphabet, and the Croats of Zagreb the *ije*-dialect and the Latin alphabet ; but the Latin alphabet is known by all educated Yugoslavs, and books are frequently printed in this alphabet in Belgrade. The Latin alphabet is used in this book, and you are recommended to use it while studying the language, as you will find it much easier to learn new words in a familiar alphabet.

# LESSON I

## ALPHABETS, PRONUNCIATION, AND STRESS ACCENT

| Latin | Cyrillic [1] | Cyrillic (written) | Pronunciation [2] (nearest English equivalents) |
|---|---|---|---|
| A a | А а | *А а* | as in r*a*ther. Examples: *a*—and, but; *Za-greb.* |
| B b | Б б | *Б б* | as English b. Examples: *baba*—old woman, grandmother; *bomba*—bomb. |
| C c | Ц ц | *Ц ц* | ts, as in ca*ts*, flo*ts*am, *ts*e-*ts*e fly. Examples: *baca*—(he) throws; *car*—tsar. |
| Č č | Ч ч | *Ч ч* | ch, as in *ch*op. Examples: *bacač*—thrower; *ček*—cheque. |
| Ć ć | Ђ ђ | *Ђ ђ* | somewhat similar to č, though nearer to the t in fu*t*ure. Example: *ćaća*—daddy. |
| D d | Д д | *Д д* | similar to English d. Examples: *da*—yes; *daća*—tax. |
| Dž dž | Џ џ | *Џ џ* | j, as in *j*ust. Example: *džak*—sack. |

[1] Students whose dictionaries are printed in the Cyrillic alphabet will notice that the order of the letters in this alphabet is somewhat different.

[2] Some words borrowed from other languages, e.g. ček (cheque), whose pronunciation is obvious, have been introduced as examples before the pronunciation of all their letters has been explained.

| Latin | Cyrillic | Cyrillic (written) | Pronunciation (nearest English equivalents) |
|---|---|---|---|
| Đ đ[1] | Ђ ђ | *Ђ ђ* | somewhat similar to dž, though nearer to the d in ver*d*ure. Examples: *đak*—schoolboy, student; *čađ*—soot. |
| E e | E e | *Є е* | as *ea* in b*ea*r. Examples: *deca*—children; *ćebe* (two syllables)—blanket. |
| F f | Ф ф | *Ф ф* | as English f. Example: *februar*—February. |
| G g | Г г | *Г г* | g as in *g*ot. Examples: *gde*—where; *čega*—of what. |
| H h | X x | *Ж х* | h, as in *h*ot; as the ch in lo*ch* before another consonant. Examples: *dah*—breath, *Hvar*. |
| I i | И и | *И и* | i as in mach*i*ne. Examples: *i*—and; *bič*—whip; *ići*—to go; *fino*—fine. |
| J j | J j | *Ј ј* | consonantal y, as in *y*oung. Examples: *ja*—I; *Rijeka*; *daje* (two syllables)—(he) gives. |
| K k | К к | *К к* | as English k. Examples: *kad*—when; *baka*—granny. |
| L l | Л л | *Л л* | as English l. Examples: *ali*—but; *leći*—to lie down; *hlad*—coolness, shade. |
| Lj lj | Љ љ | *Љ љ* | as in co*lli*ery. Examples: *biljka*—plant; *dalje* (two syllables)—farther. |

[1] Also sometimes written Dj, dj ; or Gj, gj.

| Latin | Cyrillic | Cyrillic (written) | Pronunciation (nearest English equivalents) |
|---|---|---|---|
| M m | М м | *M м* | as English m. |
| | | | Examples: *milja*—mile; *imam*—(I) have. |
| N n | Н н | *N н* | as English n. |
| | | | Examples: *nađem*—(I) find; *kamen*—stone; *ne*—no, not. |
| Nj nj | Љ љ | *Љ љ* | as in pinion, canyon. |
| | | | Examples: *fenjer*—lantern; *njima*—to them; *lenj*—lazy. |
| O o | О о | *O о* | nearer to the aw in shawl than to the o in bone. |
| | | | Examples: *o*—about, concerning; *deo* (two syllables)—a part; *molim*—please; *kao* (two syllables)—as. |
| P p | П п | *П п* | as English p. |
| | | | Examples: *poći*—to start off; *panj*—tree-stump; *polje* (two syllables)—field. |
| R r | Р р | *Р р* | trilled r, as a consonant or vowel. |
| | | | Examples: *reč*—word; *brada*—chin, beard; *par*—pair; *crn*—black; *brdo* (two syllables)—hill, mountain. |
| S s | С с | *C c* | always as in soft, loss. |
| | | | Examples: *kosa*—hair; *nos*—nose; *sada*—now. |
| Š š | Ш ш | *Ш ш* | sh, as in hush. |
| | | | Examples: *loš*—bad; *škola*—school. |

| Latin | Cyrillic | Cyrillic (written) | Pronounciation (nearest English equivalents) |
|---|---|---|---|
| T t | T т | *Т т* | similar to English t. Examples : *tako*—so, thus ; *metar*—metre ; *rt*—promontory. |
| U u | У y | *У y* | as oo in b*oo*t. Examples : *u*—in, into ; *kuća*—house ; *jug*—south. |
| V v | B в | *В в* | as English v. Examples : *hvala*—thank you ; *krov*—roof ; *vrt*—garden. |
| Z z | З з | *З з* | as English z. Examples : *prozor*—window ; *zelen*—green ; *voz*—train. |
| Ž ž | Ж ж | *Ж ж* | as the s in treasure. Examples : *žeđ*—thirst ; *koža*—skin ; *nož*—knife. |

The combination *aj* gives the diphthong *i* as in English
'mine', so that *maj* (the month of May) sounds similar to
English 'my'; *ej* gives *ay* as in English 'rayon', so that *kej*
(quay) is pronounced 'kay'; *oj* gives *oy* as in English 'toy',
so that *boj* (battle) sounds similar to English 'boy'. Vowels
in combinations such as *ou* in *pouka* (instruction), *au* in *pauk*
(spider), *ae* in *trinaest* (thirteen), *ao* in *imao* (had) are pronounced separately: po-u-ka; pa-uk; trina-est; ima-o.
Exceptions occur in a few words borrowed from foreign
languages, e.g. *kauč*, which means, and is pronounced like,
English 'couch'. A few words contain what appear to be
double vowels, e.g. *poorati* (to plough down); these vowels
are pronounced separately, as in English 'co-operate'. As in
English, vowels may be long or short, but whereas in English
there is a distinct difference in the pronunciation of long and
short vowels (compare the sound of 'a' in 'father' and

' fat '), in Serbo-Croat the difference is only one of length ; vowel length is therefore not generally indicated in this Grammar, but your pronunciation will of course benefit if you listen for it when you hear the language spoken ; you will notice, for example, that the *a* in *dan* (day) is somewhat longer than in *san* (sleep).

The spelling of Serbo-Croat is phonetic : almost every word is written exactly as it is pronounced. Every letter is pronounced. With regard to the position of the stress accent only one rule can be given : the last syllable of a word is never stressed. In words of two syllables the first syllable will therefore always be stressed. In this book the vowel of the stressed syllable in words of more than two syllables is printed in heavy type, thus : Jug**o**slavija, *srpskohrvatski*.

The so-called ' musical intonation ' of spoken Serbo-Croat, which is more noticeable in some regions than in others, is a study for the specialist rather than for the average student ; but a note on this will help the student to model his intonation on that of a Yugoslav when he hears the language spoken. The voice either rises or falls on stressed syllables and on most words of one syllable. This rising or falling does not depend on the sense of phrases or sentences. (Contrast the English: ' Stealing? Yes, stealing !', where the voice may rise or fall on the syllable ' steal' according to whether the word ' stealing' occurs in question or answer.) The signs used by phoneticians to indicate the rising or falling of the voice on long vowels are : ′ (*vino*—wine) and ⌢ (*râdnica*—workwoman) respectively, and on short vowels ˋ (*gospòdin*—Mr., gentleman) and ˶ (*gòspođa*—Mrs., lady). Thus besides indicating intonation these signs show vowel length and the position of the stress accent. (Long *un*accented vowels are indicated thus : ā.) As the rising or falling of the voice can hardly be detected in short vowels, the signs ˋ and ˶ may be regarded simply as marking a short stressed vowel.

In this book the intonation signs are supplied for the words printed in the Cyrillic alphabet in the following lists and the verse on p.9, and for the verses on pp. 82 and 100-1.

| | | |
|---|---|---|
| One | jedan | jèдан |
| Two | dva | двȃ |
| Three | tri | трȋ |
| Four | četiri | чѐтири |
| Five | pet | пȇт (longer ' e ' than in English ' pet ') |
| Six | šest | шȇст |
| Seven | sedam | сȅдам |
| Eight | osam | ȍсам |
| Nine | devet | дȅвȇт |
| Ten | deset | дȅсȇт |
| Eleven | jedanaest | jeдàнаест (four syllables— je-da-na-est) |
| Twelve | dvanaest | двàнаест (three syllables) |
| Thirteen | trinaest | трѝнаест |
| Fourteen | četrnaest | чѐтр̏наест (four syllables) |
| Fifteen | petnaest | пѐтнаест |
| Sixteen | šesnaest | шèснаест |
| Seventeen | sedamnaest | седàмнаест |
| Eighteen | osamnaest | осàмнаест |
| Nineteen | devetnaest | девѐтнаест |
| Twenty | dvadeset | двáдесȇт |
| | | |
| First | prvi | пр̑вȋ |
| Second | drugi | дру̏гȋ |
| Third | treći | трȅћȋ |
| Fourth | četvrti | чѐтвр̑тȋ |
| Fifth | peti | пȇтȋ |
| Sixth | šesti | шȇстȋ |

| Seventh | sedmi | сȇдмӣ |
| Eighth | osmi | ȏсмӣ |
| Ninth | deveti | дèвȇтӣ |
| Tenth | deseti | дèсȇтӣ |

| Monday | ponedeljak | понèдељак |
| Tuesday | utorak | у̀торак |
| Wednesday | sreda | срȅда |
| Thursday | četvrtak | четвр̀так |
| Friday | petak | пȅтак |
| Saturday | subota | су̀бота |
| Sunday | nedelja | нȅдеља |

| January | januar | jȁнyāp |
| February | februar | фȅбруāр |
| March | mart | мȁрт |
| April | april | àпрӣл | (*N.B.—Not* pronounced as in English !) |
| May | maj | мȁj | (See page 4.) |
| June | jun | jȳн |
| July | jul | jȳл |
| August | avgust | àвгуст |
| September | septembar | сȅптȇмбар |
| October | oktobar | òктōбар |
| November | novembar | нòвȇмбар |
| December | decembar | дèцȇмбар | (*N.B.*—pronounced 'detsembar') |

(Note that the days of the week and the months are not given initial capital letters in Serbo-Croat.)

| Good morning | Dobro jutro | Дòбро jу̏тро (At the end of a word *o* sounds similar to the vowel in English 'got'.) |
| Good day | Dobar dan | Дòбар дȁн |
| Good evening | Dobro veče | Дòбро вȅче |

| Good night | Laku noć | Ла̏ку но̏ћ |
| Please | Molim | Мо̏ли̑м (You may say ' Molim ? ' if you want someone to repeat something.) |
| Thank you | Hvala | Хва́ла |
| Thank you very much | Hvala lepo | Хва́ла ле̑по |
| Good ; all right | Dobro | До̀бро |
| Excuse me | Izvinite me | Изви́ните ме |
| Goodbye | Zbogom | Збо̏гом |
| Au revoir | Do viđenja | До виђе̑ња |
| Good journey | Srećan put | Сре̏ħан пу̑т |

| Yugoslavia | Jugoslavija | Југо̀сла̄вија[1] |
| Slovenia | Slovenija | Сло̀ве̄нија |
| Croatia | Hrvatska | Хр̀ва̄тска̄ |
| Serbia | Srbija | Ср̀бија |
| Macedonia | Makedonija | Макѐдо̄нија |
| Bosnia | Bosna | Бо̏сна |
| Hercegovina | Hercegovina | Хѐрцеговина |
| Dalmatia | Dalmacija | Да̀лма̄ција |
| Montenegro | Crna Gora | Цр̑на̄ Го̀ра |
| The Sanjak | Sandžak | Са̏нџак |

| Ljubljana | Ljubljana | Љу̀бља̀на |
| Zagreb | Zagreb | За́греб |
| Belgrade | Beograd | Бео̀град |
| Skoplje | Skopje (formerly Skoplje) | Ско̏пје (Ско̏пље) |

| Sarajevo | Sarajevo | Са̀рајево |
| Mostar | Mostar | Мо̀ста̄р |
| Dubrovnik | Dubrovnik | Ду̀бро̀внӣк |
| Cetinje | Cetinje | Цѐтиње |
| Novi Pazar | Novi Pazar | Но̏вӣ Па̀за̄р |

| | | |
|---|---|---|
| Great Britain | Velika Britanija | Ве̏лика̄ Брѝта̄нија |
| England | Engleska | Енгле̄ска̄ |
| Scotland | Škotska | Шко̏тска̄ |
| Northern Ireland | Severna Irska | Се̏верна̄ И̑рска |
| Wales | Vels [2] | Ве̑лс |

Learn by heart the following verse from 'Primorski pejzaž'[3]. ('Приморски пејзаж' — 'Seaside Landscape'), by Gvido Tartalja (Гвидо Тартаља, b. 1899).

| | |
|---|---|
| Mala kuća kamena | Ма̏ла ку̏ћа ка̏мена |
| | A-little house, stone, |
| sa tri mala prozora : | са три̏ ма̏ла про̏зора : |
| | with three little windows : |
| zeleni im [4] kapci, | зе̏лени им ка̀пци, |
| | green their shutters, |
| i krov sav od plamena, | и кро̏в са̏в од пла̏мена, |
| | and the-roof all of flame, |
| a na krovu vrapci. | а на кро̀ву вра́пци. |
| | and on the-roof sparrows. |

[1] Because the stressed vowel is short and an unstressed vowel long, one may get the impression that the long vowel is stressed.

[2] Most foreign geographical names and names of people are spelled phonetically, as nearly as possible, when the Cyrillic alphabet is used, and sometimes in the Latin alphabet. Thus 'Shakespeare' is 'Шекспир', and 'Bernard Shaw' 'Бернард Шо'. Double consonants very rarely occur, so 'Addison' becomes 'Адисон'. A more accurate Serbo-Croatian phonetic spelling of 'Wales' would be 'Velz', but the letter 's' occurring at the end of names taken from English is usually written 's' (Cyrillic 'с'), e.g. Dickens : 'Dikens', 'Дикенс'.

[3] *Pejzaž* is borrowed from French 'paysage'. Notice that initial capital letters are not used as freely in titles as they are in English.

[4] The actual meaning of *im* is 'to them'. You will find that this construction need not be imitated, as the possessive adjectives corresponding to English 'my' etc. are generally used.

## LESSON II
### THE PRESENT TENSE

The present tenses of all except three verbs [1] have one of the following three types of endings :

|            |         | 1     | 2     | 3     |
|------------|---------|-------|-------|-------|
|            |         |       | Singular |    |
| 1st person |         | -am   | -im   | -em   |
| 2nd        | „       | -aš   | -iš   | -eš   |
| 3rd        | „       | -a    | -i    | -e    |
|            |         |       | Plural |     |
| 1st        | „       | -amo  | -imo  | -emo  |
| 2nd        | „       | -ate  | -ite  | -ete  |
| 3rd        | „       | -aju  | -e    | -u [2] |

Examples :

| imam | (I) have | govorim | (I) speak | idem | (I) go |
|------|----------|---------|-----------|------|--------|
| imaš | (thou) hast | govoriš | | ideš | |
| ima | (he, she, it) has | govori | | ide | |
| imamo | (we) have | govorimo | | idemo | |
| imate | (you) have | govorite | | idete | |
| imaju | (they) have | govore | | idu | |

There is only one present tense ; *govorim* may also mean ' I am speaking ' and *idem* ' I am going '.

The Serbo-Croatian personal pronouns have been omitted here because they are seldom used as the subjects of verbs unless they are necessary for the sake of clarity or emphasis.

The 2nd person singular (*imaš*—thou hast) is used only in addressing a person with whom one is familiar, or a child.

---

[1] These three exceptions are : jesam—I am (see p. 23) ; hoću—I will (see p. 62) ; mogu—I can (see p. 21).

[2] A few verbs of this type have 3rd person plural ending -*eju*, e.g. umeju—they know how ; razumeju—they understand.

Otherwise the 2nd person plural is used for both singular and plural.

The negative particle *ne* precedes the verb to form the negative : ne razumem—I don't understand. But *imam* has a negative form : nemam, nemaš, etc.—I haven't, thou hast not, etc.[1]

## VOCABULARY

(Words occurring in the lessons will not usually be repeated in these Vocabularies, but can be found in the General Vocabulary at the end of the book.)

| | |
|---|---|
| čitam—I read, am reading | putujem—I travel |
| gledam—I watch, look at | radim—I work |
| jedem—I eat | sedim—I sit |
| pevam—I sing | spavam—I sleep |
| pijem—I drink | stanujem—I live, reside |
| pišem—I write | učim—I study |
| pušim—I smoke | ustajem—I get up |
| | |
| ali—but | oni—they (masc.) |
| brzo—quickly | ovde—here |
| često—often | pažljivo—carefully |
| dobro—well, good | polako—slowly |
| glasno—loudly | ponekad—sometimes |
| i—and | rano—early |
| kad *or* kada—when | stalno—constantly |
| kod kuće—at home | suviše—too, too much |
| leti—in summer | uvek—always |
| obično—usually | veselo—merrily |
| on—he | zimi—in winter |

[1] In the present tense of only two other verbs does the negative particle combine with the verb : nisam—I am not ; neću—I will not. (See Lessons V and XI.)

Exercise : Complete the present tenses of the verbs given in the Vocabulary.[1]

Read aloud and translate : 1. Pevaju veselo kad putuju. 2. Sedim ovde. 3. Ne spavamo dobro. 4. On stalno jede i pije. 5. Ne čitate, ne pišete i ne učite. 6. Gledaju pažljivo. 7. Stanujemo ovde. 8. Ne pijem. 9. Uvek pevaju glasno. 10. Sede kod kuće i čitaju. 11. Ne putujem zimi, ali često putujem leti. 12. Čitam brzo ali pažljivo. 13. Obično radim kod kuće. 14. On ponekad govori suviše brzo. 15. Zimi ne ustajemo rano. 16. Stalno radi. 17. Puše kad rade. 18. Pišem pažljivo. 19. Sedim kod kuće i čitam. 20. Oni čitaju suviše brzo.

Translate : 1. We're travelling quickly. 2. I read when I'm eating. 3. We're studying slowly and carefully. 4. He sings loudly and merrily when he's working. 5. You don't live here. 6. He doesn't understand when I speak. 7. They work here but they sleep at home. 8. We're speaking slowly. 9. You read well. 10. We sing when we work, but we don't sing too loudly. 11. He's always speaking. 12. In the winter we sit at home. 13. In the summer they usually travel. 14. I don't smoke. 15. He often gets up early. 16. They usually sit here. 17. You're speaking too quickly. 18. You don't write. 19. He works and [2] they watch. 20. I'm getting up.

---

[1] Rules will be given later (p. 37) to help you to decide which type of present tense ending a verb will take, and a list of useful verbs with their present tense endings will be found in the Appendix.

[2] Use *a*, which has also, to some extent, the meaning ‘ but ’.

## LESSON III

## THE USES OF THE CASES. MASCULINE NOUNS

In the extract from a poem given on p. 9 *mala kuća* is translated as ' *a* little house ', and *krov* as ' *the* roof '. There is, in fact, no definite or indefinite article [1] in Serbo-Croat. From the context it will usually be clear whether ' a ' or ' the' should be supplied when translating into English. Here *krov* might equally well have been translated ' *a* roof '.

This extract also provides an example of a noun in two forms : *krov, krovu.* Serbo-Croatian nouns are declined; that is, their endings vary according to the function of the noun in the sentence. *Krov* and *krovu* (the form used in the poem after the preposition *na*—on) represent two ' cases ' in the declension of *krov*. There are seven cases in Serbo-Croat, and the declensions vary according to the gender and type of the noun ; but in each declension the endings of nouns may be the same in two or more cases, and case-endings are often the same in nouns of different genders.

There are three genders : masculine, feminine, and neuter. Most nouns ending in a consonant in the singular of the first case—the nominative (the form which is given in dictionaries and vocabularies)—are masculine : *lekar*—doctor ; *grad*—city ; most nouns ending in -*o* and nearly all ending in -*e* are neuter : *selo*—village ; *dete*—child. Nouns denoting male and female living creatures are usually masculine and feminine respectively, as one would expect ; but nouns denoting young creatures are often neuter.

Genders of nouns will be given in the Vocabularies only when they do not conform to these general rules.

---

[1] The numeral *jedan* (one) is sometimes used where the indefinite article would be used in English.

## The Principal Uses of the Cases

The <u>Nominative</u> is the case of the subject of the verb : *krov* gori—*the roof* is burning ; *kuća* je mala—*the house* is small. Note that the nominative case is used after the verb ' to be ', as well as before it, in sentences such as ' *učitelj* je *Englez* '—' *the teacher* is *an Englishman* '.

The <u>Genitive</u> case is generally used, without a preposition, when in English a noun would be preceded by the preposition ' of ' : putovanja *Jugoslovena*—the travels *of a Yugoslav* ; krovovi *kuća*—the roofs *of the houses* ; litar *mleka*—a litre *of milk*. The genitive case is used after many prepositions, e.g. bez—without ; blizu—near ; do—to ; iz—out of ; od— from, of.[1]

The <u>Dative</u> is the case of the indirect object of a verb (usually preceded in English by the preposition ' to ') : pišem *učiteljima*—I'm writing *to the teachers*.

The <u>Accusative</u> is the case of the direct object of a verb : pišem *roman*—I'm writing *a novel* ; vidim *krov*—I see the roof. The accusative case is used after certain prepositions, e.g. kroz—through ; niz—down. Some prepositions which may also govern other cases govern the accusative when they indicate *motion towards* ; e.g. *na* has the meaning of ' on to ' or ' to ', and *u* has the meaning of ' into ' or ' to ' when followed by the accusative : idem u kupatilo—I'm going into the bathroom ; pada na krov—it's falling on to the roof.

The <u>Vocative</u> is the case used in addressing people : Dobar dan, *gospodine* !—Good day, *sir* !

The <u>Instrumental</u> case is used to denote the instrument employed in performing an action : putujemo *automobilom*— we're travelling *by car* ; pišete *perom*—you're writing *with a*

---

[1] You will learn the prepositions gradually, with the cases which they govern ; but a list, intended principally for reference, is given in the Appendix.

*pen.* Notice that no preposition is used with the noun in the instrumental case in such sentences. But when ' with ' has the sense of ' together with ', and the noun following it is seen as *accompanying* some action or some other noun, the preposition *sa* (with) is used, with the instrumental case : idem sa Jovanom —I'm going with John ; čaj sa šećerom—tea with sugar.

The <u>Locative</u> case is used only after certain prepositions. When followed by the locative case, *na* means ' on ' or ' at ', and *u* means ' in ' : sede *na krovu*—they're sitting *on the roof* ; čitam *u vrtu*—I'm reading *in the garden.* Compare the sentences in which these prepositions are followed by the accusative case, above.

Two examples of the declensions of masculine nouns are given here, to illustrate the difference between those whose stem [1] ends in a ' hard ' consonant and those with a stem ending in a ' soft ' consonant. The ' soft ' consonants are : C, Č, Ć, Đ, J, LJ, NJ, Š, Ž, sometimes R, T, and Z ; also the combination ŠT.

Where a hard consonant is followed by the vowel *o* in the masculine (and neuter) noun declensions, a soft consonant will be followed by the vowel *e*, except in the vocative singular of masculine nouns, as shown below.

The study of these declensions may seem at first a formidable task, and perhaps you will prefer to learn them by repeatedly practising phrases and sentences in which the various cases are used : e.g. u gradu (locative)—in the city ; vozom (instrumental)—by train ; vidim Engleze (accusative plural)—I see the Englishmen. For rapid progress in the language you are advised to memorise the declensions as soon as possible. Note any similarities between the case endings.

---

[1] The stem is that part of the noun to which the case endings are suffixed. In masculine nouns it is usually simply the nominative singular—the form which the dictionary supplies.

Hard : prozor (window).  Soft : čekić (hammer)

| | Singular | | Plural |
|---|---|---|---|
| Nominative | prozor | čekić | prozori,[1] čekići |
| Genitive | prozora | čekića | prozora, čekića, etc. |
| Dative | prozoru | čekiću | prozorima |
| Accusative | prozor | čekić | prozore |
| Vocative | prozore | čekiću | prozori |
| Instrumental | prozorom | čekićem | prozorima |
| Locative | prozoru | čekiću | prozorima |

The accusative singular of a masculine noun denoting a living creature takes the ending -a (like the genitive) instead of having the same form as the nominative, e.g. *sin* (son) has accusative singular *sina*; *konj* (horse) has accusative singular *konja*; *Jugosloven* (a Yugoslav), accusative singular *Jugoslovena*. (Notice the changes in the position of the stress accent in this and some other words.)

Most masculine nouns of one syllable, and some of more than one syllable, insert in the plural the syllable -*ov*- after a hard consonant, or -*ev*- after a soft consonant, between the stem and the plural endings, e.g. krov, pl. krovovi, krovova, krovovima, etc.; nož (knife), pl. noževi, noževa, noževima, etc.[2]

The declensions of ' sin ' (son) and ' muž ' (husband) are therefore :

| | Singular | | Plural | |
|---|---|---|---|---|
| Nom. | sin | muž | sinovi | muževi |
| Gen. | sina | muža | sinova | muževa |
| Dat. | sinu | mužu | sinovima | muževima |
| Acc. | sina | muža | sinove | muževe |

[1] In the poem on p. 9 *prozora* is in the genitive singular after the number 3. This will be explained in Lesson XIV.

[2] The nominative plural of these nouns will be given in the Vocabularies.

|       | Singular |        | Plural    |           |
|-------|----------|--------|-----------|-----------|
| Voc.  | sine     | mužu   | sinovi    | muževi    |
| Instr.| sinom    | mužem  | sinovima  | muževima  |
| Loc.  | sinu     | mužu   | sinovima  | muževima  |

Exercise : With the masculine nouns already given in this lesson, and those in the Vocabulary below, practise using the cases, in both singular and plural, as follows :

Genitive after *bez* (without) ; *blizu* (near).

Dative after *pišem* (I'm writing to) ; *govorim* (I'm speaking to).

Accusative after *vidim* (I see) ; *volim* (I like).

Vocative after *zbogom* [1] (good-bye).

Instrumental after *putujem* (I'm travelling—e.g. by train) ; and after *putujem sa* (I'm travelling with).

Locative after *na* and *u* (on, in).

Accusative and Dative after the verb *dajem* (I'm giving).

Examples : bez krova—without a roof ; blizu prozora— near the window ; pišem lekarima—I'm writing to the doctors ; vidim profesore—I see the professors ; volim šećer— I like sugar ; zbogom, Jovane !—good-bye John ! ; putujem brodom—I'm travelling by boat ; putujem sa mužem—I'm travelling with (my [2]) husband ; na krovu—on the roof ; u džepu—in a pocket ; dajem pasoše studentu—I'm giving the passports to the student.

## VOCABULARY

| | |
|---|---|
| automobil—car | čaj—tea |
| bioskop—cinema | dosta—enough |
| breg (pl. bregovi)—hill | džep (pl. džepovi)—pocket |
| brod (pl. brodovi)—ship | gde—where |

[1] A contraction of *sa Bogom*—'with God' (*Bog*—'God').

[2] The possessive adjectives ('my', etc.) are omitted when the identity of the possessor is obvious.

gospodin [1]—Mr., gentleman

grad (pl. gradovi)—town, city

hleb—bread

je—is

jezik—language, tongue

komad—piece

lekar—doctor

mladić—young man

pasoš—passport

pod (pl. podovi)—floor

profesor—professor

roman—novel

slušam—I'm listening to (with accusative)

student—student

šećer—sugar

voz (pl. vozovi)—train

zašto—why

Read and translate : 1. Mladić sedi u vozu i čita. 2. Imam komad hleba. 3. Piju čaj bez šećera. 4. Sedimo blizu prozora. 5. Ne pušimo u bioskopu. 6. Gospodin Petrović ima automobil i konja. 7. Jovan je sa gospodinom Petrovićem. 8. Studenti ne uče. 9. Profesor ima pasoš u džepu. 10. Mladići imaju noževe u džepovima. 11. Vidim gospodina Pavlovića kroz prozor. 12. Dajemo pasoše gospodinu Petroviću. 13. Idemo u Beograd. 14. Imam sina u Beogradu. 15. Zbogom, gospodine Pavloviću ! 16. Studenti ne slušaju profesora kad govori. 17. Profesor ne ide sa studentima u bioskop. 18. Ne čitam romane. 19. Ne putujemo brodom. 20. Zašto sedite na podu ? 21. Ne vide Jovana. 22. Sedim na bregu i gledam krovove. 23. Govorimo sa mladićem. 24. Razumem jezik. 25. Hvala. Dosta !

Translate : 1. Good morning,[2] Mr. Petrović ! 2. We're writing to the doctor. 3. Mr. Pavlović is a doctor. 4. He writes novels. 5. The students are sitting on the floor and smoking. 6. The sugar is in the tea. 7. He doesn't like towns. 8. He's not going to Belgrade without a passport. 9. Where's John ? 10. He's sitting near the window and reading. 11. We drink tea without sugar. 12. I'm travelling to Zagreb with

---

[1] The declension of the plural form of *gospodin* will be explained on p. 139.

[2] See p. 7.

Mr. Petrović. 13. We're travelling by train. 14. They are looking at the horse. 15. He's giving the passport to Mr. Pavlović. 16. Why aren't you sitting ? 17. He always travels by boat. 18. Good-bye, John. 19. Where is the town ? 20. I don't understand the language. 21. They don't smoke in the cinema. 22. I haven't (any) [1] sugar. 23. The hills are (su) near the town. 24. I don't see John on the ship. 25. The students aren't listening : they're asleep (they're sleeping).

---

[1] Use the genitive case without a preposition to denote 'any' or 'some' of a substance or liquid.

# LESSON IV

## NEUTER NOUNS. 'I CAN' AND 'I MUST'

Compare the declension of neuter nouns, given below, with that of masculine nouns. You will see that they are very similar, but that neuter nouns are somewhat simpler : their vocative and accusative are always the same as their nominative cases. There is the same difference as in masculine nouns between ' hard ' and ' soft ' stems. (Notice that sometimes *r* is hard, sometimes soft : jezero—lake ; more—sea.) No syllable *ov* or *ev* is ever inserted in the plural.

Hard : brdo (high hill).  Soft : polje (field)

|  | Singular | | Plural | |
|---|---|---|---|---|
| Nom. | brdo | polje | brda | polja, etc. (as for ' brda ') |
| Gen. | brda | polja | brda | |
| Dat. | brdu | polju | brdima | |
| Acc. | brdo | polje | brda | |
| Voc. | brdo | polje | brda | |
| Instr. | brdom | poljem | brdima | |
| Loc. | brdu | polju | brdima | |

A few neuter nouns have lost a syllable -*en*- or -*et*- in the nominative, vocative and accusative singular, e.g. *ime* (name) has singular : ime, imena, imenu, ime, ime, imenom, imenu ; and plural : imena, imena, imenima, imena, imena, imenima, imenima. Similar nouns are pleme (tribe), vreme (time), seme (seed). Dugme (button) has singular : dugme, dugmeta, dugmetu, dugme, dugme, dugmetom, dugmetu ; and plural : dugmeta, dugmeta, dugmetima, dugmeta, dugmeta, dugmetima, dugmetima. (Notice the position of the stress accent.) *Dete* (child) is declined in the singular like *dugme* ; its plural will be discussed later (p. 140). All nouns with the ' diminutive ' ending -*če* are declined like *dugme*, e.g. unuče—little grandson (from unuk—grandson). *Nebo* (sky, heaven) is declined like *brdo* in the singular, but has a syllable *-es-* inserted in the plural : *nebesa*, etc.

Exercise : Practise using the various cases, singular and plural, of the neuter nouns given in the Vocabulary at the end of this lesson, as you practised using masculine nouns (p. 17).

We mentioned in Lesson II that the present tenses of three verbs are irregular. One of these is *mogu*—I can : mogu, možeš, može, možemo, možete, mogu.

*Moram*—I must—is regular (like *imam*).

These and many other verbs which are generally followed by an infinitive in English, e.g. I must *travel*; he can *go*, may be (and usually are) followed instead by the conjunction *da*— ' that ', and the present tense : moram da putujem (literally ' I must that I travel ') ; može da ide (' he can that he goes ').

*Da* and a present tense may also correspond to an English infinitive with the sense of ' in order to ', e.g. I'm going to Belgrade (in order) *to see* the town—idem u Beograd da vidim grad.

## VOCABULARY

ili—or
jasno—clearly
jezero—lake
kupatilo—bathroom
leto—summer
meso—meat
more—sea
ogledalo—looking-glass
ormar—cupboard
pero—pen
pivo—beer
pozorište—theatre

predgrađe—suburb
proleće—Spring
provodim—I spend (time)
restoran—restaurant
selo—village
sir—cheese
stan (pl. stanovi)—flat, apartment
tražim—I look for, seek
vino—wine
više—more
volim—I like, love
želim—I wish

Read and translate : 1. Jovan sedi u vozu i gleda brda i polja. 2. Volim da idem u pozorište. 3. Uvek pišem perom. 4. Ne možete da čitate. 5. Sedimo blizu prozora da gledamo more. 6. Oni ne vole pivo ; više vole vino. 7. Jovan obično provodi proleće i leto u selu blizu jezera. 8. Stanujem u stanu u predgrađu Londona. 9. Želim da vidim Dubrovnik. 10. Morate da čitate glasno. 11. Ne može da razume. 12. Kupatilo je ovde. 13. Ogledalo je u kupatilu. 14. Imam pero, ali ne mogu da pišem. 15. Ne govorite dosta jasno. 16. Profesori stanuju blizu pozorišta, i često idu u pozorište. 17. Sedimo ovde, pijemo pivo i pušimo. 18. Često ustajem rano i idem u selo. 19. Zimi volim gradove ; leti više volim selo. 20. Oni jedu hleb sa sirom ili mesom.

Translate : 1. We're looking for a restaurant. 2. Where's the professor ? 3. He's singing in the bathroom. 4. I can't understand when you speak. 5. The wine is with the beer in the cupboard. 6. I generally spend the spring and summer near a lake. 7. They are looking at the horses in the fields. 8. I'm looking for a looking-glass. 9. They can't write without pens. 10. We're going to the theatre. 11. They wish to travel by car to (na) the seaside (sea). 12. John wishes to speak the language well. 13. I must go into the fields. 14. I can't work when you're singing. 15. He's often in the theatre : he likes the theatres in London. 16. They live in a flat in a suburb of Zagreb. 17. We work in the villages near the sea. 18. I can see the lakes. 19. I'm giving (to) the child a piece of meat. 20. He's eating a piece of bread with the meat.

## LESSON V

### THE PRESENT TENSE OF THE VERB 'TO BE'. QUESTIONS

The present tense of the verb 'to be' has two forms—a full form and a short form. The short forms are 'enclitic', which means that they must always be preceded by another word or words at the beginning of a sentence, after a punctuation mark, or after any pause in a sentence. (Only two other verbs—both auxiliary verbs—have enclitic forms.[1]) The personal pronouns are therefore placed here before the short forms of this verb. Only when there is special emphasis on both pronoun and verb are these pronouns used with the *full* forms of this verb.

| Full Form | Short (enclitic) Form | |
|---|---|---|
| jesam | ja sam | I am |
| jesi | ti si | thou art |
| jest | on, ona, ono je | he, she, it is |
| jesmo | mi smo | we are |
| jeste | vi ste | you are |
| jesu | oni, one, ona su | they (m., f., n.) are |

The short, or enclitic, form is the one generally used: studenti su u Beogradu—the students are in Belgrade; on je ovde *or* ovde je—he is here. In the second of these alternatives (ovde je) notice that as the pronoun *on* (he) was omitted, the enclitic verb *je* could not be left in its original position; the adverb *ovde* was therefore placed before the enclitic verb.

When a conjunction, such as *kad* (when), *gde* (where), *da* (that) stands at the beginning of a sentence or clause, any enclitic verb in this sentence or clause must follow it immediately: ne znam gde je Jovan—I don't know where John

---

[1] These are the verbs which help to form the future tense and the conditional (pp. 62 and 116).

is ; ja sam u Zagrebu kad su studenti u Dubrovniku—I am
in Zagreb when the students are in Dubrovnik ; znamo da je
lekar u selu—we know that the doctor is in the village. But
this rule does not apply to the conjunctions *i* (and) and *a*
(and/but) ; in fact, enclitic verbs can never be placed
immediately after these conjunctions.

The full forms, jesam, etc., have three uses :

1. For emphasis : (ja) jesam Englez—I *am* an Englishman.
2. In questions, followed by the word *li* (the ' interrogative
particle ') : jesam li (ja)—am I ? ; jeste li (vi)—are you ?
The third person singular is an exception to this rule ; its
short form is used in the interrogative : je li (on, ona, ono)—
is he ? is she ? is it ? (The personal pronoun will be omitted
unless it is necessary for the sake of clarity or emphasis.)
3. In answering questions with a simple ' Yes, I am ', ' Yes,
he is ', etc. (It is unnecessary then to use the word *da*—
' yes '.) Jeste li (vi) Englez ? Jesam—Are you an Englishman ? Yes, I am. Jesu li (oni) blizu prozora ? Jesu.—Are
they near the window ? Yes, they are. Je li (on) Hrvat ?
Jest.—Is he a Croat ? Yes, he is.

If any other word or words occur in the answer to a question,
the enclitic form of this verb must be used in this answer (as
in most other statements), and not the full form : Jeste li
Jugosloven ? Ne, ja sam Englez—Are you a Yugoslav ? No,
I'm an Englishman. (Note that the pronoun *ja*, which it is
usually better to omit, was necessary after the comma, in order
that the enclitic verb *sam* should not stand at the beginning
of its sentence.) Jesu li u kupatilu ? Ne, ovde su.—Are they
in the bathroom ? No, they are here (here are).

Questions may also be introduced with the conjunction *da
li*—' whether '. The enclitic form of the verb ' to be ' is then
used : Da li su automobili na putu ? Are the cars on the
road ? (*or* Jesu li automobili na putu ?).

Questions are similarly expressed, in either way, with all

other verbs : Imaju li šećera ? *or* Da li imaju šećera ?—Have they some (or any) sugar ? Čekate li ? *or* Da li čekate ?—are you waiting ?

The interrogative particle *li* is unnecessary if any interrogative word occurs in the sentence : ko je ovde ?—who is here ? ; gde je kuća ?—where is the house ?

The negative of the present tense of ' to be ' is :

| | |
|---|---|
| (ja) nisam | (I) am not |
| (ti) nisi | (thou) art not |
| (on, ona, ono) nije | (he, she, it) is not |
| (mi) nismo | (we) are not |
| (vi) niste | (you) are not |
| (oni, one, ona) nisu | (they) are not |

There are no restrictions or rules applying to the use of this negative form. Thus a negative answer to the question ' Da li su ovde ? ' (*or* ' Jesu li ovde ? ')—Are they here ?—could be ' Nisu ', or ' Ne, nisu ', or ' Ne, nisu ovde ', or ' Ne, oni nisu ovde '. The forms without the pronoun are preferable.

Exercise : Using the present tense of the verb ' to be ' compose statements (positive and negative), questions and answers, for every person, on the following model : Ja sam student. Nisam student. Da li sam student ? Jesam li student ? Jesam. Nisam.

Read and translate : 1. Da li ste lekar ? Ne, nisam ; ja sam profesor. 2. Da li ste vi lekar ? Jesam. 3. Studenti nisu u Beogradu ; oni su u selu. 4. Jesu li ovde ? Jesu. 5. Da li je gospodin Pavlović u Dubrovniku ? Jest. 6. Vi ste Jugosloveni ; mi nismo. 7. Ne znam gde je selo. 8. Znamo da su Jovan i profesor u Londonu. 9. Gde su pasoši ? Ovde su. 10. Ko ste vi ? 11. Niste gospodin Pavlović. 12. Da li smo u Beogradu ? Nismo. 13. Jesu li na brodu ? Jesu. 14. Da li znate gde ste ? 15. Ne ; ne znam gde sam.

Translate : 1. Who is Milan ? 2. He's a Yugoslav. 3. Are

they in Belgrade ? 4. No, they're not ; they're in Sarajevo.
5. He's not in the car ; he's here. 6. We don't know where
the boat is. 7. I don't travel when Jovan is in London. 8. He's
not a doctor. 9. Are we in a village ? 10. Are the students
here ? 11. Yes, they are ; they're with Mr. Petrović. 12. Are
you a Yugoslav ? No, I'm not. 13. You aren't Croats.
14. I know that (they) are here. 15. Is Jovan with the doctor ?
Yes, he is.

## VOCABULARY

avion—aeroplane
da—yes
dalje—farther
do—to, as far as (with gen.)
dolazim—I come
Englez—Englishman
gore—above
hajdemo—let's go
hotel—hotel [1]
hvala—thank you
jer—because
kažem—I say, tell
kod—with, at (French
  ' chez '—with gen.)
kofer—box, case
mesto—place, space
metnem—I put
mislim—I think

mnogo—much, many (with
  gen.)
naravno—of course
ne—no
prtljag—luggage
putovanje—travel, travelling
razgovor—conversation
ručak—luncheon
ručam—I lunch
sad, sada—now
sasvim—quite
tamo—there
u redu—all right (in order)
vagon-restoran—dining-car
vrlo—very
zajedno—together
zatim—then, after that
znam—I know

Read and translate :

### Razgovor u vozu

Imate li dosta mesta ? (gen. after *dosta*).
Imam, hvala. Mogu da metnem kofer tamo gore.

[1] *N.B.* Stress the first syllable.

Imate mnogo prtljaga.

Imam, jer putujem u Dubrovnik, gde obično provodim proleće i leto ; stanujem u hotelu blizu mora.

Vi ste Jugosloven ?

Nisam, ja sam Englez.

Dobro govorite.

Učim jezik ovde i kod profesora u Londonu.

Vi dolazite sada iz Londona ?

Da. Volim putovanje. Često putujem avionom, ali više volim vozove. A vi, gospodine, vi ste iz Beograda ?

Ne, ja sam iz Zagreba. Ja sam Hrvat.

Da li vi idete ponekad u London ?

Često. Tamo imam sina. On je student. Ah, dobro ! Kažu da možemo sada da idemo u vagon-restoraṇ na (for) ručak. Hajdemo !

Translate :

### Conversation in a train

You haven't enough room.

No, we haven't. We've too much (suviše, with gen.) luggage.

You can put the box up there (there up).

Good ! Now it's (omit ' it ') all right.

You speak very well. Are you Yugoslavs ?

No, we're not. We're Englishmen. But we spend a lot (mnogo) of time here. We're coming from Dubrovnik and travelling to Sarajevo ; then to Belgrade.

Good ; we can travel together as far as Sarajevo.

Do you know whether we can lunch on the train ?

Of course. In the dining car.

Do you know where the dining car is ?

I think that it's (omit ' it ') quite near.

I'm going for luncheon now. And you ?

Yes. Let's go.

## LESSON VI

### FEMININE NOUNS. SOME NOTES ON CONSONANT CHANGES AND 'MOVEABLE A'

Most feminine nouns end -*a* in the nominative singular. There is no difference in declension between feminine nouns with stems ending in hard consonants and those ending in soft consonants, e.g. the ending of the instrumental singular is always -*om*, even when preceded by a soft consonant. There is also no difference between the accusative singular of feminine nouns denoting living creatures and of those denoting inanimate objects.

|  | žena (woman) | |
|--|----------|-------|
|  | Singular | Plural |
| Nom. | žena | žene |
| Gen. | žene | žena |
| Dat. | ženi | ženama |
| Acc. | ženu | žene |
| Voc. | ženo [1] | žene |
| Instr. | ženom | ženama |
| Loc. | ženi | ženama |

Feminine nouns ending -ica in the nominative singular have vocative singular -*ice* : gospođica (Miss, young lady), vocative : gospođice.

Practise using the following nouns, where appropriate, in the genitive, dative, accusative, vocative, instrumental and locative cases (singular and plural), as you practised the declensions of masculine and neuter nouns in Lessons III and IV : kuća (house), soba (room), stolica (chair), torba (bag, basket), šolja (cup), čaša (tumbler), crkva (church), gospođa (Madam, lady), drugarica (friend, f.), studentkinja (student, f.).

---

[1] Occasionally the form of the vocative is the same as that of the nominative, particularly in girls' names and nouns denoting relationships, e.g. tetka Olga ! (Aunt Olga !), mama ! (mummy !).

In nouns of all three genders whose stems end in the consonants *k*, *g*, or *h*, these consonants change to *c*, *z*, and *s* respectively when they occur before the vowel *i*; e.g. *putnik* (traveller) has nominative plural *putnici*, and dative, instrumental, and locative plural *putnicima*; *ruka* (hand) has dative and locative singular *ruci*; *knjiga* (book) has dative and locative singular *knjizi*; *snaha* (daughter-in-law) has dative and locative singular *snasi*.[1]

Other nouns in which these changes take place are: vojnik (soldier), reka (river), slika (picture), biblioteka (library).

Translate: govorim sa putnicima; vojnici su ovde; imam šolju u ruci; brod je na reci; putnici pevaju; slike su u knjizi; putujem sa vojnicima; jeste li u biblioteci?

Translate: The church isn't in (na) the picture; the picture is in (u) the book; the travellers are on a boat on the river; I'm speaking with the soldiers; we're writing to the soldiers; he has a glass in (his) hand; the books are in the library.

In some nouns (of all genders) whose stem ends in two consonants these consonants are separated in the genitive plural by the vowel *a*, e.g. *devojka* (girl) has genitive plural *devojaka*; *pesma* (poem, ballad, song)—*pesama; pismo* (letter)—*pisama.* Some masculine nouns insert *a* between two final consonants in the nominative singular (and in the accusative singular when this is the same as the nominative singular, i.e. when the noun denotes an inanimate object) as well as in the genitive plural, e.g. nom. and acc. sing. *ritam* (rhythm), gen. pl. *ritama* (but gen. sing. *ritma*, dat. sing. *ritmu*, etc.). No general rules can be given regarding the words in which these changes take place, but they will be indicated wherever necessary in this book.

Translate: in rhythm; in a song; many rhythms; many songs; enough letters; to a girl; of the girls.

[1] The form *snahi* also occurs.

A certain number of feminine nouns have nominative singular ending in a consonant,[1] e.g. *stvar* (thing, matter; affair). Their declension is very simple :

|       | Singular | Plural    |
|-------|----------|-----------|
| Nom.  | stvar    | stvari    |
| Gen.  | stvari   | stvari    |
| Dat.  | stvari   | stvarima  |
| Acc.  | stvar    | stvari    |
| Voc.  | stvar    | stvari    |
| Instr.| stvari   | stvarima  |
| Loc.  | stvari   | stvarima  |

There is an alternative instrumental singular ending, *-ju* (*stvarju*), which is generally used when no preposition precedes the noun.

Other feminine nouns declined like *stvar* are : noć (night ; instr. sing. noću : ' by night '), reč (word ; instr. sing. *rečju*), varoš (small town), vest (item of news ; vesti—' the news ').

The gender of nouns belonging to this declension will be indicated in the Vocabularies ; otherwise it may be assumed that nouns ending in a consonant in the nominative singular are masculine.

### VOCABULARY

Dalmacija—Dalmatia
dan—day
danju—by day
gubim—I lose
Engleskinja—Englishwoman
fijoka—drawer
Jugoslavija—Yugoslavia
karta—map
klupa—bench, seat

ključ (pl. ključevi)—key
kuhinja—kitchen
ležim—I'm lying
muzika—music
negde—somewhere
o (with loc.)—about, concerning
polica—shelf
pred (with instr.)—in front of

[1] A list is given in the Appendix.

salon—drawing-room       ulica—street
sigurno—certainly         verovatno—probably
te—so ; and so          vidim—I see
trava—grass           vrt (pl. vrtovi)—garden

Read and translate : 1. Čitate li vesti ? Ne čitam vesti, čitam roman. 2. Gde su knjige ? One [1] su u sobi. 3. Da li su na policama ? Nisu. Šolje i čaše su na policama. 4. Jesu li u ormaru ? Jesu. 5. Jeste li u kući ? Nisam. Ja sam na ulici. 6. Je li kuća blizu ulice ? Jest. 7. Da li je gospodin Petrović u varoši ? Nije. Ne znam gde je. 8. Vidite li gospodina Petrovića ? Da. On je u vrtu sa gospođom Petrović. [2] 9. Razumete li ? Ne razumem. 10. Imamo li hleba ? Nemamo. 11. Gde je sir ? Znam da je sir u torbi na polici u kuhinji. 12. Imate li slike Jugoslavije ? Imam. One su u knjizi. 13. Da li imate knjigu sa slikama ? Imam ; ovde je. 14. Gledate li slike ? Da. Gledam mnogo slika. 15. Da li putujete u Jugoslaviju ? Da. Često putujem u Dubrovnik. 16. Da li obično slušate mnogo pesama u Dalmaciji ? Da. Tamo mnogo pevaju. 17. Vi pišete mnogo pisama. 18. Jesu li putnici u crkvi ? Nisu ; oni govore sa vojnicima. 19. Mislim da vi radite noću. Ne, ja radim danju, a spavam noću. 20. Razumete li sada ? Da, sada razumem dobro.

Translate : 1. Is he reading a novel ? No, he's reading the news. 2. Are you looking at pictures ? Yes ; they're in a book. 3. Does he sleep well ? No, he studies by night. 4. Where are the books ? They're not here. 5. Are they on the shelves ? I don't know. 6. I think that Mrs. Petrović knows where they are, so I'm looking for Mrs. Petrović now. 7. Do you understand when I speak ? I usually understand when you don't

---

[1] The pronoun is in the feminine plural because it refers to a feminine plural noun (*knjige*).

[2] Surnames of men are declined, but not of women. Foreign surnames after *gospodin* need not be declined.

speak too quickly, but I don't understand Mr. Petrović. 8. Is
he a Yugoslav ? Yes, he is. 9. Is Mrs. Petrović an Englishwoman ? No, she's not. 10. Where is she ? She's with
Mr. Petrović. 11. Where are they ? Are they in the house or
in the garden ? 12. I think that they're in the garden in front
of the house. 13. Are you listening to the rhythm of the song ?
Yes ; I like music. 14. I know that the woman is an Englishwoman. 15. Yes ; and the husband is, I think, a Yugoslav.

Read and translate : Ne mogu da vidim gospođu Petrović.
Možda je u kuhinji. Ne, nije. Mislim da je u salonu : traži
knjige o Dalmaciji i slike Dubrovnika. Ne zna gde su : ona
stalno gubi stvari. Kaže da zna da su knjige negde sa kartama
i slikama, i misli da su u fijoci, ali sada ne zna gde je ključ od
fijoke. Traži ključ. Sigurno misli da Milan zna gde je ključ,
jer ona sada traži Milana ; gleda kroz prozor ; ali on verovatno čita u biblioteci, gde obično provodi dan. Ne, on sedi
na klupi u vrtu pred kućom ; knjige o Dalmaciji leže na travi.

Translate :

‘ Mrs. Petrović, where are you ? Are you in the kitchen ? ’
‘ No, I'm not. I'm here.’
‘ Where ? Are you in the drawing-room ? ’
‘ Yes, I am. I'm looking for the book about Yugoslavia—
the book with the pictures. Do you know where it is ? I'm
constantly losing things.’
‘ I know that it's with the maps ; I think that they're in the
drawer. Have you the key, please ? Thank you. No, they're
not here.’
‘ Where's John ? Perhaps (možda) he knows where it is.’
‘ I don't think he's [1] in the house. He usually spends the
day in the library. Why are you looking through the window ? ’
‘ I'm looking for John ; perhaps he's in the garden. Yes,
there he is. He's sitting on the grass with the book in (his)
hand.’

[1] Say : ‘ I think that he is not.

## LESSON VII

### THE COMPOUND PAST TENSE.   NOTES ON THE FORMATION OF THE PRESENT TENSE

Only one past tense is in common use in Serbo-Croat. This tense can therefore be said to correspond to all the past tenses in use in English. Like all but one of the English past tenses, this is a compound tense. It is always composed of the present tense of the verb ' to be ' and a participle—usually called the active past participle. This past tense, e.g. *ja sam pevao,*[1] may therefore correspond to English ' I sang ', ' I have sung ', ' I was singing ', ' I had sung '.

In order to form the active past participle (*pevao*) it is necessary to look at the infinitive of the verb. The infinitive of most verbs ends in the syllable *-ti*, preceded by one of the vowels *a, e, i,* or *u,* e.g. *pevati*—to sing ; *videti*—to see ; *biti*—to be ; *čuti*—to hear. The active past participle, which has masculine, feminine and neuter, singular and plural forms, is formed by substituting one of the following endings for the *-ti* ending of the infinitive :

|        | Singular | Plural |
| ------ | -------- | ------ |
| Masc.  | -o [2]   | -li    |
| Fem.   | -la      | -le    |
| Neut.  | -lo      | -la    |

Examples :

(From pev*ati*) : pevao, pevala, pevalo ; pevali, pevale, pevala.

(From vid*eti*) : video, videla, videlo ; videli, videle, videla.

(From b*iti*) : bio, bila, bilo ; bili, bile, bila.

(From č*uti*) : čuo, čula, čulo ; čuli, čule, čula.

---

[1] *N.B.*—To be pronounced as three syllables, with the *o* as in English ' got '.

[2] This *o*—a vowel which one does not normally associate with masculine endings—was formerly *l*. (See p. 112.)

The only general exception to this rule is that in the *ije*-dialect verbs with infinitive ending *-jeti* have masculine nominative singular of this participle ending *-io* (*vidjeti*, *vidio*, *vidjela*). *Umreti*—to die, is exceptional : active past participle *umřo*, *umrla*, *umrlo*, etc. ; the *ř* in the masculine nominative singular is usually printed thus to indicate that it is a separate syllable : *um-r-o*.[1]

This participle agrees with the subject of the verb in gender and number. Examples of this tense in use are, then :

   vojnik je bio—the soldier was (has been, was being, had
      been).
   žena je pevala—the woman sang (has sung, etc.).
   selo je gorelo—the village burned, etc. (*goreti*—to burn).
   putnici su videli—the travellers saw, etc.
   devojke su imale—the girls had (*imati*—to have).
   putovanja su počela—the journeys began (*početi*—to begin).

Ja sam pevao—I sang (masc.) ; ja sam pevala—I sang (fem.) ; mi smo pevali—we sang (masc., or people of both sexes) ; mi smo pevale—we sang (fem.) ; vi ste pevali—you sang (masc. pl. ; or people of both sexes ; or one man or *one woman* with whom one is not familiar enough to address her as *ti* : *ti si pevala*) ; oni su pevali—they sang (masc., or masc. and fem.) ; one su pevale—they sang (fem.).

Participles agreeing with two or more masculine subjects or with two or more feminine subjects are masculine plural or feminine plural respectively ; but in sentences with two or more subjects which are all neuter or of mixed genders the active past participle will be masculine plural : vino i pivo su bili u ormaru—the wine and beer were in the cupboard ; žena i dete su pevali—the woman and child were singing. (This rule also applies to adjectives.)

---

[1] Active past participles of certain verbs may sometimes be regarded as adjectives : ona je iznemogla—she is exhausted (iznemoći—to become exhausted).

As the auxiliary verb is enclitic and therefore cannot stand at the beginning of a sentence or clause, it will when necessary follow the participle instead of preceding it, as in the second of each of the following pairs of examples :

ja sam video brod [1]—video sam brod—(I) saw the ship.

mi smo bili u vrtu—bili smo u vrtu—(we) were in the garden.

ona je pevala pesmu—pevala je pesmu—(she) was singing a song.

ovde su ručali—ručali su ovde—(they) lunched here.

Exercise : Form active past participles from the following verbs, and practise the formation of their past tenses :

| | |
|---|---|
| čitati—to read | razgovarati—to talk, converse |
| gledati—to look at | razumeti—to understand |
| govoriti—to speak | ručati—to lunch |
| kazati—to tell | sedeti—to be sitting |
| ležati—to be lying | slušati—to listen, listen to |
| metnuti—to put | spavati—to sleep |
| misliti—to think | stanovati—to live, reside |
| morati—to be obliged, to have to | tražiti—to look for, seek |
| | učiti—to study |
| pisati—to write | ustajati—to get up |
| piti—to drink | voleti—like, love |
| pušiti—to smoke | znati—to know |
| putovati—to travel | želeti—to wish, desire |

The rules for forming the interrogative and negative of the present tense of ' to be ' apply similarly to this past tense, i.e. questions are asked :

jeste li videli ?—did you see ? (have you seen ?, etc.).

je li pevao ?—did he sing (was he singing ?, etc.).

*or* da li ste videli ? da li je pevao ?

[1] After a subject or adverbial phrase consisting of three or more words, or several syllables, the active past participle often precedes the auxiliary verb, e.g. Gospodin Jovan Petrović *video je* brod.

Negative :

    (ja) nisam video—I didn't see (haven't seen, etc.).

    (mi) nismo videli—we didn't see, etc.

As the negative form of the present tense of ' to be ' is not enclitic it will never be necessary to place the negative auxiliary verb (*nisam, nisi, nije,* etc.) after the participle.

Exercise : Translate—did you speak ? was he writing ? did she smoke ? were they talking ? have you understood ? was I sitting ? were they listening ? was she sleeping ? were you studying ? did he know ? Give both positive and negative answers to these questions, e.g. da, govorio sam (*or* ja sam govorio) ; ne, nisam govorio.

Questions in the negative usually have an element of surprise in them, and questions of this kind may be introduced by *zar* : zar niste videli crkvu ?—do you mean to say you didn't see the church ? ; zar je on ovde ?—is he really here ?

The active past participles of verbs whose infinitive does not end in *-ti* preceded by a vowel are less easily deduced from the infinitive, and must usually be learned together with the infinitive. These infinitives end either *-ći* or *-sti,* e.g. *ići*—to go ; *tresti*—to shake. *Ići* has active past participle *išao, išla, išlo ; išli, išle, išla ; moći*—to be able—has *mogao, mogla, moglo ; mogli, mogle, mogla ; tresti* has *tresao, tresla, treslo ; tresli, tresle, tresla.* Notice that in these participles the vowel *a* is inserted in the masculine singular only, before the final *o.*

Since the infinitives of most of the verbs which you have already met have been given in this chapter, you may have noticed that it is not always possible to deduce from the infinitive which of the three types of present tense endings a verb will take. You will therefore need to learn the infinitive, the first person singular of the present tense, and the masculine singular form of the active past participle of verbs ending *-ći* or *-sti,* and the infinitive and first person singular of the present tense of most other verbs ; e.g. *ići, idem, išao ; tresti, tresem, tresao, jesti* (to eat), *jedem, jeo ; videti, vidim ; imati, imam ; kazati, kažem.* You will find that everything you need in order to form the tenses you will be using has then been supplied. A list of common verbs, giving these necessary parts, will be found in the Appendix. Verbs with the infinitive endings *-iti, -nuti,* and *-ovati* have not been included as these always have present tenses *-im, -nem,* and *-ujem* respectively, e.g. *misliti, mislim ; metnuti, metnem ; putovati, putujem.*[1]

Notice, however, that verbs like *piti* (to drink), *liti* (to pour) whose infinitive consists of only two syllables, have present tense ending *-jem* : *pijem, lijem* ; and other verbs formed from these by means of prefixes have the same endings in the present tense, e.g. *upiti* (to drink in, absorb), *upijem.* The present tense of the verb ' to be ' is of course an exception.

## VOCABULARY

adresa—address
bolje—better
dakle—so ; well then
daleko—far away
dok—while
dugo—for a long time
iako—although
inostranstvo—abroad
izbrojiti—to count out
izgled—view
izgovoriti—to pronounce

izvaditi—to draw out
kafana—café
kasno—late
koliko—how much, how many (with gen.)
kupiti—to buy
leći, legnem, legao, legla—to lie down
ljudi—people
međutim—however
mleko—milk

---

[1] In the Vocabularies given in this Grammar the first person singular of the present tense and the active past participle (masc. sing., and—where it may be helpful—fem. sing.) are given when these cannot be deduced from the infinitive. It can be assumed that verbs with infinitive ending *-ati* have present tense ending *-am,* etc., unless the present tense ending is indicated.

moći, mogu, mogao, mogla—
  to be able

napolju—outside

naprotiv—on the contrary

na žalost [1]—unfortunately

nešto—something

novac (gen. novca)—money

odmah—immediately

oko (preposition, with gen.)—
  around

platiti—to pay

po (prepn. with loc.)—on, in,
  about

posle (prepn. with gen.)—
  after

pre nego što (conjunction)—
  before

primetiti—to notice

pružiti—to pass, offer

raditi—to work, do

reći, reknem, rekao, rekla—to
  say

rezervirati (-am)—to reserve

sa (with gen.)—from, from off

samo—only

srećom—fortunately

stanica—station

stići, stignem, stigao, stigla—
  to arrive

suviše—too much

šofer—driver

šta ?—what ?

šteta—a pity

taksi—taxi

te—and so

teško meni !—dear me !

učiniti—to do

unapred—in advance

uzeti, uzmem—to take

večerati—to have supper

već—already

za (with acc.)—for

zaboraviti—to forget

Read and translate : 1. Dugo smo stanovali u Ljubljani.
2. Kad sam ja govorila, on nije razumeo. 3. Da li ste tražili
gospođu Simić ? 4. Nismo bili ovde. 5. Bili smo u vrtu kad
je on stigao. 6. Dok ste vi spavali on je radio. 7. Često smo
putovali kad sam ja bila dete. 8. Niste pisali pismo. 9. Da li
ste primetili izgled sa prozora ? 10. Jovan je išao sa vojnicima.
11. Sedeli su u kafani, razgovarali, pili i pevali. 12. Da li ste
mislili da sam zaboravila knjige ? 13. Zar niste spavali posle
putovanja ? 14. Bile smo u varoši, i kupile mnogo stvari.

---

[1] In this, and in a few other phrases, the stress accent falls on the
preposition.

15. Srećom sam čitala pažljivo kad sam primetila da je [1] profesor u biblioteci. 16. Niste razumeli jer niste slušali. 17. Ustajali smo rano kad smo bili u selu. 18. Selo je gorelo, a oni su samo gledali. 19. Već su ručali. 20. Nije mogao da jede, ali je pio mleka.

Translate : 1. Unfortunately I wasn't reading when I saw the professor in the library. 2. Did he say you're working too much ? 3. No, on the contrary ; he said I must work more. 4. The café was in front of the hotel. 5. I can't·pay for the taxi. 6. She said that she was an Englishwoman. 7. He didn't always get up early. 8. You haven't noticed the view from the windows. 9. He's already forgotten the address. 10. I haven't understood. 11. I couldn't understand when they spoke. 12. We've already lunched on the train. 13. Have you forgotten the passports ? 14. She arrived by aeroplane. 15. The travellers were looking at the hills and lakes. 16. The church was near the hotel. 17. I saw the hotel when we were in the train. 18. Were they sitting on chairs or on the floor ? 19. They only talked and smoked. 20. He said he liked the rhythm of the songs.

Read and translate : Gospodin Nikolić je unapred rezervirao sobe u hotelu. Bilo je kasno kad je stigao vozom, sa gospođom Nikolić, na stanicu. Uzeli su taksi ali na žalost, kad su govorili sa šoferom on je rekao : » Ne razumem.« Šteta, jer su mislili da govore [2] vrlo dobro. Međutim, izgovorili su adresu hotela dosta jasno, te su uskoro stigli u hotel ; bio je blizu stanice. Gospodin Nikolić nije znao

---

[1] In ' reported speech ' the tense used is that which the speaker actually uses : she said the book was on the shelf—rekla je da *je* knjiga na polici (because what she actually said was ' the book is on the shelf '). This rule applies to similar clauses after any verb indicating that something went on in the mind of the subject· of this verb.

[2] See note to Serbo-Croatian sentence 15, above.

koliko da plati za taksi, te je izvadio nešto novca [1] iz džepa i pružio šoferu. Verovatno šofer nije uzeo suviše, jer je pažljivo izbrojio novac.

Mogli su da vide park oko hotela, iako je bila noć. Ljudi su sedeli, pili i razgovarali napolju u kafani pred hotelom. Gospodin i gospođa Nikolić želeli su samo da spavaju; brzo su večerali u hotelu i odmah legli.

Translate :

' What did you do when you arrived at the station ? '

' We took a taxi. We thought we knew the language very well, but the driver didn't understand when we spoke. Fortunately he did understand the address of the hotel ; it was not far from the station. I offered the driver some money, but I don't know how much he took.'

' Dear me ! You see that it's better to know the language well before you travel abroad.' [2]

' I know. But I don't think that he took too much, because he counted the money very carefully.'

' So you arrived at the hotel.'

' Yes,—a hotel with a café and (with) a park. Of course, we couldn't see the park by night. We had reserved the rooms in advance. We had already dined on the train and only wanted to sleep, so we lay down immediately, and slept for a long time.

---

[1] nešto novca (literally ' something of money ')—some money.
[2] Use *po* with the locative.

## LESSON VIII
### ADJECTIVES

Adjectives agree with the nouns which they qualify in gender, number, and case.

Most adjectives in Serbo-Croat have two forms—definite and indefinite. Before a definite adjective the definite article 'the' may be understood, and before an indefinite adjective the indefinite article 'a': *mladi student*—the young student (definite); *mlad student*—a young student (indefinite). In practice, however, the definite form of the adjective is used far more than the indefinite form, and many adjectives (including all those whose masculine nominative singular always ends in -*i*, such as the numerous adjectives with the characteristic Slavonic -*ski* ending) have only a definite form. Some adjectives have only an indefinite form.

The declension of definite adjectives differs in form from that of indefinite adjectives only in the masculine and neuter singular. In the feminine singular, and throughout the plural, the difference is only one of intonation or vowel length.

DEFINITE

|  | Masculine | Singular Feminine | Neuter |
|---|---|---|---|
| Nom. | mladi | mlada | mlado |
| Gen. | mladog(a) | mlade | mladog(a) |
| Dat. | mladom(e) | mladoj | mladom(e) |
| Acc. | mladi, mladog(a) | mladu | mlado |
| Voc. | mladi | mlada | mlado |
| Instr. | mladim | mladom | mladim |
| Loc. | mladom(e) | mladoj | mladom(e) |

The vowels enclosed in brackets are usually dropped. Not all adjectives which are declined as definite adjectives have masculine nominative singular ending -*i*.

### Plural

|  | Masculine | Feminine | Neuter |
|---|---|---|---|
| Nom. | mladi | mlade | mlada |
| Gen. | mladih | mladih | mladih |
| Dat. | mladim | mladim | mladim |
| Acc. | mlade | mlade | mlada |
| Voc. | mladi | mlade | mlada |
| Instr. | mladim | mladim | mladim |
| Loc. | mladim | mladim | mladim |

### INDEFINITE

|  | Masc. sing. | Neut. sing. |
|---|---|---|
| Nom. | mlad | mlado |
| Gen. | mlada | mlada |
| Dat. | mladu | mladu |
| Acc. | mlad, mlada | mlado |
| Voc. | — | — |
| Instr. | mladim | mladim |
| Loc. | mladu | mladu |

In the masculine singular the forms of the accusative which resemble the genitive are used when the adjective qualifies a noun denoting a living creature : imam malog sina—I have a little son ; *but* : imam mali nož—I have a (or the) little knife.

The stem of the adjective *mlad* ends in a hard consonant. The declension of adjectives with stems ending in a soft consonant differs from that of *mlad* only in the masculine and neuter singular, in those cases where the hard consonant was followed by the vowel *o* :

|  | Masc. sing. | Neut. sing. |
|---|---|---|
| Nom. | vruć (hot) | vruće |
| Gen. | vrućeg(a) | vrućeg(a) |
| Dat. | vrućem(u) | vrućem(u) |

|       | Masc. sing.        | Neut. sing. |
|-------|--------------------|-------------|
| Acc.  | vruć, vrućeg(a)     | vruće       |
| Voc.  | vruć               | vruće       |
| Instr.| vrućim             | vrućim      |
| Loc.  | vrućem(u)          | vrućem(u)   |

In many adjectives the vowel *a* is inserted to form an extra
syllable when the adjective would otherwise end in two consonants—i.e. *only* in the masculine nominative singular, and
in the masculine accusative singular when this has the same
form as the nominative (that is, when it qualifies a noun
denoting an inanimate object). Adjectives of this kind are
usually declined only as definite adjectives, e.g. *dobar* (good)
has genitive *dobrog(a)*, plural *dobri*. Hence: dobar dan—
good day; *but* dobro jutro—good morning (neuter). Both the
masculine and feminine singular of such adjectives will be
given in vocabularies here, e.g. *dobar, dobra.*

The rule for the agreement of adjectives with *vi* is the same
as that given in Lesson VII for the agreement of the active
past participle : *vi ste dobri*—you are good—may refer to one
man or one woman with whom one is not familiar, or to masc.
pl. or masc. and fem. pl.[1]

Adjectives used ' predicatively '—i.e. after parts of the verb
' to be ' and not followed by a noun—are if possible [2] in the
indefinite form : he is young—*on je mlad.*

Demonstrative adjectives are declined as definite adjectives
with hard stems, but differ from other adjectives in their
masculine nominative singular endings, having *-aj* instead of
the usual *-i*. English has only two forms : ' this ' and ' that ',
with their plurals ' these ' and ' those ', but Serbo-Croat has
three : *ovaj (ova, ovo)*—this ; *taj (ta, to)*—that (not far from

[1] See also Lesson VII (p. 34) for rules for the agreement of an
adjective with two or more nouns.
[2] i.e. unless the adjective has only a definite form.

the speaker) ; *onaj (ona, ono)*—that (farther away) ; plurals :
*ovi, ove, ova ; ti, te, ta; oni, one, ona. Taj* is declined (masc.) :
*taj, toga, tome, taj* (or *toga*), etc. ; (fem.) : *ta, te, toj*, etc.

Exercise : Insert demonstrative adjectives, or appropriate
adjectives from the Vocabularies on pages 46 and 48 in the
Serbo-Croatian sentences at the end of Lessons III, IV,
and VI.

Used as demonstrative *pronouns*, as the subject of the verb
' to be ', only the neuter singular forms *ovo, to, ono* are used,
whatever the gender and number of the noun to which they
refer, e.g. ovo je bila lepa crkva—this was a beautiful church ;
ono su stare stvari—those are old things.

The possessive adjectives *njegov* (his, its), *njen* [1] (her), *njihov*
(their) are now usually declined as definite adjectives (with
hard stems) : *u njihovom selu*—in their village. *Naš* (our) and
*vaš* (your) are also definite adjectives (but with soft stems) :
*u vašem gradu*—in your city. *Moj* (my) and *tvoj* (thy) may
also be declined as definite adjectives with soft stems, e.g. *moj,
mojeg(a), mojem(u)*, etc., or as follows :

|  | Singular | | | Plural | | |
|---|---|---|---|---|---|---|
|  | Masc. | Fem. | Neut. | Masc. | Fem. | Neut. |
| Nom. | moj | moja | moje | moji | moje | moja |
| Gen. | mog(a) | moje | mog(a) | mojih | mojih | mojih |
| Dat. | mom(e), mom(u) | mojoj | mom(e), mom(u) | mojim | mojim | mojim |
| Acc. | moj, moga | moju | moje | moje | moje | moja |
| Voc. | moj | moja | moje | moji | moje | moja |
| Instr. | mojim | mojom | mojim | mojim | mojim | mojim |
| Loc. | mom(e), mom(u) | mojoj | mom(e), mom(u) | mojim | mojim | mojim[2] |

[1] Also *njezin.*   [2] All plural *-im* suffixes have also a (rare) *-ima*
form.

Another possessive adjective, *svoj*, is declined like *moj*. *Svoj* should be used in place of the other possessive adjectives when the thing possessed belongs to the subject of the sentence, e.g. žena nosi svoju torbu—the woman is carrying her (own) bag. ' Žena nosi njenu torbu ' would mean ' the woman is carrying her (another woman's) bag '

Possessive pronouns (mine, etc.) have the same form as possessive adjectives : *moja je*—it's mine (referring to a feminine object).

The possessive adjective is often omitted with nouns denoting relatives, or parts of the body, if the identity of the possessor is obvious.

Exercise :  Insert possessive adjectives before the nouns in the Serbo-Croatian sentences at the end of Lessons III, IV, and VI.

Possessive adjectives may be formed from proper names of people, or nouns denoting persons, by adding -*ov* after a hard consonant, or -*ev* after a soft consonant, to the stems of names or nouns with masculine or neuter forms, and -*in* to the stems of those ending -*a*. *Jovanov* (John's) is thus formed from *Jovan*, *Pavlov* (Paul's) from *Pavle*, *kraljev* (the king's) from *kralj*, *babin* (granny's) from *baba*. These adjectives agree (like other adjectives) with the nouns which they qualify, and are declined as definite or indefinite adjectives : video sam Pavlovu sestru—I've seen Paul's sister ; bili smo u Jovano- vom (*or* Jovanovu) selu—we were in John's village. These possessive adjectives can be formed only from names or nouns which are not themselves qualified by an adjective (or posses- sive adjective) ; the genitive must otherwise be used : to je kuća njegove babe—that's his grandmother's house (the house of his grandmother) ; knjige mladog Jovana—young John's books.

Most adverbs of manner are the same in form as the neuter

singular, nominative, of the corresponding adjectives : *običan*—usual ; *obično* (neut. sing.)—usually ; *dobar*—good ; *dobro*—well ; *pažljiv*—careful ; *pažljivo*—carefully. But adjectives whose masculine nominative singular ends *-ski* or *-čki* have similar adverbial endings, e.g. *prijateljski*—friendly ; in a friendly manner.

Names of countries ending *-ska* or *-čka*, e.g. *Engleska* (England), *Nemačka* (Germany), are feminine adjective forms : the noun *zemlja* (country) is understood after them. They are therefore declined as adjectives : *u Engleskoj*—in England. Adjectives formed from the names of countries or from other place names are written with small initial letters, e.g. *engleski*.

## VOCABULARY

avionska pošta—air mail

brz—quick, fast

cigareta—cigarette

crn—black ; red (of wine)

dajte—give (imperative)

dopisnica—postcard

dosadan (f. dosadna)—boring

drag—dear

gluv—deaf

haljina—dress

jedan (f. jedna)—one

jeftin—cheap

kaput—coat

ljubazan (f. ljubazna)—kind, amiable

majka—mother

marka—postage stamp

mi—to me

most—bridge

narodni—national, folk

nov—new

olovka—pencil

poslati, pošljem—to send

predavanje—lecture

preko—across (with gen.)

preporučen—registered (of letters, etc.)

prijatelj (f. prijateljica)— friend

primiti—to receive

rečenica—sentence

rukav—sleeve

sestra—sister

sinoć—last night

Srpkinja—Serbian woman

srpskohrvatski (or hrvatskosrpski)—Serbo-Croatian

šešir—hat
širok—wide
tako—so, thus
učtiv—polite
važan (f. važna)—important
veliki—large

vrh—top, summit
zaista—really, indeed
zanimljiv—interesting
zelen—green
živeti, živim—to live

Read and translate : 1. Čitali su njegovu novu knjigu u mojoj sobi. 2. Da li ste videli njenu zelenu haljinu, i njen crni kaput sa širokim rukavima ? 3. Uvek putujem brzim vozom. 4. Gde je vaša kuća ? Da li je u ovom predgrađu ? 5. Njegovo predavanje je bilo zanimljivo. 6. Zar niste videli novi most preko one reke ? 7. Mlade Srpkinje su pevale svoje. narodne pesme. 8. Dajte ovaj šešir onoj staroj gospođi. 9. Onaj grad je vrlo lep. 10. Jovanov sin stanuje u našem stanu u Londonu. 11. Sestrina kuća nije velika, ali je u lepom selu. 12. Te knjige su sada njihove. 13. Sinoć sam govorio s vašim sestrama u bioskopu. 14. Zašto pišete ove srpskohr-vatske rečenice tako brzo ? 15. Stalno puši jeftine cigarete i pije crno vino. 16. Ovo je naša majka a to je moj sin. 17. Slušali su profesorovo predavanje vrlo pažljivo, jer je bilo važno. 18. Na žalost predavanja onog starog profesora su često suviše dosadna. 19. Primio sam ovo pismo od svoga prijatelja u Engleskoj. On mi uvek piše na srpskohrvatskom.[1] 20. Ne mogu da pišem ovom jeftinom olovkom.

Translate : 1. He's going to the theatre with my sister. 2. You can't talk with that deaf old gentleman. 3. Have you received good news from your son ? 4. John's mother has bought this new.house. 5. We usually work in our rooms. 6. I must read your new book ; I've heard that it's very interesting. 7. She likes to lunch in a good hotel. 8. He bought one [2] stamp for his registered letter. 9. These young

---

[1] ' in Serbo-Croatian '. The noun *jeziku* (locative case) is understood.

[2] Decline *jedan, jedna, jedno* as a definite adjective.

Englishwomen are learning our language. 10. You can see their village from the top of that high hill. 11. That's the woman in the green coat. 12. This is an important letter. 13. You are really very kind, dear Mrs. Petrović! 14. We travelled by fast train and soon arrived at a big station. 15. I don't like living (to live) in large towns. 16. I've sent your postcard by air mail. 17. You really must see his new car and chauffeur! 18. He's talking to (with) an amiable and polite young lady. 19. They've received registered letters from their friends abroad (*u*, with loc.). 20. Did you know that our old doctor now lives in this village?

## VOCABULARY

advokat—solicitor, lawyer
ako—if
brži—quicker
dakle—so, well then
evo (with gen.)—here is, here are
  (eto, eno—there is, there are)
hartija—paper
hitan (f. hitna)—urgent
juče—yesterday
koštati, koštam—to cost
koverat (gen. koverta)—envelope
lak—easy, light
list—sheet (of paper), leaf
molim, molim vas—please

naročito—particularly
ništa—nothing
ništa ne mari—it doesn't matter
pošta—post office; mail
potreban (f. potrebna)—necessary
sitan (f. sitna)—very small
sitnina—small change
strpljiv—patient
svakako—certainly
što brže—as quickly as possible
tačno—exactly, punctually
treba—it is necessary
unutrašnjost—interior
zaboga!—heavens!

Read and translate:

### U pošti

Molim vas, gospođice, dajte mi jednu marku za pismo i jednu za dopisnicu.

Za inostranstvo ili za unutrašnjost ?

Ovo pismo je za inostranstvo a dopisnica za unutrašnjost.

Hoćete li poslati svoje pismo običnom ili avionskom poštom ?

Koliko dana putuju pisma do Engleske ?

Ne znam tačno, gospodine, ali je svakako brže avionom.

Avionskom poštom dakle, molim vas, jer je hitno. Šta mislite, treba li da pošaljem pismo preporučeno ?

Ne, nije potrebno ako nije naročito važno. Evo vaših maraka : ovo je marka za vaše pismo, gospodine, a ovo je za vašu dopisnicu.

Hvala. Koliko koštaju ? Na žalost nemam sitnog novca.

Ništa ne mari. Ja imam dosta sitnine.

Translate : I'm going to the post office ; I can take your postcards if you wish. What do you think, is it better for me to send (better that I send) my letters by air mail, and registered ? They're particularly important, and I want them to arrive (want that they arrive) as quickly as possible. Don't you think that young girl (*gospođica*) in the post office is very kind and polite ? She told me (*mi*) [1] in Serbo-Croat, very patiently, how many days it takes for letters (how many days letters travel) to England by ordinary post and by air mail when I bought these stamps there yesterday ; she speaks very clearly and I easily understood when she said how much my stamps cost. Heavens ! I'd forgotten that I must write to my solicitor. Please give me my pen and a sheet of paper and an envelope.

[1] The order of words is : Ona mi je . . .

# LESSON IX

## THE ASPECTS OF THE VERB

Most verbs in Serbo-Croat, as in other Slavonic languages, have two forms, or ' aspects ' : perfective (pf.) and imperfective (ipf.). The perfective aspect is used when the action expressed by the verb is limited in duration, or when the verb denotes a completed action—whether this completion is actual or foreseen. The imperative ' Drink up your tea ' suggests that the action of drinking is to be completed ; therefore ' drink up ' corresponds to a Serbo-Croatian perfective verb ; similarly the uses of the verb ' learn ' in the following : ' I've learned these words,' ' I'll learn these words,' ' I'd learn these words if I were you,' suggest a completed action, and a Serbo-Croatian perfective verb would be used in these sentences.

The imperfective aspect is used to express actions which are continuous, or repeated,[1] or whose completion is not stated or foreseen. ' Drink your tea ' does not necessarily mean that the whole of the tea is to be drunk, but that the person addressed is to drink an unspecified quantity, for an unspecified length of time. The verb ' drink ' must here, therefore, be an imperfective verb. Similarly the verb in the sentence ' I've studied these words ' does not imply a completed action ; ' studied ' would therefore be an imperfective verb, where the verb ' learned ' was perfective. But ' I've been learning these words ' again suggests an incomplete action, and an imperfective verb must be used to express ' been learning '. It follows that the compound past tense (Lesson VII) may correspond to different English past tenses, according to which aspect of verbs is used. (It will be realised that an apparent deficiency of other tenses is compensated for in the same way.)

---

[1] Except after adverbs meaning ' whenever ', ' each (every) time that ', when a perfective verb is generally used.

As an example, *piti* is an imperfective verb, meaning not only ' to drink ' but ' to be drinking ' ; the corresponding perfective verb is *popiti*—to drink up. ' Pio sam čaj ' means, therefore, ' I was drinking (the) tea ' ; ' popio sam šolju čaja ' means ' I drank (the whole of) a cup of tea '.

The imperfective aspect must be used when the verb of a simple sentence or of a principal clause is in the present tense.[1] The reason for this will be understood when it is realised that these verbs, in English, always have either a continuous or a frequentative sense : he's writing ; he writes (e.g. for a living)—*on piše* (from *pisati*, pres. *pišem*, ipf.).[2]

But the present tense of a perfective verb may be used in subordinate clauses : I asked (requested) my son to write (that he *writes*) a letter : Zamolio sam svoga sina da *napiše* pismo. *Napisati*, pres. *napišem*, is the perfective verb corresponding to the imperfective *pisati*, *pišem*.

The perfective and imperfective aspects of the verbs given as examples so far in this lesson have been similar in formation : the prefixes *po* and *na* have changed the imperfective verbs *piti* and *pisati* respectively into perfective verbs. There are many other prefixes having the same function. They are known as ' prepositional ' prefixes : most of them have the same form as corresponding prepositions, and they often add the meaning of the preposition to that of the verb to which they are prefixed, e.g. *upiti* means ' to drink in, to absorb '.

When a verb has one simple form (i.e. without a prepositional prefix) and a corresponding form with a prepositional prefix, as in the examples already given, the former will always be imperfective and the latter perfective.

---

[1] In narrative writers frequently use the present tense (the ' historic present ') for describing events which have taken place in the past. The aspects of the verbs used are then the same as they would be if the writer were using the past tense.

[2] For this reason only imperfective verbs were given in Lesson II.

Other examples are :

**uč**iti, **uč**im (ipf.)—to study, to be learning ; **nauč**iti (pf.)—
to learn.

**pi**tati, pitam (ipf.) ; **zapi**tati (pf.)—to ask.

**mo**liti, molim (ipf.) **zamo**liti (pf.)—to request, beg, pray.

The endings of the present tense will be the same in both
aspects of these verbs.

Some verbs have two simple forms, one perfective and one
imperfective. Notice that when verbs exist in such pairs they
differ both in the infinitive and in the present tense endings,
and the verb with the infinitive ending -*ati* is imperfective :

**da**ti, dam (pf.) ; **da**vati, dajem (ipf.)—to give.

**di**gnuti, dignem (pf.) ; **di**zati, dižem (ipf.)—to raise.

**ku**piti, kupim (pf.) ; **ku**povati, **ku**pujem (ipf.)—to buy.

**me**tnuti, metnem (pf.) ; **me**tati, mećem (ipf.)—to put.

**pu**stiti, pustim (pf.) ; **pu**štati, puštam (ipf.)—to let go, leave.

**sta**viti, stavim (pf.) ; **sta**vljati, stavljam (ipf.)—to place.

Both perfective and imperfective forms of most verbs must
be learned.

A few verbs, such as *vìdeti, vidim*—to see ; *čuti, čujem*—to
hear, are used both as perfective and imperfective verbs : da
li ste čuli tu reč ?—did you hear that word ? čujem muziku—
I hear the music.

*Reći (reknem ; rekao, rekla)*—to say—is perfective : šta ste
rekli ?—what did you say ? *Kazati (kažem)*—to say, tell, and
*govoriti*—to speak—are imperfective : šta kažete ?—what are
you saying ?

## VOCABULARY

bacati, bacam (ipf.) ; **ba**citi
(pf.)—to throw

čovek—man (pl. ljudi)

divan (f. divna)—lovely

doći, dođem, došao, došla
(pf.)—to come

drug (pl. drugovi)—companion, friend

još—still, yet
kući—(to) home [1]
milicajac (gen. milicajca)—
policeman
ostaviti (pf.) ; ostavljati, ostavljam (ipf.)—to leave, abandon
otići, otidem, otišao, otišla (pf.)—to go off, go away
otputovati (pf.)—to start on a journey
parče (gen. parčeta)—piece
pitati, pitam (ipf.)—to ask [2]
pojesti, pojedem, pojeo (pf.)—to eat, eat up
pročitati (pf.)—to read, read to the end

račun—bill
radnja—shop
siromašan (f. siromašna)—poor
stranica—page of a book
škola—school
takav (f. takva)—that sort of, such
ući, uđem, ušao, ušla (pf.)—to enter (with u and acc.)
umoran (f. umorna)—tired
ustati, ustanem (pf.)—to get up
zaspati, zaspim (pf.)—to fall asleep
zatražiti (pf.)—to ask for

Read and translate : 1. Zašto tako polako pijete čaj ? 2. Čovek je brzo popio pivo i zatražio račun. 3. Kad ste kupili taj šešir ? 4. Zašto uvek kupujete takve šešire ? 5. Da li ste naučili srpskohrvatske reči na ovoj stranici ? 6. Na žalost naši mladi studenti uče polako. 7. Dala sam njene stare haljine onoj siromašnoj ženi. 8. Njihovi drugovi su otputovali sinoć. 9. Zašto dajete svome malom detetu čaj ? 10. Pojeo je parče hleba sa sirom i otišao u pozorište. 11. Kad smo ušli u njegovu sobu on je gledao kroz prozor. 12. Zamolio sam ga (him) da dodje rano kući. 13. Zapitala je milicajca gde je pošta. 14. Da li ste odmah zaspali ? 15. Znam da ste kupili novu kuću. 16. Moji sinovi, moj muž i ja obično ustajemo rano, ali danas smo ustali kasno. 17. Da li ste pročitali ovu

[1] This use of the dative without a preposition, after verbs denoting ' motion towards ', is very rare.
[2] The person asked is in the accusative case.

knjigu ? Ne, još je (it : fem. acc.) čitam. 18. Idete li često u pozorište ? 19. Jovan je juče otišao u školu bez svojih knjiga. 20. Napisao sam mnogo pisama.

Translate : 1. He usually puts his things on the floor, but he has put these important letters in a drawer. 2. I'm studying carefully, but I can't say that I've learned the language. 3. I'm asking you (*vas*) whether you know where my letters are (where are my letters). 4. I have asked the girl whether she knows where the doctor lives. 5. She asked (i.e. requested) her friend to give (that she gives) the driver some money. 6. I'm eating the bread. 7. He didn't eat much. 8. She said : 'Please give me your hat.' 9. I'm leaving these things in my mother's house. 10. Your son left his books in our library. 11. Did you really throw that lovely hat into the river ? 12. He always throws his old things away. 13. Your child is sleeping in my room. 14. We were tired, and soon fell asleep. 15. I don't usually drink, but before luncheon I drank one glass of wine. 16. I've bought the envelopes and now I'm buying stamps. 17. They asked (i.e. requested) Mr. Nikolić to write (that he writes) a book about his travels. 18. Aren't you giving the child any milk ? 19. My wife has gone to a shop to buy (that she buys) a new coat. 20. Are you writing letters ?

## LESSON X

### THE ASPECTS OF THE VERB (CONTINUED). FURTHER NOTES ON ADJECTIVES

In the previous lesson it was mentioned that prepositional prefixes often add the meaning of the corresponding preposition to that of the verb to which they are prefixed. So *pred* (before), prefixed to *videti* gives *predvideti*—to foresee ; and *pod* (under), changing its form to *pot-*,[1] and prefixed to *pisati*, gives *potpisati*—to sign. Verbs which have acquired a new meaning in this way, and have become perfective in the process, have another (often longer) form for their imperfective aspect with the new meaning. Study the following examples :

videti (vidim)—to see (a simple verb, ipf.).
predvideti (predvidim)—to foresee (the simple verb compounded with a prepositional prefix, pf.).
predviđati (predvidam)—to foresee, to be foreseeing (ipf.).
pisati (pišem), ipf.—to write.
potpisati (potpišem), pf.—to sign.
potpisivati (potpisujem), ipf.—to sign, to be signing.

Notice therefore that a verb is not necessarily perfective if it has a prepositional prefix.

Examples were given at the end of the last lesson of simple verbs which exist in pairs, one perfective and the other imperfective. A prepositional prefix will give a new meaning to both the perfective and the imperfective verbs, without altering their aspects, e.g. :

dopustiti, pf. ; dopuštati, ipf.—to allow.
prodati, pf. ; prodavati, ipf.—to sell.
predstaviti, pf. ; predstavljati, ipf.—to introduce, to present.

---

[1] See p. 111.

Present tense endings are of course the same as for the simple forms of these verbs.

The student need not fear that he will have to devise these forms himself. This would be impossible. A good dictionary will supply them all, and in both aspects; but an understanding of their formation will be found helpful in understanding their use and meanings. Knowledge of the prepositions will of course often help in understanding the meaning of a verb, though prepositions do not always retain their meanings when prefixed to verbs.

The prefix *za-* often suggests the beginning of an action: plakati, plàčem—to weep (ipf.); zaplakati—to burst into tears (pf.); pevati, pevam—to sing (ipf.); zapevati—to begin to sing, to burst into song (pf.).

The prefix *po-* usually only serves to render an imperfective verb perfective, e.g. piti (ipf.), popiti (pf.).

The following verbs should be particularly noted:

sesti (sednem; seo, sela)—to sit down, pf. If this verb is followed by a preposition which may govern either the accusative or another case according to whether 'motion towards' is implied or not,[1] the preposition will here take the accusative case: seo je na pod—he sat down on the floor.

sedeti (sedim)—to be sitting, is imperfective, to be used where no motion is implied: sedeo je na podu (loc.)—he was sitting (or sat) on the floor.

Similarly, leći (legnem; legao, legla)—to lie down, is perfective: legao je na krevet (acc.)—he lay down on the bed. ležati (ležim)—to lie, to be lying, is imperfective: ležao je na krevetu (loc.)—he was lying on the bed.

These verbs, and some other verbs, have also 'frequentative' forms: sedati (sedam) means 'to keep sitting down', or 'to sit down one after another'; legati (ležem) means 'to

[1] See pp. 14 and 15.

keep lying down ', etc. Prepositions following these verbs will govern the accusative case.

The perfective present of *biti* (to be) is : budem, budeš, bude, budemo, budete, budu. Compare :

rekao mu (to him) je da je poslušan—he told him that he was (is) obedient ; rekao mu je da bude poslušan—he told him to be obedient.


*Ići*—to go.

*Ići* is a simple imperfective verb. It has many forms with prepositional prefixes which alter its meaning and its aspect. The imperfective form of these has an entirely different root, e.g. *otići* (from *od ići*)—to go away, to go off (pf.) has imperfective *odlaziti* (*odlazim*).

Most of the compounds of *ići* are in such common use that the student is advised to learn these here :

ići (idem ; išao, išla), ipf.—to go.

doći (dođem ; došao, došla), pf.—to come.

dolaziti (dolazim), ipf.—to come, to be coming.

izići *or* izaći (iziđem *or* izađem ; izišao *or* izašao, etc.), pf.— to go out. (Followed by the preposition *iz*—out of, and the genitive case.)

izlaziti (izlazim), ipf.—to go out, to be going out.

naći (nađem ; našao, etc.), pf.—to find.

nalaziti, ipf.—to find, to be finding.

otići (otidem *or* odem ; otišao, etc.), pf.—to go away.

odlaziti, ipf.—to go away, be going away.

poći (pođem ; pošao, etc.), pf.—to start off.

polaziti, ipf.—to start off, to be starting off.

preći (pređem ; prešao, etc.), pf.—to cross over. (Used as a transitive verb, or followed by the preposition *preko*— across, and the genitive case.)

prelaziti, ipf.—to be crossing over.

prići (priđem ; prišao, etc.), pf.—to go up to, to approach. (Followed by the dative case.)

prilaziti, ipf.—to approach, to be approaching.

proći (prođem ; prošao, etc.), pf.—to pass, to go past. (Used as a transitive verb, or with the preposition *pored*—past, and the genitive case.)

prolaziti, ipf.—to pass, to be passing.

sići (siđem ; sišao, etc.), pf.—to descend. (Often followed by the preposition *sa* and the genitive case.)

silaziti, ipf.—to descend, to be descending.

ući (uđem ; ušao, etc.), pf.—to enter. (Followed by the preposition *u* and the accusative case.)

ulaziti, ipf.—to enter, to be entering.

Do not confuse *poći*—'to start off' (i.e. when going some-where) with *početi* (pf., present *počnem* ; ipf. *počinjati*, present *počinjem*), which means 'to begin' : pošao sam u jedan sat— I started (off) at one o'clock (one hour) ; počeo sam da pišem (ipf.) pismo—I began to write the (or 'a') letter. (The verb in the clause following 'to begin' and 'to finish'—*svršiti*, pf. ; *svršavati*, *svršavam*, ipf.—is always imperfective.) Remember that *stići* (stignem ; stigao, stigla), pf.—to arrive, is not a compound of *ići*. Its imperfective form is *stizati*, *stižem*.

*Further Notes on Adjectives.*

*Kakav* (fem. *kakva*) means 'what sort of ?' or 'what a !' : kakva je klima u vašoj zemlji ?—what is the climate like in your country ? Kakva klima !—What a climate !

*Ovakav, takav, onakav* (fem. *onakva*, etc.) mean 'this sort of', 'that sort of', and 'that sort of' (referring to something farther away) respectively. Of these, *takav* is the most frequently used : takav čovek je opasan—a man like that is dangerous.

*Koji ?* asks 'which ?' : koje dete ?—which child ?

*Sav* (fem. *sva*) means ' all ', ' the whole ': sav grad je goreo—the whole town was burning.[1]

All these adjectives are declined as definite adjectives. *Sav* has neuter *sve*, genitive (masc. and neut.) *svega*, dat. and loc. *svemu*. The masculine plural *svi* may be used to mean ' everybody ': svi su bili zadovoljni—everybody was satisfied. The neuter singular *sve* can have the meaning of ' everything ': sve je gotovo—everything is ready.

Translate : 1. In what sort of car is he travelling ? 2. What kind of books do you like ? 3. What a man ! 4. Why does he always drink that sort of wine ? 5. I don't read novels of that kind. 6. With which woman were you talking ? 7. Which man did you see ? 8. Are they all here ? 9. He's finished everything. 10. She writes letters to everybody.

## VOCABULARY

Austrija—Austria
bife (masc.)—buffet
carinik—customs officer
čekati (ipf.)—to wait, await
činovnik—an official
dok ne—until
drugi (adj.)—another, other, second
granica—frontier
hodnik—corridor
hteti (ipf.)—to want, wish
i ... i ... —both ... and ...
jugoslovenski (adj.)—Yugoslav

kondukter—guard
kupe (masc.)—compartment
kutija—box
nekoliko—some, a few, several (with gen. pl.)
odgovoriti (pf.), odgovarati (ipf.)—to answer
otvoriti (pf.), otvarati (ipf.)—to open
peron—platform
pogledati (pf.)—to glance
pospan—sleepy
prijatan (fem. prijatna)—pleasant

[1] *Ceo* (see Lesson XVIII) and *čitav* (fem. *čitava*) also mean ' the whole '.

progovoriti (pf.)—to utter
red—order, row (u redu—in
   order, all right)
sam (adj.)—alone

stanični—belonging to the
   station
sve dok ne—right until
tu—there

Notes: *Ne* combines with verbs which have a negative form, e.g. dok nemam—until I have ; sve dok nisam stigao—right until I arrived. The present tense of *hteti* is given in the next lesson.

Read and translate : Kad je naš voz prolazio kroz Austriju mogli smo da legnemo. Odmah smo zaspali. Spavali smo sve dok nismo stigli na granicu. Tu smo hteli da iziđemo iz voza i da popijemo čašu piva u bifeu na staničnom peronu, ali kondukter je rekao da moramo sedeti u svome kupeu ; kazao je da carinik i drugi činovnici dolaze u voz pre nego što voz pređe granicu. Dakle, seli smo i čekali. Uskoro je došao jedan jugoslovenski činovnik i zatražio naše pasoše. Kada je otišao, moj drug je pogledao u hodnik i rekao : » Dolazi carinik. Moramo reći da imamo ove kutije engleskih cigareta.« Carinik—vrlo učtiv i ljubazan čovek—ušao je u naš kupe, pogledao na naš prtljag, progovorio nekoliko reči na srpskohrvatskom i izišao.

Translate : I talked with the other travellers, but I was very tired for I had already been travelling a long time, and when they got out of the train and I was alone in the compartment I lay down and fell asleep. I slept while the train was passing through Austria, but when we arrived at the Yugoslav frontier the guard came into my compartment. 'The customs officer and other officials are coming,' he said. 'Thank you,' I answered sleepily, and began opening my cases. However, this wasn't necessary. When the customs officer came he only glanced at my luggage, said 'All right', and went out, although I was just going[1] to say 'I have this large box of cigarettes'. A second Yugoslav came and asked for my passport. He spoke a few words in Serbo-Croat and I understood everything. Both the customs officer and the other official were very agreeable and polite. Although it was night and I was so tired I thought that my journey in Yugoslavia had begun very pleasantly.

1. iako sam već hteo da . . .

## LESSON XI

### THE FUTURE TENSE

This tense is another compound tense, as in English. It is composed of an auxiliary verb and an infinitive. The auxiliary verb is the present tense of the verb *hteti*. Like the present tense of the verb ' to be ' the present tense of *hteti* has both full and short forms.

> Full Form
> hoću      I want (I will, I shall)
> hoćeš
> hoće
> hoćemo
> hoćete
> hoće

The short, enclitic, forms are used only when the verb is used as the auxiliary verb in forming the future tense. They are obtained by dropping the first syllable *ho-*, and (being enclitic) must of course be preceded by another word in a sentence or clause :

> Short (Enclitic) Form
> ja ću      I shall
> ti ćeš
> on, ona, ono će
> mi ćemo
> vi ćete
> oni, one, ona će

The future tense of every verb is therefore formed in the same way :

| ja ću imati— | ja ću biti— | ja ću ići— |
| I shall have | I shall be | I shall go |
| ti ćeš imati | ti ćeš biti | ti ćeš ići |

| on, ona, ono će imati | on, ona, ono će biti | ona ona, ono će ići |
| mi ćemo imati | mi ćemo biti | mi ćemo ići |
| vi ćete imati | vi ćete biti | vi ćete ici |
| oni, one, ona će imati | oni, one, ona će biti | oni, one, ona će ići |

The above will be the order of the auxiliary verb and the infinitive provided the verb is preceded by some other word : Olga će videti slike—Olga will see the pictures ; sutra ću biti u Zagrebu—tomorrow I shall be in Zagreb ; ovde ćemo čekati—we will wait here (here we will wait).

But if the verb stands at the beginning of the sentence or clause the enclitic auxiliary verb must follow the infinitive ; the infinitive and auxiliary then usually form one word : the -ti ending of the infinitive drops, and the enclitic auxiliary is suffixed.

Thus *ja ću biti, ti ćeš biti*, etc., become :

> bićи I shall be
> bićeš
> biće
> bićemo
> bićete
> biće

Similarly *ja ću imati* becomes *imaću ; mi ćemo imati* becomes *imaćemo ; vi ćete videti* becomes *videćete ; oni će govoriti* becomes *govoriće.*[1]

When the enclitic auxiliary verb follows the infinitive of verbs like *rasti*—to grow (in which the consonant *s*, instead of a vowel, precedes the -ti ending), in order to form the future in this way the following change takes place :

> ja ću rasti becomes rašću
> ti ćeš rasti „ rašćeš

[1] Sometimes, especially in the *ije*-dialect, these are written *bit ću, imat ću, imat ćemo, videt ćemo*, etc.

on će rasti     becomes rašće
mi ćemo rasti     „     rašćemo
vi ćete rasti     „     rašćete
oni će rasti     „     rašće

The infinitives of verbs like *ići* (with the ending *-ći*) do not combine with the auxiliary verb when this follows them. The alternative form to *ja ću ići* is therefore *ići ću*.

Exercise : Give the future tense of the following verbs, both with and without the nominative personal pronoun : putovati, jesti, doći, voleti.

In the future tense the choice of aspect will depend upon whether or not the action denoted by the verb is foreseen as a limited, completed action :

Sutra ću pisati pisma—tomorrow I shall write letters (ipf.).

Sutra ću napisati pismo—tomorrow I shall write a letter (pf.).

The negative of the present tense of *hteti* is :

neću     I do not want to ; I shall not
nećeš
neće
nećemo
nećete
neće

The negative of the future tense is therefore :

| neću biti—I shall not be | neću jesti—I shall not eat | neću ići—I shall not go |
|---|---|---|
| nećeš biti | nećeš jesti | nećeš ići |
| neće biti | neće jesti | neće ići |
| nećemo biti | nećemo jesti | nećemo ići |
| nećete biti | nećete jesti | nećete ići |
| neće biti | neće jesti | neće ići |

As negative auxiliary verbs are not enclitic it will never be necessary to reverse the order of the infinitive and the auxiliary verb in the negative.

When *neću* etc. are followed by the conjunction *da* and the present tense of a verb, the sense is rather 'I do not want to ', e.g. neću da idem—I don't want to go.

The interrogative of the future tense is formed in the same way as that of the compound past tense : if there is not already an interrogative word in the sentence either the question may be introduced by *da li*, in which case the short form of the auxiliary verb will be used; or the full form of the auxiliary verb may be followed by the interrogative particle *li* :

Da li će doći ? *or* Hoće li doći ?—will he come ?

Da li ćete putovati avionom ? *or* Hoćete li putovati avionom ?—will you travel by aeroplane ?

The negative interrogative, like other 'surprise' questions (see Lesson VII), is usually introduced by *zar* : zar nećete pušiti ?—won't you really smoke ? ; zar neće doći ?—won't he come ?

Exercise : Give the negative, and negative interrogative, of the future tense of the following verbs : videti, rasti, moći, prekinuti (to interrupt).

Remember in reported speech to use the tense which the speaker actually used (Lesson VII) : she said that she would come (she said : 'I will come ')—rekla je da će doći ; we promised we would be there (we promised : 'We shall be there ')—Obećali smo da ćemo biti tamo. Note that the conjunction 'that ', which is often omitted in English, cannot be omitted in Serbo-Croat.

## VOCABULARY

bašta—garden

članak (gen. članka)—article (e.g. in newspaper)

dockan (adverb)—late

docnije—later

doručak (gen. doručka)—breakfast

gladan (f. gladna)—hungry

imenik—directory

izabrati, izaberem (pf.)—to choose

jabuka—apple tree

jelovnik—menu

molim vas—please (I pray you)

možda—perhaps

na vreme—in time, punctually

obećati, obećam (pf.)—to promise

očekivati, očekujem (ipf.)—to expect

onda—then

paket—packet

planina—mountain

po—on, about (with loc.)

pod—under [1]

podne (neut. indeclinable)—noon

posetiti (pf.)—to visit

posle—after (with gen.)

posle (adverb)—afterwards

povrće (neut.)—vegetables

prenoćiti (pf.)—to spend the night

prvo—firstly

siguran (f. sigurna)—sure, certain

sladoled—ice cream

telefonirati (pf. and ipf.)—to telephone

telefonski (adj.)—telephone

večeras—this evening

voće (neut.)—fruit

zadatak (gen. zadatka)—task

završiti (pf.)—to finish

1. This preposition, like the prepositions *među*—among, *nad*—over, and *pred*—in front of, may be followed by the accusative or instrumental cases, according to whether motion towards, or position, is indicated : metnuo sam pismo među knjige (acc.)—I put the letter among the books ; but : pismo je među knjigama (instr.)—the letter is among the books.

Read and translate : 1. Kad će poći voz za Beograd ? Poći će odmah. 2. Jovan je obećao da će doći kući posle ručka. 3. Da li ćemo morati prenoćiti u Ljubljani ? 4. Ona će sedeti u njihovoj lepoj bašti i čitati ove knjige. 5. Dete će popiti veliku šolju mleka pre nego što zaspi. 6. Večeras nećemo ići u pozorište : bićemo suviše umorni. 7. Da li ćete posetiti gospođu Petrović pre nego što odete u bioskop ? 8. Sutra ćemo telefonirati starom profesoru. 9. Zar ti studenti neće biti na predavanju gospodina Petrovića ? Biće vrlo zanimljivo. 10. Pročitaću ova važna pisma pre nego što legnem. 11. Zar nećete otići na stanicu da pitate kad polazi voz ? 12. Neću zaspati dok ne završim ovaj zadatak. 13. Očekivao sam da će lekar stići na vreme, ali nije. 14. Putovaćemo noću, a spavaćemo danju. 15. Gde ćete sesti ? Blizu prozora ili blizu ormara ? 16. Proći ćemo pored vaše kuće posle podne ; da li ćete biti na prozoru ? 17. Izići ćemo iz voza kad stignemo na stanicu. 18. Hoćete li napisati dopisnu kartu mome sinu ? 19. Ja ću metnuti svoje stvari pod vaše. 20. Već je dockan : kada ćemo večerati ?

Translate : 1. When shall we arrive in Zagreb ? 2. I won't read my letters before breakfast. 3. He'll be sitting under the big apple tree in our garden this afternoon. 4. We'll put this telephone directory under these other big books. 5. Please will you post this little package when you go to (na) the post ? 6. When will they come out of the cinema ? Do they usually come out late ? 7. He'll eat up that ice cream. 8. Will the travellers see those beautiful lakes and mountains as they pass through Slovenia, or do they travel by night ? 9. Will this be a good book for their son ? 10. This train will soon start ; it usually starts punctually. 11. Won't the soldiers be able to sleep here ? 12. Will you give these things to your sister, please ? 13. We shan't get out of the train : the Yugoslav officials will come into our compartment. 14. Won't your students go to (na) that lecture ? 15. Will the professor write an article about the book which (koju) he has been reading ?

## Vocabulary

dobiti, dobijem (pf.)—to get, win, earn

ispod—under, from under (with gen.)

izvući, izvučem ; izvukao, izvukla (pf.)—to pull out

kovčeg—chest, trunk

navečer—in the evening

nepoznat—unknown
ostaviti (pf.)—to leave,
  abandon
pešice *or* peške—on foot
postelja—bed

prvi—first
put—road, journey
staza—path
strpati (ipf.)—to cram
supa—soup

Read and translate the following passage, an extract (adapted) from a short story in the *ije*-dialect by the Croatian writer Milan Begović (1876–1948). It is continued at the end of the next lesson.

Kad je došla kući, Jeca je ušla u svoju sobu, izvukla ispod postelje kovčeg i na brzu ruku [1] strpala u kovčeg ono malo stvari [2] što (which) su bile njezine. Sve što je dobila od gospođe Lucije ostavila je u ormaru. Onda je otišla na stanicu da pita kad polazi prvi voz za Drniš. Ona će ići kući, svakako će ići. Putovat će preko Drniša. Stići će navečer u Drniš, gdje [3] će morati prenoćiti, jer neće moći da ide pješice [4] preko planine, po nepoznatim stazama.

1. na brzu ruku—hastily. 2. Literally: ' that little (few) of things ', i.e. 'those few things '. 3. *gde* in the *e*-dialect. 4. *pešice* in the *e*-dialect.

Translate: Are you hungry? We'll go into this little restaurant. My husband said that he would be here; perhaps he'll come later. Where shall we sit? Will you sit on this chair? I'll put this big bag under my chair: is that all right? Here's the menu; what will you choose? I'm sure you'll be able to eat plenty of meat and vegetables after your long journey; but first we'll take soup; we'll think about (*na*, with acc.) fruit and cheese afterwards—the cheese is probably good here. We've plenty of time. Afterwards we won't go on foot; we'll take a taxi and go to the theatre.

## LESSON XII

## PERSONAL PRONOUNS.   WORD ORDER

### Declension of Personal Pronouns

#### Singular

|        | 1st person | 2nd person | Masc. | Fem. | Neut. |
|--------|------------|------------|-------|------|-------|
| Nom.   | ja         | ti         | on    | ona  | ono   |
| Gen.   | mene, me   | tebe, te   | njega, ga | nje, je | njega, ga |
| Dat.   | meni, mi   | tebi, ti   | njemu, mu | njoj, joj | njemu, mu |
| Acc.   | mene, me   | tebe, te   | njega, ga | nju, ju, je | njega, ga |
| Voc.   | —          | ti         | —     | —    | —     |
| Instr. | mnom       | tobom      | njim(e) | njom | njim |
| Loc.   | meni       | tebi       | njemu | njoj | njemu |

Third person header spans Masc., Fem., Neut. columns ("3rd person").

#### Plural

|        | 1st | 2nd | Masc. | Fem. | Neut. |
|--------|-----|-----|-------|------|-------|
| Nom.   | mi  | vi  | oni   | one  | ona   |
| Gen.   | nas | vas |       | njih, ih |   |
| Dat.   | nama, nam | vama, vam |   | njima, im |   |
| Acc.   | nas | vas |       | njih, ih |   |
| Voc.   | —   | vi  |       | —    |       |
| Instr. | nama | vama |      | njima |      |
| Loc.   | nama | vama |      | njima |      |

The genitive, dative, and accusative cases of these pronouns
each have two forms (the feminine accusative singular has
three). These are their full and their short, enclitic, forms.
The difference between these forms in the genitive and accusative plural of the first and second person (*nas* and *vas*) is not

shown in printing: the vowel of their full form is long, and that of their short form short.

The full forms must be used when the pronoun stands at the beginning of a sentence or clause, or if it is emphasised, e.g. I'll give this book to you, for I don't give my books to him—Vama ću dati ovu knjigu (or Daću vama ovu knjigu), jer ne dajem svoje knjige njemu.

The full forms are also used after prepositions: [1] *blizu mene*—near me; *na njemu*—on him; *u njima*—in them.

With these exceptions the form of the personal pronoun to be used is always the short, enclitic form. The feminine accusative singular has two short forms: *ju* and *je*. Of these, *ju* is used only when this pronoun immediately precedes the verb *je*; otherwise the form *je* is always used.

## WORD ORDER

In the passages and sentences given so far in this book the order of words will have been seen to be much the same as in English, except for the rule that an enclitic verb or pronoun cannot stand at the beginning of a sentence or clause. Generally speaking there is greater flexibility of word order in Serbo-Croat than in English; owing to the fact that the cases have special forms the meaning of a sentence will be clear whatever the order of the words, whereas in English it would be impossible to reverse the positions of the subject and object of a sentence such as 'the dog bit the man'.

But there are definite rules regarding the position of enclitic pronouns and enclitic verbs. The student is recommended to learn by heart the examples given below rather than to try to memorise the rules, and to refer frequently to this section.

---

[1] Occasionally the stress accent may be placed on the preposition and the enclitic form of the pronoun used; then the preposition is sometimes lengthened, e.g. *pred* (in front of) becomes *preda*. Also 'on to him', usually *na njega*, may be written *na nj*.

### The Position of the Enclitic Pronoun

When the enclitic pronoun is the direct or indirect object of a verb which is *not* an enclitic verb, the enclitic pronoun precedes the verb :

Ja ga vidim—I see him.

Sada ga vidim—Now I see him.

But if no other word precedes this pronoun in the sentence or clause the enclitic pronoun must follow the verb :

Vidim ga—I see him.

When there is more than one enclitic pronoun in the sentence or clause the pronoun in the accusative case always follows the pronouns in other cases :

Ja mu ga dajem—I'm giving it to him (I to–him it am–giving).

*or* Dajem mu ga.

When the verb is negative the negative particle *ne* always immediately precedes the verb :

Ja ga ne vidim—I don't see him.

*or* Ne vidim ga.

Ja mu ga ne dajem—I'm not giving it to him.

*or* Ne dajem mu ga.

Negative forms of auxiliary verbs, as mentioned earlier, are not enclitic verbs, so the rules given above apply also when the negative forms of auxiliary verbs are used :

Ja ga nisam video—I didn't see him.

*or* Nisam ga video.

Ja mu ga neću dati—I shall not give it to him.

*or* Neću mu ga dati.

Exercise : Translate each of the following sentences with and without the nominative personal pronoun, and using only enclitic pronouns in the other cases : I like him ; I don't like him ; he likes her ; he didn't like her ; she's giving it to me ;

she's not giving it to you; she did not give it to him; I'm giving it to her.

Put the above sentences into the plural.

### THE POSITION OF THE ENCLITIC VERB

The principal rules to observe are:

1. The enclitic verb can never stand at the beginning of a sentence or clause.

2. In a subordinate clause the enclitic verb must immediately follow a conjunction or relative pronoun introducing the clause, except when the conjunction is *i* (and) or *a* (and *or* but). The conjunction in most frequent use is *da* (that), and the student is advised always to pause after using this conjunction and ask himself whether there will be an enclitic verb in the clause following it.

> Znam da je vaša sestra ovde—I know that your sister is here.
>
> Mislimo da su kuće bile blizu crkve—We think that the houses were near the church.
>
> Da li verujete [1] da će vaš drug doći ?—Do you believe that your friend will come ?

(But: Znam da vaša sestra nije ovđe; mislimo da kuće nisu bile blizu crkve; da li verujete da vaš drug neće doći ?— because the negative forms of auxiliary verbs are not enclitic.)

Exercise: Translate—I think that the house is (was) here; we know that the doctor will (will not) come; he believes that his friend is (is not) in the train; I know that your book is (was) on the table; they say that their sister is (was) in the kitchen.

### THE POSITION OF THE ENCLITIC PRONOUN IN RELATION TO THE ENCLITIC VERB.

When an enclitic pronoun is the direct or indirect object of a verb in a compound tense in which there is an enclitic

---

[1] From *verovati*—to believe.

auxiliary verb the pronoun immediately follows the auxiliary verb, except when the verb is *je*. Enclitic pronouns precede the verb *je*.

Ja sam ga video juče—I saw him yesterday.

*or* Video sam ga juče.

*or* Juče sam ga video.

Mi ćemo vam pisati sutra—We shall write to you to-morrow.

*or* Pisaćemo vam sutra.

*or* Sutra ćemo vam pisati.

On će mi ga dati—He will give it to me.

*or* Daće mi ga.

*But :* On me je video jutros—He saw me this morning.

*or* Video me je jutros.

*or* Jutros me je video.

Note that as the enclitic pronoun precedes the verb *je* this verb, although enclitic, will not always immediately follow a preceding conjunction : Znam da me je Jovan video—I know that John saw me.

## VOCABULARY

dočekati (pf.)—to wait for (until the expected person comes)

doneti, donesem (pf.)—to bring

kafa—coffee

karta—ticket

kuda—whither

obećati, obećam (pf.)—to promise (used with dative of person)

pas (gen. psa)—dog

povesti, povedem (pf.)—to take, lead (a person)

pozvati, pozovem (pf.)—to invite

ponuditi (pf.)—to offer

rečnik—dictionary

slobodan, slobodna—free, at liberty

večera—supper, dinner

voditi (ipf.)—to take, lead (a person)

zahvaliti (pf.)—to thank (used with dative of person)

Read and translate : 1. Nećemo je videti sutra. 2. Mi ga nismo čuli kad je ulazio u kuću. 3. Ja sam je gledao ali me ona nije primetila. 4. Našli smo ih u parku i zamolila sam ih da dodju sutra. 5. Sada ću otići da ga tražim. 6. Juče mi je rekao da će ići u pozorište sa mnom. 7. Mi ih nećemo pozvati na ručak. 8. Da li mu je rekla da ju je njegov drug pozvao na večeru ? 9. Mi ćemo vas dočekati na stanici. 10. On joj je dao svoju adresu. 11. Ona mi je obećala da će biti poslušna. 12. Doneo je stolice za njih i za mene. 13. Da li su vas razumeli kad ste govorili srpskohrvatski ? 14. Daćemo im ove rečnike kad ih vidimo. 15. Oni nisu bili kod mene kad ste ih tražili.

Translate : 1. I went to look for him but I didn't find him. 2. She sang a lovely song : did you hear it ? 3. He told me that he wouldn't come. 4. We thanked them when they invited us to luncheon, but told them we should not be free. 5. I'll give him her address ; she said she would give it to me. 6. He offered her a cigarette but she didn't take it. 7. I was looking at his pockets ; there are (*ima*) a lot of things in them. 8. There's your coat : I put it on the chair. 9. They promised us at ' Putnik ' [1] that they would give us the tickets tomorrow. 10. My dog won't go with him, but perhaps he'll go with you. 11. She wants to take us with her (so sobom). 12. I didn't understand him when he was talking with them. 13. Are you really giving this to *me* ? 14. To me it's not clear why they didn't write to him. 15. They said they'd wait for us at the station, but I don't see them.

## VOCABULARY

| | |
|---|---|
| danas—today | odlučiti (pf.)—to decide |
| galama—noise, hubbub | otvoriti (pf.)—to open |
| muzej—museum | potreban, (f. potrebna)— |
| naglas—aloud | necessary |

[1] ' Putnik '—the Yugoslav travel agency.

**probuditi** (pf.)—to awaken
**sijati** (ipf.)—to shine
**spremati** (ipf.), **spremiti** (pf.)—to prepare

**sunce**—sun
**ustati, ustanem** (pf.)—to get up
**vodić**—guide book

Translate : The noise in the street awoke us early, and we got up immediately. ' I'll prepare the coffee,' John said to me. ' Where have you put it ? ' ' I think that I put all the necessary things in your case. Didn't you see them when you opened it last night ? Here they are ! While you prepare it we'll decide where (whither) we will go today. Have you the guide book ? Give it to me, please. Thank you. Here's a picture of that beautiful church ; we saw it yesterday, you know, when we were passing. Perhaps we shall be able to go into it today. We must go to this museum, too.' [1] I read about it aloud while John was preparing the coffee. ' We must visit it this afternoon,' [2] I said to him. He passed me a cup. ' Oh, this is very pleasant ! The sun's shining and the coffee is good. We'll drink it up and go out to see the town.'

1. Use *i* (and, too) before the phrase ' to this museum '.
2. Say ' after noon '.

## VOCABULARY

**čim**—as soon as
**izleteti, izletim** (pf.)—to fly out
**krenuti, krenem** (pf.)—to start off
**mariti za** (ipf., with acc.)—to care about
**misao** (f. ; gen. sing. misli, nom. pl. misli, like *stvar*)—thought

**odavna, odavno**—for a long time past
**polazak** (gen. **polaska**)—departure
**policija**—police
**poludeti, poludim** (pf.)—to go mad
**pre** (with gen.)—before
**prema** (with loc.)—towards
**prizemlje**—ground floor

smeti, smem (ipf.)—to dare, to be allowed

svejedno—' all one ' (i.e. ' it doesn't matter ')

trčati, trčim (ipf.)—to run

vikati, vičem (ipf.)—to shout

za (with instr.)—after, following after

želja—wish, desire

This passage, for reading and translation, is a continuation of the passage in the *ije*-dialect given in the previous lesson. The forms of words which differ in the *e*-dialect are given in brackets in the notes below.

Poslije [1] podne, malo prije [2] polaska voza, Jeca je uzela kovčeg. Našla je Luciju u prizemlju i rekla joj :

— Ja idem kući.

— Ti si poludjela ! [3] A moje dijete ? [4]

— Svejedno. I moje [5] čeka [6] na me odavna.

— Ti ne smiješ [7] ići — vikala je Lucija. — Poslat ću za tobom policiju. Ja te ne puštam !

Ali Jeca je izletjela [8] iz kuće i trčala prema stanici.

Čim je sjela [9] u vagon, voz je krenuo. S njom su putovali drugi putnici, ali ona nije marila za njih. Živjela [10] je u njoj samo jedna misao i želja : da stigne što prije [11] tamo, gdje [12] je njen Jovo.

1. (posle). 2. (pre). 3. (poludela). 4. (dete). 5. i moje— ' mine, too '. 6. Translate ' has been waiting '. The present tense is used because the action is still continuing. 7. (smeš). 8. (izletela). 9. (sela). 10. (živela). 11. što prije (što pre)— as soon as possible. 12. (gde).

# LESSON XIII

## THE REFLEXIVE PRONOUN. REFLEXIVE VERBS

The reflexive pronoun is the same for every person, singular and plural, and therefore corresponds to all English reflexive pronouns—myself, thyself, himself, herself, itself, ourselves, yourselves, themselves. It is declined :

| | |
|---|---|
| Gen. | sebe |
| Dat. | sebi, si |
| Acc. | sebe, se |
| Instr. | sobom |
| Loc. | sebi |

The rules for the use of the full and enclitic forms of the personal pronouns apply to the accusative forms *sebe* and *se* of this pronoun.

When in English a personal pronoun in one of the above cases refers to the same person as the subject of the sentence the reflexive pronoun should be used in Serbo-Croat. Compare : ' I am taking him with me '—Vodim ga sa sobom (i.e. ' with myself '), and ' Will you come with me ? '—Hoćete li doći sa mnom ?

As the reflexive pronoun *se* is an enclitic pronoun like other short forms of personal pronouns, in the accusative case its place in the sentence will be determined accordingly :

Ona se umiva—She's washing herself.

*or* Umiva se.

Vi ćete se izgubiti—You'll lose yourself.

*or* Izgubićete se. (' Izgubiti se ' also means ' to disappear '.)

In the 3rd person singular of the compound past tense the auxiliary verb *je* is often omitted after *se* :

On se je ubio—He killed himself.

*or* On se ubio.

*or* Ubio se.

Do not confuse this reflexive pronoun with the *adjective* 'myself', 'himself', etc., which is *sam, sama*, etc. (The vowel is longer than in the verb *sam*.) She saw them herself (i.e. 'she herself saw them')—videla ih je sama. This adjective also means 'alone' (see p. 60).

Exercise : Translate with and without nominative personal pronouns : I am (was) washing myself ; he is (was) washing himself ; I lost myself ; she lost herself ; I ask myself (i.e. I wonder) ; he asked himself ; he asked her (acc.) himself.

Translate the above sentences also in the plural.

Many verbs which are not reflexive in English are reflexive in Serbo-Croat. The verb ' to return ', for example, is always transitive in Serbo-Croat, and where it would be used intransitively in English the reflexive pronoun must be expressed as its object in Serbo-Croat :

Moj sin će vam vratiti vašu knjigu—My son will return your book to you.

Moj sin će se vratiti sutra—My son will return tomorrow (i.e. . . . will bring himself back).

The reason for the use of the reflexive pronoun with some other verbs is not usually so obvious, e.g. bojati se, bojim se (ipf.)—to fear ; sećati se, sećam se (ipf.), setiti se, setim se (pf.)—to remember. The noun or pronoun following these verbs is in the genitive case :

Bojim se učitelja—I'm afraid of the teacher.
Bojali ste se kiše—You were afraid of the rain.
Sećam se onih dana—I remember those days.

Smejati se, smejem se [1] (ipf.)—to laugh, and smešiti se, smešim se (ipf.)—to smile, are also reflexive verbs :

---

[1] This verb, like verbs meaning ' to ridicule ', is followed by the dative case when it means ' to laugh at '.

On se smeje—He's laughing.

*or* Smeje se.

Zašto se smešite ?—Why are you smiling ?

The verbs *diviti se, divim se* (ipf.)—to admire, and *čuditi se, čudim se* (ipf.)—to wonder at, take the dative case :

Divim se vašoj hrabrosti—I admire your courage.

The verbs *dogoditi se* and *desiti se* (pf.), *događati se* and *dešavati se* (ipf.) mean ' to happen ' and are, of course, used only in the 3rd person :

Ovo se dešava svaki dan—This happens every (each) day.

Kad se (je) to dogodilo ?—When did that happen ?

Other reflexive verbs will be found in the lists in the Appendix.

Verbs are often used reflexively in Serbo-Croat where in English the passive voice would be used :

Naslov se piše ovde—The title is written here (The title writes itself here).

Ove pesme su se pevale u Dalmaciji—These songs were sung in Dalmatia (These songs sang themselves . . . ).

The reflexive pronoun may also mean ' each other ' :

Da li su se videli ?—Did they see each other ?

## Vocabulary

glumac (gen. glumca)—actor
glumica—actress
kako—how
komedija—comedy
kupati (se) (ipf.)—to bathe
lice—face
nadati se (ipf.)—to hope
najzad—at last

naljutiti se (pf.)—to get angry
niz, niza (with acc.)—down
obala—coast, shore
obradovati se, obradujem se (pf.) [1]—to be delighted
penjati se, penjem se (ipf.)—to climb

[1] Followed by *što* (' that ').

poneti, ponesem (pf.)—to bring, fetch

popeti se, popnem se (pf.)—to climb

potrčati, potrčim (pf.)—to run off

pozdraviti (pf.)—to greet

prekjuče—the day before yesterday

prevariti (pf.)—to deceive

prevariti se—to make a mistake

radovati se, radujem se (ipf.) [1]—to rejoice, be delighted

roditelj—parent

sastati se, sastanem se (pf.)—to meet

skočiti (pf.)—to jump

starica—old woman

strog—stern, severe

šala—joke, jest

šuma—forest, wood

taman, tamna—dark

toliko—so much

uvideti, uvidim (pf.)—to realise

uz (with acc.)—up, alongside, along with

viđati (ipf.)—to see sometimes, frequently, regularly

zato što—because

zaustaviti (pf.)—to stop, bring to a halt

zbog (with gen.)—because of

zemlja—earth, ground ; country

zgrada—building

zid (pl. zidovi)—wall

zvati, zovem (ipf.)—to call

Read and translate : 1. Oni se ne sećaju vaših roditelja. 2. Englezi se nisu smejali ovoj šali, jer je nisu razumeli. 3. Sebi je ostavio vrlo veliki komad mesa. 4. Nadam se da se ona starica neće naljutiti na mene. 5. Naš prijatelj gospodin Petrović nije kupio kuću za sebe nego za svoju sestru. 6. Pitam se da li sam se prevarila. 7. To se nije desilo juče ; desilo se prekjuče. 8. Zar niste mogli da se vratite na vreme ? 9. Jovan se umivao dok se njegov otac kupao. 10. Mladići su najzad uvideli da su se izgubili u šumi. 11. Pozdravili su se kad su se sastali. 12. Piše ovde da se ne sme ući u ovu zgradu. 13. Kaže se (it is said) da je i majka onoga glumca bila velika glumica. 14. Penjali su se uz onaj zid kad sam ih video.

[1] Followed by *što* (' that ').

15. Putnici su poneli sve svoje stvari sa sobom. 16. Radujem se što ste došli. 17. Odmah smo se zaustavili. 18. Kako se zove ono selo‑koje (which) se nalazi ('is situated') blizu šume? 19. Moj sin se bojao vašeg velikog psa, gospodine. 20. Ja se nisam mogao setiti njegovog imena.

Translate: 1. Mila has disappeared. 2. I don't know whether she will come back. 3. I hope they'll take me with them. 4. Why were you laughing? 5. I wasn't laughing; I was only smiling. 6. She's naturally afraid of him because of his stern face. 7. 'Wine (gen.), Mila!' they shouted when Mila was serving in the café. 8. Do you remember the night when we got lost in that dark forest? 9. I've bought this picture for myself, because I admired it so much. 10. Fortunately that doesn't often happen. 11. As soon as she had read his letters she returned them to me. 12. It happened when we were at your home.[1] 13. A comedy by (od) Marin Držić is being given (is giving itself) at the theatre; we must see it. 14. What do they say (what is said) about this book? 15. They didn't see each other often, although they liked each other (very) much. 16. The car stopped in front of a large building and the driver got out. 17. He climbed up the wall, jumped on to the ground, and ran off along the path.[2] 18. Our little village is situated ('finds itself') on the coast. 19. What is your name?[3] 20. I was delighted when I received the good news about you.

1. Use kod with the genitive of the personal pronoun 'you'. 2. 'along the path': use the instrumental case, without a preposition. 3. Say: How (kako) do you call yourself?

## VOCABULARY

al': ali—but
Ana—Anna
berberin—barber

jedva—scarcely
kafanski—belonging to the café

kao da—as if, as though

ministarstvo—ministry

momak (gen. momka)—lad

natrag—back, in reverse direction

neko—somebody

nositi (ipf.)—to carry

obrijati, obrijem (pf.)—to shave

obući, obučem ; obukao, obukla (pf.)—to put on (clothes)

okrenuti, okrenem (pf.)—to turn

oriti se (ipf.)—to resound

ošišati (pf.)—to cut (hair)

pa—and so, and then

slatko—sweetly

služiti (ipf.)—to serve

srce—heart

sutradan—the next day

točiti (ipf.)—to pour out (wine, etc.)

tuđ—somebody else's, foreign

tužiti za (ipf. ; with instr.)— to grieve for

tvrdo—firmly, soundly

učiniti se (pf.)—to seem

uputiti (pf.)—to direct

vrata (neut. pl.)—door

vući, vučem ; vukao, vukla (ipf.)—to pull, draw

Re-read the remarks on ' musical intonation ' in Lesson I, and translate and learn by heart the following verse from a poem by the Serbian poet Đura Jakšić (1832–78) :

> Vína, Mîlo ! òrilo se
> Dòk je Míla óvde bíla.
> Sâd se Mila izgùbila—
> Túđe rûke víno nòsē.
> Ana tòčī
> Ana slûžī
> Àl' za Mílōm sȑce tûžī.

Read and translate the following passage from a short story by the Serbian humorist and dramatist Branislav Nušić. (1864–1938). It is continued in Lessons XV and XVII.

Tu noć, u kafani, Petronije je vrlo slatko i vrlo tvrdo spavao. A sutradan probudio se pre nego što su se probudili kafanski momci i jedva je čekao da se otvore vrata. Otišao je zatim kod berberina, ošišao se, obrijao se, obukao crni kaput i uputio se Terazijama [1] u ministarstvo. Kad je došao do ministarstva učinilo mu se kao da ga neko vuče za (by) kaput natrag, pa se okrenuo da vidi ko je to.

[1] Terazije (f. pl.)—a street in Belgrade.

## LESSON XIV
### CARDINAL NUMERALS

| | | | |
|---|---|---|---|
| 1 | jedan, jedna, jedno | 21 | dvadeset i jedan (jedna, jedno) |
| 2 | dva, dve, dva | 22 | dvadeset i dva (dve, dva) |
| 3 | tri | 23 | dvadeset i tri |
| 4 | četiri | 30 | trideset |
| 5 | pet | 31 | trideset i jedan, etc. |
| 6 | šest | 40 | četrdeset |
| 7 | sedam | 50 | pedeset |
| 8 | osam | 60 | šezdeset |
| 9 | devet | 70 | sedamdeset |
| 10 | deset | 80 | osamdeset |
| 11 | jedanaest [1] | 90 | devedeset |
| 12 | dvanaest | 100 | sto or stotina |
| 13 | trinaest | 101 | sto jedan, etc. |
| 14 | četrnaest | 200 | dvesta or dve stotine |
| 15 | petnaest | 300 | trista or tri stotine |
| 16 | šesnaest | 400 | četiri stotine |
| 17 | sedamnaest | 500 | pet stotina |
| 18 | osamnaest | 600 | šest stotina, etc. |
| 19 | devetnaest | 1,000 | hiljada or tisuća |
| 20 | dvadeset | 2,000 | dve hiljade, etc. |

The numeral ' one '—*jedan, jedna, jedno*, is declined as a definite adjective, agreeing with the noun following it : imam jednog sina—I have one son (note again the endings of adjective and noun when the noun denotes a masculine living creature) ; našla je samo jedan dućan—she found only one shop ; u jednoj kući—in one house ; na jednom mestu—at one place. This numeral has also plural forms, to be used with the few nouns which have only plural forms in common use, such as novine (f. pl.)—newspaper,[2] vrata (n. pl.)—door, kola

---

[1] This is a contraction of *jedan na deset* (one on to ten).

[2] Another word for ' newspaper ' is *list* (masc. sing.), pl. *listovi*.

(n. pl.)—cart, car; and some parts of the body, e.g. grudi (f. pl.)—chest, leđa (n. pl.)—back.

Jedne novine—one newspaper; u jednim novinama—in one newspaper; jedna vrata su otvorena—one door is open.

It has already been mentioned (Lesson III) that the numeral *jedan, jedna, jedno* is sometimes used where the indefinite article is used in English. According to the context, 'jedna žena je pevala' might mean 'a woman was singing' or 'one woman was singing'.

Unless it is one of those nouns used only in their plural form, the noun following the numerals 21, 31, 41, etc., is always in the singular: 41 guests—četrdeset i jedan gost; to 21 women—dvadeset i jednoj ženi; in 31 villages—u trideset i jednom selu.

The noun following the cardinal numerals 2, 3, 4; 22, 23, 24; 32, 33, 34, etc., is always in the genitive singular: tri sina—three sons; dvadeset i četiri žene—24 women; trideset i dva pisma—32 letters. Note that the numeral 2 has masculine, feminine, and neuter forms, to agree with the gender of the noun following it, and that this numeral and the noun will usually have the same endings: dva pasoša—two passports (m.); dve sestre—two sisters; dva jezera—two lakes (n.). An adjective qualifying a noun in the genitive singular after the numerals 2, 3, 4; 22, 23, 24; 32, 33, 34, etc., takes the endings of the genitive singular of the indefinite form of the adjective declensions; again, then, when the numeral is *dva, dve, dva* the endings will usually be the same for numeral, adjective, and noun: dva dobra sina—two good sons; dve vesele devojke—two merry girls; dva mala sela—two little villages; četrdeset i četiri velika grada—44 large cities.

The same rule applies to the agreement of the active past participle when a noun following the numerals 2, 3, 4, 22, 23, 24, etc., is the subject of a verb in the compound past tense:

dva dobra sina su radila—two good sons were working ; but the masculine plural ending *-i* (radili) may also be used when the subject is masculine.

All other cardinal numerals (5 to 20, 25 to 30, etc.) are followed by the genitive plural : devet inteligentnih sinova— 9 intelligent sons ; petnaest udatih žena—15 married women ; dvadeset i sedam visokih brda—27 high mountains. The active past participle used in the past tense following these will take the usual plural endings : devet sinova su bili ; petnaest žena su bile ; dvadeset i sedam brda su bila.

As *stotina* (hundred), *hiljada* and *tisuća* (thousand) are feminine nouns, it will now be clear why 400, for example, is *četiri stotine* (gen. sing.), while 500 is *pet stotina* (gen. pl.).

With the exception of *jedan*, which must be treated as an adjective, cardinal numerals are not declined after prepositions, and the noun following them will always be in the genitive (singular or plural) whatever the case the preceding preposition would otherwise govern.

Compare : u jednom selu ; u dva sela ; u devet sela ; s [1] jednim sinom ; sa dva sina ; sa dvadeset sinova. See p. 9 : sa tri mala prozora.

The numerals 2, 3, and 4 may be declined, but are seldom used in their declined forms. The declension of *dva, dve, dva* is :

| Nom. | dva (m., n.) | dve (f.) | Acc. | dva (m., n.) | dve (f.) |
|------|--------------|----------|------|--------------|----------|
| Gen. | dvaju | dveju | Instr. | dvama | dvema |
| Dat. | dvama | dvema | Loc. | dvama | dvema |

' Both ' may be either *oba* (m.), *obe* (f.), *oba* (n.), or *obadva* (m.), *obadve* (f.), *obadva* (n.). These are declined like *dva, dve, dva*, but as the rules given above regarding the use of *dva, dve, dva* apply also to these words they are not often used in their declined forms.

---

[1] Abbreviated from *sa*.

The declension of *tri* and *četiri*, for all three genders, is :

Nom. and acc. : tri, četiri.
Gen. : triju, četirju.
Dat., instr., loc. : trima, četirma.

Examples of the use of these numerals when declined are : stanovnici dvaju (triju) velikih gradova—the inhabitants of 2 (3) large towns ; drži ga dvema (obema) rukama—he is holding it with two (both) hands. Here the numerals are declined because no preposition precedes them ; it will be noticed that they no longer govern the genitive singular, but that adjectives and nouns following them are in the same case as the numeral itself, and in the plural.

Once, twice, three times are *jedanput, dvaput, triput,* or *jedan put, dva puta, tri puta* ; 4 times, 5 times, etc., are *četiri puta, pet puta*, etc.

*Nijedan* means ' not one ', and takes a negative verb : nijedna žena nije došla—not one woman came.

### VOCABULARY

Božić—Christmas
čestitka—greetings card
dinar—Yugoslav coin
dnevno—daily
dopadati se (ipf.)—to be
  pleasing to
funta—pound
hrana—food
kućica—cottage

minut—minute
nedelja—week
pročitati (pf.)—to read
različit—different, various
težak, teška—heavy, difficult
turist—tourist
voda—water
vodič—guide

Read and translate : 1. Napisao je šest važnih pisama za pedeset minuta. 2. Zašto imate četiri telefonska imenika ? 3. Rezervirali smo pet lepih soba—jednu za mene i moga muža i četiri za Jovana i njegovih sedam mladih drugova.

4. Videćete dvadeset i jednu zgradu : dve velike kuće i devet-
naest malih kućica. 5. Njena dva sina su spremala (spremali)
ručak, dok je ona sedela u bašti sa svoje tri prijateljice.
6. Njegova žena mi je rekla da je on bio pet nedelja u
Engleskoj i da je pušio pedeset engleskih cigareta dnevno.
7. Izgubili smo hiljadu dinara ; sad imamo samo trideset
i jednu englesku funtu u džepu. 8. Nema (there isn't) dosta
mesta za ovih petnaest velikih paketa u jednim kolima. 9. Bilo
je (there were) osamnaest studenata a samo četrnaest stolica ;
četiri studenta su dakle sedela (sedeli) na podu. 10. Obećala
je da će pevati deset narodnih pesama. Radujem se, jer mi
se mnogo dopadaju jugoslovenske narodne pesme.

Translate each of the following sentences twice : the
second time with the numerals which are in brackets.

1. I'll take the 3 (5) young girls with me. 2. He returned
with 4 (6) heavy packages. 3. I think you've read these 2 (5)
important articles : will you return them to him ? 4. She
received 51 (57) greeting-cards at Christmas ; she always
receives a lot. 5. We have enough food for 30 (32) poor
women. 6. He says he has read all 3 (8) pages of this letter
in 4 (14) minutes. 7. One guide (2 guides) went to the museum
with the 11 (22) weary tourists. 8. They bathe in the calm
water of this lake 3 (5) times daily. 9. I'm learning these
words ; I've already learned 100 (102) new words today.
10. Did you notice those 2 (6) men ? [1]  Each of them is
travelling with 3 (5) different passports !

[1] men—*ljudi*, has genitive plural *ljudi*. (*Čovek* has no regular plural
form.)

## LESSON XV

### ORDINAL NUMERALS. THE DATE. THE DAY OF THE WEEK. THE TIME OF DAY

The Ordinal Numerals are declined like definite adjectives with stems ending in a hard consonant (with the exception of *treći*, which has a ' soft ' ending), agreeing like adjectives with the nouns which they qualify.

| | | | | |
|---|---|---|---|---|
| 1st | prvi, prva, prvo | 19th | devetnaesti |
| 2nd | drugi, druga, drugo [1] | 20th | dvadeseti |
| 3rd | treći, treća, treće | 21st | dvadeset prvi, etc. |
| 4th | četvrti, četvrta, četvrto | 30th | trideseti |
| 5th | peti, etc. | 40th | četrdeseti |
| 6th | šesti | 50th | pedeseti |
| 7th | sedmi | 60th | šezdeseti |
| 8th | osmi | 70th | sedamdeseti |
| 9th | deveti | 80th | osamdeseti |
| 10th | deseti | 90th | devedeseti |
| 11th | jedanaesti | 100th | stoti |
| 12th | dvanaesti | 200th | dvestoti |
| 13th | trinaesti | 300th | tristoti |
| 14th | četrnaesti | 400th | četiristoti |
| 15th | petnaesti | 500th | petstoti, etc. |
| 16th | šesnaesti | 1,000th | hiljaditi |
| 17th | sedamnaesti | 1,001st | hiljadu prvi |
| 18th | osamnaesti | 2,000th | dvehiljaditi |

The Serbian forms of the names of the months, which are very similar to English, were given in Lesson I. They are repeated here with the Croatian forms alongside them, for in this respect Croatian differs from Serbian. (For the sake of

---

[1] Also means ' the other '. ' Another ' with the sense of ' one more ' is *još jedan* (see p. 53) : dajte mi još jednu šolju čaja.

simplicity and consistency the Serbian forms are used in this book.)

| januar  | siječanj[1] | jul       | srpanj   |
|---------|-------------|-----------|----------|
| februar | veljača     | avgust    | kolovoz  |
| mart    | ožujak      | septembar | rujan    |
| april   | travanj     | oktobar   | listopad |
| maj     | svibanj     | novembar  | studeni  |
| jun     | lipanj      | decembar  | prosinac |

Answering the question ' Koji je danas ? ', in which the word *datum* (date) is understood (Koji je datum danas ?— What is the date today ?), the day and month are in the nominative case, and the ordinal numeral is masc. sing., agreeing with *dan* (day), which is understood : (Danas je) prvi januar—(Today is) 1 January ; treći april—3 April ; dvadeset osmi februar—28 February.

To answer the question ' when ? ' the ordinal numeral and the name of the month are in the genitive case—a case which is used for many other expressions denoting ' time when ' : Kad se to desilo ?—When did that happen ? (Desilo se) trinaestog avgusta—(It happened) on the 13th August ; tridesetog oktobra—on the 30th October ; trećeg decembra— on the 3rd December.

In answer to either type of question the year is expressed thus : Hiljadu devet stotina šezdeset druge godine (1962), i.e. *hiljadu* (thousand) is in the accusative,[2] *devet stotina*— nine hundreds (*stotina* is genitive plural after *devet*), and *šezdeset druge*, the ordinal numeral (62nd), is in the genitive

---

[1] The vowel *a* in the final syllable of siječanj, ožujak, travanj, svibanj, lipanj, srpanj, rujan, prosinac, septembar, oktobar, novembar, and decembar is ' moveable ' (e.g. gen. siječnja, decembra).

[2] The accusative singular of *stotina* and *hiljada* is often used when one would expect some other case.

singular, feminine, agreeing with the noun *godine* (genitive singular of *godina*—year).

1389 : hiljadu tri stotine osamdeset devete godine.
1773 : hiljadu sedam stotina sedamdeset treće godine.
1895 : hiljadu osam stotina devedeset pete godine.[1]

Today is the 25th December 1984—Danas je dvadeset peti decembar hiljadu devet stotina osamdeset četvrte godine.

He came on the 8th September 1951—Došao je osmog septembra hiljadu devet stotina pedeset prve godine.

The date on a letter is usually written thus : 8.XII.1965.

The question ' Koji je dan danas ? ' asks the day of the week, and the answer will be ' Danas je ponedeljak '—' Today is Monday ' (see p. 7, Lesson I).

' Hour ' is either *sat* (nominative *and* genitive plural *sati*) or *čas* (pl. *časovi*).

' Koliko je sati ? '—' What time is it ? ' means literally ' How many is (it) of hours ? '

4 o'clock—četiri sata *or* četiri časa (four hours); 5 o'clock— pet sati *or* pet časova.

*Pola* or *po*, both of which mean ' half ', are used as follows to express the half hour : 4.30—pola pet *or* četiri i po.

' Quarter ' is *četvrt* :

3.15—tri i četvrt (*or* tri i petnaest).

3.45—četvrt do četiri (*or* tri i četrdeset i pet, *or* petnaest do četiri).

12.35—dvanaest i trideset i pet (*or* dvadeset i pet do jedan).

The answer to ' u koliko sati ? '—' at what time ? ' is : u jedan sat (acc.)—at 1 o'clock ; u pola osam—at half past seven (*pola* is indeclinable) ; u dvadeset do devet—at 20 to 9 ; u podne—at noon ; u ponoć—at midnight (*ponoć* is fem.).

---

[1] It is also possible to use *u* with the locative : u hiljadu osam stotina devedeset petoj godini—in 1895.

## Vocabulary

čudan, čudna—strange
desni—right-hand
desno—on the right
ili . . . ili—either . . . or
junak—hero
levi—left-hand
levo—on the left
najmanje—at least
napustiti (pf.)—to leave, abandon
poginuti, poginem (pf.)—to perish, be killed
prazan, prazna—empty

prst—finger
prsten—ring (on finger)
radio (gen. radija)—radio
roditi se (pf.)—to be born
slučaj—case, event (u svakom slučaju—in any case)
spisak (gen. spiska)—list
stati, stanem (pf.)—to stop, stand still
tek—only, not before
večeravati (ipf.)—to have supper, dine

Read and translate : 1. Došao je u pola šest a otišao u četvrt do osam. 2. Stići ću vozom u pet i dvadeset. 3. Desilo se ili petnaestog ili šesnaestog aprila. 4. U koliko sati polazi prvi voz za Beograd ? U dva i trideset i pet. 5. Pročitao sam njegov treći roman, a sada čitam četvrti ; mnogo mi se dopadaju. 6. Rodio se tridesetog novembra hiljadu devet stotina dvadeset druge godine ; u svakom slučaju on ima najmanje četrdeset godina. 7. Da li je danas jedanaesti ili dvanaesti februar ? 8. Ustao je tek u deset sati i napustio kuću u četvrt do jedanaest. 9. Moji roditelji stanuju u petoj kući desno. 10. Nadamo se da ćete doći u sedam i trideset, jer večeravamo obično u osam.

Translate : 1. It happened on the 1st December. 2. What is the date today ? I think it's the 31st November. 3. It can't be ; November has only 30 days. 4. I opened the first ten envelopes ; the fifth and seventh were empty. 5. Many Serbian heroes were killed at Kosovo in 1389. 6. What is the time ? I think it's half past 5. 7. They dined at a quarter to 8.

8. You'll find the book on the third shelf; give it to me, please. 9. We'll listen to the news on the wireless at 6 o'clock. 10. Isn't it strange, this clock always stops at midnight, or perhaps at mid-day; anyway, at 12 o'clock. 11. He went away from home at ten past four on the ninth of August and did not return. 12. Does she wear the ring on the third finger of her left (hand) or of her right hand? 13. You're first on the list, I'm second, she's third and he's fourth. 14. He was born on the 3rd April 1945. 15. Ours is the fourth house in the second street on the left.

## VOCABULARY

baš—just, exactly

brijati, brijem (ipf.)—to shave

čekaonica—waiting-room

dugačak, dugačka—long (of things)

još jedan—one more

kancelarija—office

milo—dear, pleasing (milo mi je—I am glad)

ministar (gen. ministra)—minister

ministrov—minister's

nozdrva—nostril

pamet (f.)—mind, intelligence

pasti, padnem; pao, pala (pf.)—to fall (pasti na pamet, with dat.—to occur to)

povući, povučem; povukao, povukla (pf.)—to draw, pull

prag—threshold

pripaliti (pf.)—to light, ignite

raspoložen—disposed; in a good mood

ravnodušno—indifferently

stojati, stojim (ipf.)—to stand

taman—just, just when

Read and translate:

Taman je hteo da pređe prag, a njemu je palo na pamet da se pita koji je datum danas. Je li možda trinaesti? Bio je prvi april, hvala Bogu. Ušao je u čekaonicu. Već kad je pošao da se brije kupio je nekoliko dobrih cigareta i metnuo u džep.

Ponudio je najpre momku, koji (who) je stojao pred ministro-vim vratima, cigaretu, pustio ga da pripali i povuče dva tri dima,[1] pa je tek onda počeo :

— Je li već došao g.[2] ministar ?

Momak je prvo povukao dugačak jedan dim, pustio ga kroz nozdrve i odgovorio ravnodušno :

— Neće danas dolaziti u kancelariju !

— A, tako !

Baš je Petroniju bilo milo što neće ministar doći danas u kancelariju. On je ponudio momku još jednu cigaretu i otišao vrlo raspoložen.

(Branislav Nušić, contd.)

---

[1] *dim* (smoke) here means ' puff '.
[2] Abbreviation for *gospodin*.

## LESSON XVI

# THE COMPARATIVE AND SUPERLATIVE FORMS OF ADJECTIVES

The endings of the comparative forms of adjectives, corresponding to the English -er, may be :

|  |  | Singular |  |  | Plural |  |
|---|---|---|---|---|---|---|
|  | m. | f. | n. | m. | f. | n. |
| *either* 1. | -iji | -ija | -ije | -iji | -ije | -ija |
| *or* 2. | -ši | -ša | -še | -ši | -še | -ša |
| *or* 3. | -ji | -ja | -je | -ji | -je | -ja |

These are suffixed to the stem of the adjective. A ' moveable *a* ' in the last syllable of the masc. nom. sing. of the positive form of an adjective, e.g. *prijatan* (and in the acc. sing. when this is the same as the nominative) will then of course be dropped.

The first group of endings, -*iji*, etc., is taken by most adjectives :

jeftin—cheap : jeftiniji, jeftinija, jeftinije (sing.) ; jeftiniji, jeftinije, jeftinija (pl.)—cheaper.

prijatan—pleasant : prijatniji, etc.—pleasanter ; star—old : stariji, etc.—older.

The second group, -*ši*, etc., is taken by only three adjectives : lak—easy : lakši, lakša, lakše (sing.) ; lakši, lakše, lakša (pl.) ; lep—beautiful, nice : lepši ; mek—soft : mekši.

The commonest adjectives taking the third group of endings, -*ji*, etc., are given in a list below. In studying this list you should notice the following points : the consonant *j* usually coalesces with, or ' softens ' a consonant immediately preceding it, bringing about a change of consonant ; when it is preceded by two consonants the former of which is *s* or *z*, these are usually also ' softened ' ; the consonant *l* is inserted when *j* would be preceded by *b*, *p*, *v*, or *m*.[1] If you learn the positive and comparative (masc. nom. sing.) forms of each of the following adjectives you will be learning these rules automatically.

beo,[2] bela, belo (sing.) ; beli, bele, bela (pl.)—white.
belji, belja, belje (sing.) ; belji, belje, belja (pl.)—whiter.
besan, besna, besno ; besni, besne, besna—furious.
bešnji, bešnja, bešnje ; bešnji, bešnje, bešnja—more furious.
blag—mild : blaži, etc.—milder.
bled—pale : bleđi.
brz—quick : brži.
crn—black : crnji.
čest—frequent, dense : češći.
čvrst—firm : čvršći.
drag—dear : draži.
dug—long : duži.
gluv—deaf : gluvlji.
grub—rough, coarse : grublji.
gust—dense : gušći.
jak—strong : jači.
kriv—crooked ; guilty : krivlji.
krut—stiff : krući.
lud—stupid, mad : luđi.
ljut—angry : ljući.
mlad—young : mlađi.
skup—expensive : skuplji.
suv (*or* suh)—dry : suvlji (suši).
tesan—tight : tešnji.
tih—quiet : tiši.
tup—blunt : tuplji.
tvrd—hard : tvrđi.

[1] These consonant changes will be discussed again in Lesson XVIII. You will not find examples of all of them in the comparative forms of adjectives.　　　　　　　　[2] See Lesson XVIII.

The following adjectives also take these endings, but first drop their final syllable. The same consonant changes then take place:

blizak (fem. bliska)—near, close: bliži

dalek—far; dalji

debeo (fem. debela)—thick, fat: deblji

dubok—deep: dublji

dugačak (fem. dugačka)— long (of things): duži

gladak (fem. glatka)—smooth: glađi

kratak (fem. kratka)—short: kraći

nizak (fem. niska)—low: niži

plitak (fem. plitka)—shallow: plići

redak (fem. retka)—rare, sparse: ređi

sladak (fem. slatka)—sweet: slađi

širok—broad: širi

tanak (fem. tanka)—slender: tanji

težak (fem. teška)—heavy, difficult: teži

uzak (fem. uska)—narrow: uži

žestok—violent, fiery; žešći

The comparative forms of four adjectives are irregular:

dobar—good: bolji, bolja, bolje, etc.—better.

zao (zla, zlo) or rđav—bad: gori, gora, gore, etc.—worse.

veliki—large: veći, veća, veće, etc.—larger.

malen or mali—small: manji, manja, manje, etc.—smaller.

Whatever is the type of the adjective in its positive form, it will become a definite adjective with a soft stem in its comparative form; hence the neuter singular (nom.) always ends -*e*, the genitive singular, masc. and neut., will always end -*eg* or -*ega*, and dative singular -*em* or -*emu* (see Lesson VII).

Most adjectives in the neuter singular may be used as adverbs: lepo—nicely; dobro—well; brzo—quickly, etc.[1] The neuter singular of the comparative form of an adjective will therefore be the comparative form of the corresponding

---

[1] But adjectives ending -*ski* have corresponding adverbs ending -*ski*.

adverb : brže—more quickly ; manje—less ; dalje—farther ; lakše—more easily. *Više* is used as the comparative of the adverb *mnogo* (' much '), and like *mnogo* is followed by the genitive singular or genitive plural :

mnogo vode—much water ; više vode—more water (gen. sing.).

mnogo žena—many women ; više žena—more women (gen. pl.).

The superlative of all adjectives, and of their corresponding adverbs, is formed by prefixing *naj-* to the comparative form : najstariji, najstarija, etc.—oldest ; najlepši, etc.—most beautiful ; najdraži—dearest ; najbolji—best ; najbrže—most quickly ; najmanje—least, in the least ; najviše—most, most of all.

The preposition *od*, followed by the genitive case, is the usual equivalent of the English ' than ' when two nouns or pronouns are compared : ova Gramatika je teža od onog romana—this Grammar is more difficult than that novel ; on je stariji od mene—he is older than I.

Otherwise ' than ' is *nego* or *nego što* : život je mirniji u selu nego u varoši—life is quieter in the village than in the town ; vaša zemlja je još lepša nego što sam očekivao—your country is still more beautiful than I expected.

Notice the following uses of the comparative : što brže, što dalje—as fast as possible, as far as possible ; sve brže, sve dalje—faster and faster, farther and farther ; tim bolje—so much the better ; čitala je i dalje—she went on reading (' she read also further ') ; i tako dalje (abbreviated to *i t. d.*)—and so on.

### VOCABULARY

bogat—rich
breskva—peach
glasno—loudly

hrabar, hrabra—brave
inteligentan, inteligentna—intelligent

magla—fog
med—honey
obećavati (ipf.)—to promise
očigledno—obviously, evi-
dently
platno—linen
prestati, prestanem (pf.)—to
cease
prevoditi (ipf.)—to translate
rat—war
rečenica—sentence

riba—fish
saobraćaj—traffic
sigurno—certainly, surely
sledeći—next, following
slikar—painter
smokva—fig
svet—world (also ' people ')
ukusan, ukusna—nice,
delicious
voziti (ipf.)—to drive

Read and translate : 1. Ulica pored mosta nije duža od
naše ; mislim da je mnogo kraća. 2. Da li ste rekli da je
London najveći grad na svetu ? 3. Najskuplje stvari nisu uvek
i najbolje. 4. Molim vas, dajte mi jači čaj. 5. Desetog
novembra magla u Londonu je bila gušća nego obično.
6. Olgin glas je uvek mnogo tiši od Milanovog. 7. Jovan misli
da je engleski najteži jezik na svetu, ali vi sigurno mislite dȁ
je srpskohrvatski mnogo teži. 8. Da li je trideseti decembar
najkraći dan u godini ? Ne znam, ali mislim da je dvadeset
prvi jun najduži. 9. Vozili smo se najlepšim putem, iako je
bio opasniji. 10. Kažu da je med slađi od šećera, ali nije.
11. Trčala je sve brže, sve dok nije mogla da ide dalje. 12. Da
li verujete da bogatiji čovek nije zadovoljniji od siromašnog ?
13. Obećavam vam da ću vam poslati što više novca. 14. Nadam se da će more biti mirnije posle podne ; više volim da se
kupam u mirnijoj vodi. 15. Šta radite ? Učim reči, čitam
srpskohrvatske rečenice, prevodim engleske rečenice, i tako
dalje.

Translate : 1. I wonder whether that hotel is better than
this. 2. It is easier (easier is) to read than to translate. 3. There
are (*ima*, with gen.) larger and more beautiful buildings in
Belgrade now than before the war. 4. Why don't you come

more often ? 5. Peaches and figs are certainly more delicious
in your country than in ours. 6. He's evidently braver than I.
7. Do you think that Serbo-Croat is more difficult than
English ? 8. Will your two books be more expensive than
these ? 9. Did they say that he's their best painter ? I've seen
better pictures than his here. 10. It will be quieter for you
(say ' to you ') here. 11. Honey isn't sweeter than sugar, but
it's nicer. 12. We came very early, but they had arrived still
earlier. 13. When they begged her to stop she sang louder
and louder. 14. Is the water deeper here than in (*na*) that
place ? We prefer to bathe in the deepest water. 15. Here is
most (*najviše*, with gen.) traffic, because this is the widest road.
16. He spoke more clearly when he noticed that I was an
Englishman. 17. Are the cheapest newspapers the most
interesting in your country ? 18. This linen is coarser, but
fortunately I like coarse linen. 19. She's the most intelligent
woman in this office. 20. The fish in the following folk ballad
is certainly very intelligent :

### Rȉba i djèvōjka [1]

Djèvōjka sjèdī [2] krȁj [3] mȏra,
Pȁk [4] sáma sèbi gòvorī :
Ah, mȉli [5] Bȍže i drȃgī !
Ȉma l' štȍ [6] šȉrē od mȏra ?
Ȉma l' štȍ dȕžē od pȍlja ?
Ȉma l' štȍ bržē od kònja ?
Ȉma l' štȍ slȃđē od mȅda ?
Ȉma l' štȍ drȃžē od brȁta ?
Gòvorī rȉba iz vòde :
Djèvōjko, lúda budàlo' [7]!
Šȉrē je nȅbo od mȏra,
Dȕžē je mȏre od pȍlja,

Bȑžē su ȍči [8] od kònja,
Slȁđi je šèćer od mȅda,
Drȁži je drȁgi [9] od brȁta.

1. *devojka* in *e*-dialect. 2. *sedi* in *e*-dialect. 3. beside (with gen.). 4. and. 5. dear. 6. ' Ima li nešto.' 7. *budala* (always feminine in form)—fool. The stress accent in the voc. case may alternatively be on the first syllable. 8. eyes (fem. pl.). 9. dear, i.e. the beloved.

# LESSON XVII

## INTERROGATIVE PRONOUNS AND ADJECTIVES. RELATIVE PRONOUNS. EXPRESSIONS OF TIME

The Interrogative Pronouns : *ko ?*—' who ? ' and *šta ?* (or *što ?*)—' what ? '.

| | | | |
|---|---|---|---|
| Nom. | ko [1]—who ? | šta (*or* što)—what ? | |
| Gen. | koga—(of) whom ? | čega | |
| Dat. | kome—(to) whom ? | čemu | |
| Acc. | koga—whom ? | šta (*or* što) | |
| Instr. | (s) kim(e)—(with) whom ? | čim(e) | |
| Loc. | (na) kome—(on) whom ? | (na) čemu | |

(These pronouns have, of course, no Vocative Case.)

The final vowel *e*, given in brackets, is often omitted. Ko je onaj čovek ?—Who is that man ? Šta je ovo ?—What is this ? Ko su one žene ?—Who are those women ? Šta su ove stvari ?—What are these things ? Koga se bojite ?—Of whom are you afraid ? Šta kažete ?—What are you saying ? Kome ste govorili ?—To whom were you speaking ? S kime ste putovali ?—With whom did you travel ? Čime [2] ste otvorili kutiju ?—With what did you open the box ?

*Niko* (nobody) and *neko* (somebody) are declined like *ko* ; *ništa* (nothing) is declined like *šta* ; ' something ' is *nešto* in nom. and acc., and is otherwise declined like *šta*.

Notice the negative verb in the following sentences : Niko nije ovde—nobody is here ; ništa nije bolje—nothing is better. In negative sentences pronouns, verbs, and adverbs which have negative forms must all be negative : two negatives do not cancel each other out as they do in English : I saw nobody—nisam video nikoga ; I never saw anybody anywhere—nikad nisam video nikoga nigde. (Nikad *or* nikada—never ; nigde—nowhere.)

---

[1] *tko* in *ije*-dialect.　　　　[2] See Lesson III.

A preposition governing the gen., acc., instr., or loc. case of the pronouns *niko* and *ništa* is usually inserted after the prefix *ni*, e.g. ni od koga—from nobody ; ni s kim—with nobody.

*Čiji, čija, čije* (sing.), *čiji, čije, čija* (pl.) asks the question ' whose ?', and agrees with the noun following it. It is declined as a definite adjective with a ' soft ' stem (see p. 42). Čija karta ?—whose ticket ? čija je ova karta ?—whose is this ticket ? čiji šeširi ?—whose hats ? čiji su ovi šeširi ?—whose are these hats ? čiju knjigu čitate ?—whose book are you reading ? čijim čekom ste platili račun ?—with whose cheque (ček, m.) did you pay the bill ? *Ničiji* means ' nobody's '.

The relative pronoun ' who ', ' which '—*koji, koja, koje* (sing.), *koji, koje, koja* (pl.) is in some parts of the country declined throughout like a definite adjective with a ' soft ' stem ; but usually its forms in certain cases in the masc. and neut. singular are the same as those of the interrogative pronoun *ko*. Notice that the declension of the relative pronoun is then very similar to that of the possessive adjective *moj* (my).

|  | Singular | | | Plural | | |
|---|---|---|---|---|---|---|
|  | Masc. | Fem. | Neut. | Masc. | Fem. | Neut. |
| Nom. | koji | koja | koje | koji | koje | koja |
| Gen. | koga | koje | koga | kojih | kojih | kojih |
| Dat. | kome | kojoj | kome | kojim(a) | kojim(a) | kojim(a) |
| Acc. | koga [1] koji [2] | koju | koje | koje | koje | koja |
| Instr. | kojim | kojom | kojim | kojim(a) | kojim(a) | kojim(a) |
| Loc. | kome | kojoj | kome | kojim(a) | kojim(a) | kojim(a) |

The final *a* given in brackets is usually omitted.

This relative pronoun agrees in number and gender with the

[1] Referring to an ' animate ' noun.
[2] Referring to an ' inanimate ' noun.

noun to which it refers (žena koja peva—the woman who is
singing ; žene koje pevaju—the women who are singing), but
its case is decided by its function in its own clause : student
koga vidite je njen sin—the student (nom. masc. sing.) whom
(acc. masc. sing.) you see is her son ; znam devojku kojoj ste
dali pismo—I know the girl (acc. fem. sing.) to whom (dat.
fem. sing.) you gave the letter ; sreo sam putnike s kojim sam
putovao—I met the travellers (acc. masc. pl.) with whom
(instr. masc. pl.) I travelled.

As in English the pronoun ' that ' is often used as a relative
pronoun (' the book that I gave you '), so *što* may be used as
a relative pronoun referring to a noun of any gender or
number ; it is declined like the similar interrogative pronoun,
again according to its function in its own clause (nom. and acc.
are always *što*) : imam knjige što ste mi pozajmili—I have the
books that (acc.) you lent to me. The relative pronoun cannot
be omitted. ' The letter you received ' must be translated
' pismo koje (*or* što) ste primili '.

*Što* is always used as the relative pronoun after *ono, sve* :
*ono što* means ' that which ', or often ' what ' in English :
I believed what she said—Verovao sam ono što je kazala ;
you have everything that is necessary—imate sve što je
potrebno.

### Expressions of Time.

The accusative case is generally used in adverbial phrases
denoting duration of time : čekao je jedan sat—he waited one
hour ; radiću godinu dana—I'll work for a year. (In sentences
such as this the nouns nedelja—week, mesec—month, and
godina—year are often followed by the genitive plural *dana*—
' of days ', e.g. ostao je mesec [1] dana—he stayed a month of
days.)

The genitive case is generally used in adverbial phrases

---

[1] *mesec* has gen. pl. *meseci*.

denoting ' time when ' : došla je idućeg dana—she came the
next day ; bio sam tamo prošle godine—I was there last year ;
ne mogu da idem ove godine—I can't go this year.

In certain phrases these cases are interchangeable : ceo [1]
dan *or* celoga dana—the whole day ; svaki dan *or* svakoga
dana—each (every) day.

' On Monday ' [2] is *u ponedeljak* (acc.), ' on Wednesday '—
*u sredu*, etc. But if the name of the day is qualified by an
adjective, the genitive case is used : next Monday—*idućeg
ponedeljka*.

The instrumental singular is used for the phrases ' on
Mondays ', ' on Wednesdays ', etc. : *ponedeljkom, sredom.*
Obično dolazi utorkom, ali prošle nedelje došao je u četvrtak—
he usually comes on Tuesdays, but last week (gen. sing.) he
came on Thursday. (Notice the use of the imperfective and
perfective aspects of the verb in this sentence.)

The instrumental plurals : *satima, mesecima, godinama,*.etc.,
mean ' for hours ', ' for months ', ' for years ' : već godinama
je bio u Jugoslaviji—he had been in Yugoslavia for years
already.

Note the following expressions :

Stići ću do pet sati—I'll arrive by 5 o'clock.

Došao je na jedan dan—he came for one day (acc.).

Doći će kroz (*or* za) jedan sat—he'll come in an hour's
time (acc.).

O Božiću (loc.)—at Christmas ; pred Božić (acc.)—just
before Christmas ; pred veče—just before evening, in the
early evening ; krajem (instr.)[3] decembra (gen.)—at the end
of December ; pocetkom[4] januara—at the beginning of
January ; ujutru *or* pre podne—in the morning ; posle
podne—in the afternoon ; uveče—in the evening ; danju—
by day ; noću—by night.

---

[1] See p. 112.  [2] See p. 7.
[3] nom. *kraj*.  [4] nom. *početak*.

## VOCABULARY

i . . . i . . . —both . . . and
istina—truth
odložiti (pf.)—to postpone
opet—again
posećivati, posećujem (ipf.)—
to visit
poverljiv—confidential
prekosutra—the day after tomorrow
razgovarati (ipf.)—to talk,
converse

sednica—meeting, assembly
sresti, sretnem ; sreo, srela
(pf.)—to meet
staviti (pf.), stavljati (ipf.)—
to place
stideti se, stidim se (ipf.)—to
be ashamed
strašan, strašna—frightful
sutradan—the next day

Read and translate : 1. Znate li o čemu je čitala u onoj knjizi koju ste joj dali ? 2. Pitam se ko će doći na večeru. Koga ste pozvali ? 3. Subotom nisam nikada slobodan ; videćemo se u četvrtak. 4. Ko je ona žena s kojom ste razgovarali kad sam vas video prošle nedelje u muzeju ? 5. Već je zaboravio sve što je učio. 6. Stići ćemo početkom aprila i ostaćemo celo proleće u Splitu, kod onih prijatelja o kojim sam vam često govorio. 7. Čiji je ovaj paket ? Ne može se pročitati adresa na njemu. 8. Čime ću pisati ? Izgubio sam i pero i olovku. 9. Niko mu nije kazao čija je ona karta, pa ju je stavio u svoj džep. 10. Šta ste odgovorili kad vas je zapitao da li vam se dopadaju njegove slike ?

Translate : 1. I don't remember the name of that man who spoke to me about you on Tuesday. Who is he ? 2. He hoped he would meet the girl whom he had seen in the train. 3. To whom did you give the letter ? 4. What's that ? Is it a page out of the book which you were reading ? 5. Whom shall we see at the theatre this evening ? 6. What was he writing with— pen or pencil ? 7. With whose son were you speaking ? 8. Nobody ever lives long in these houses. 9. I'm ashamed of this room ; nothing is ever in order in it. 10. Whose were those things that you were putting into the drawer when I came into the room ? 11. This is the longest letter I've ever received. I shall never have enough time to read it. 12. We didn't see anybody, although we were nearer than you. 13. You've been eating and drinking all day. 14. The two young men with whom I was returning from the theatre last night were Milan and his younger brother. 15. You can't believe everything he says ; what he told you this morning isn't true. 16. Who is the man whom you always visit on Wednesdays ? 17. Can you come for an hour ? I hope you'll arrive by half past four. 18. Something terrible has happened. We've lost the money that you gave us. 19. Do you know whose flat this is (whose is this flat) ? 20. I wonder what he was writing to her about.

Read and translate :

Sutradan je ministar bio u kancelariji ali je odmah otišao.
Prekosutra ministar je u kancelariji, ali neće primati.
Četvrtog dana kod ministra su dva druga ministra i „imaju neki važan razgovor" (to mu je momak poverljivo kazao), pa se ne zna da li će stići da prima.
Petog dana ministar je kazao da će primiti samo one koji imaju vrlo važan posao, koji se ne može do sutra odložiti.
Šestog dana Petronije je morao opet da se obrije. Ali tog dana opet ministar nije dolazio u kancelariju.
Sedmog dana bila je ministarska sednica, pa nije mogao ministar nikoga da primi.
Osmog dana ministar neće primati.
Devetog dana ministar je bio u kancelariji, ali je odmah otišao.
Desetog dana ministar je primio sedam ljudi, a zatim je momak rekao : oni koji su još ostali da dođu sutra.
Trinaestog dana Petronije je morao opet da se obrije, ali kad je prešao prag na ministarstvu, setio se da je već trinaesti april.

(Branislav Nušić, continued.)

## LESSON XVIII

# CONSONANT CHANGES AND OTHER NOTES ON THE FORMS OF WORDS

The rules for the commonest consonant changes, which have already been mentioned, are repeated here with further details and the rules regarding those other consonant changes which you will need to be able to apply yourself. Do not try to memorise all the rules now, but use this chapter for reference as you do the exercises. The rules are in any case more easily learned by memorising the examples.

The consonants $k$, $g$, $h$ become $c$, $z$, $s$ respectively before the vowel $i$ in noun declensions:

Masculine:

vojnik (soldier): nom pl. vojnici; dat., instr., and loc. pl. vojnicima.

bubreg (kidney): nom. pl. bubrezi; dat., instr., and loc. pl. bubrezima.

siromah (poor man): nom. pl. siromasi; dat., instr., and loc. pl. siromasima.

Feminine:

reka: dat. and loc. sing. reci.

knjiga: dat. and loc. sing. knjizi.

snaha: dat. and loc. sing. snasi (but also snahi).

Note that this change does not take place in adjective declensions: *jak* (strong): nom. pl. *jaki*.

Exceptions are *tetka*—aunt (dat. and loc. sing. *tetki*); *mačka*—cat (dat. and loc. sing. *mački*); *mazga*—mule (dat. and loc. sing. *mazgi*) and other feminine nouns whose stems end in the same consonant combinations (*tk*, *čk*, *zg*). Further exceptions are proper names, e.g. Anka (dat. Anki), Luka (dat. Luki).

This change of *k* to *c*, *g* to *z*, and *h* to *s* also takes place in the imperative of verbs before the vowel *i*. Examples will be given when the formation of the imperative is explained (Lesson XX).

Exercise : Give the nominative and dative plural of pukov-nik (colonel), radnik (worker), beleg (mark, sign), Čeh (a Czech), orah (walnut) ; and the dative singular of slika, ruka, and noga.[1]

The same consonants, *k*, *g*, *h*, become *č*, *ž*, and *š* respectively before the vowel *e* in the vocative singular of masculine nouns : vojnik has voc. sing. *vojniče* ; Bog (God) : voc. sing. *Bože* [2] ; duh (spirit) : voc. sing. *duše*.

Exercise : Give the voc. sing. of radnik, junak, pukovnik, drug, vrag (devil), siromah.

This change (*k* to *č*, *g* to *ž*, *h* to *š*) also takes place when *k*, *g*, or *h* precede the vowel *e* in the present tense of verbs. In certain verbs with the present tense endings -em, -eš, -e, -emo, -ete, -u the consonant preceding the ending -u differs from that which precedes the other endings. The consonant *ć* in the -ći ending of the infinitive of these verbs derives from the coalescing of the consonants *kt*, *gt*, or *ht* ; in the present tense the change *k* to *č*, *g* to *ž*, *h* to *š* has taken place before the vowel *e*, but not before *u : vući (vuk-ti)—vučem, vučeš, vuče, vučemo, vučete, vuku*.

Exercise : Give the present tense of peći (pek-ti)—to bake ; seći (sek-ti)—to cut ; strići (strig-ti)—to shear ; vreći (vreh-ti)—to thresh.

The same change takes place in the passive participles of these verbs before the vowel *e* (e.g. *pečen*—baked) ; this will be shown in Lesson XXI. This change also takes place in the aorist tense, which you will not need to use yourself in

---

[1] These nouns have genitive plural *ruku* and *nogu*.
[2] Nominative plural is *bogovi*—gods.

speaking or writing, but will need to recognise in your reading. Examples will be found in Chapter XXII.

Sometimes this change takes place also before the vowel *i*, e.g. *majčin* (mother's) from *majka*.

*C* sometimes changes to *č* and *z* to *ž*, before the vowels *e* or *i*. This occurs principally in the vocative singular of masculine nouns : *stric* (uncle) : voc. *striče ; knez* (prince) *: kneže* ; and, in the same nouns, before the -*evi* ending of the plural : *stričevi*. As the vowel *a* in *otac* (father) is ' moveable ', the vocative of this noun is *oče* (note that the *t* has also dropped) and plural *očevi*. The possessive adjective formed from these nouns is *stričev, knežev, očev*, etc.

### ' SOFTENING ' OF CONSONANTS

The changes which take place when the consonant *j* immediately follows certain other consonants and ' softens ' these have already been noticed, and examples of most of them occurred in the list of adjectives taking the endings -*ji*, etc., in the comparative. The full list (in alphabetical order) is : b+j — blj ; c+j — č ; d+j — đ (dj) ; g+j — ž ; h+j — š ; k+j — č ; l+j — lj ; m+j — mlj ; n+j — nj ; p+j — plj ; s+j — š ; t+j — ć ; v+j — vlj ; z+j — ž. (In the Cyrillic alphabet *lj* and *nj* each appear as one symbol : see pp. 2 and 3.)

Other examples of words in which these changes occur will be found among the passive participles in Chapter XXI, when -*jen* is suffixed to the stem of the verb. Here, to complete the list of examples of this ' softening ' of consonants, are three passive participles : *bačen*—thrown (from *baciti*) *;* *nošen*— worn (from *nositi*) *;* slomljen—broken (from *slomiti*).

The passive participle of *pustiti* (to let go) is *pušten* (from *pust-jen*). This change takes place in certain other forms of words, although *st*+*j* usually becomes *šć* (čest, češći) and always does so in feminine nouns ending -*st* and taking the instrumental singular ending -*ju*, e.g.. *opasnost* (danger) :

instr. sing. *opasnošću*. This 'softening' regularly takes place when feminine nouns with consonantal ending take the instr. sing. ending *-ju*, e.g. ljubav (love) : ljubavlju. ·

Exercise : From p. 96 and the passive participles given above find examples to illustrate all the changes which take place when *j* 'softens' a preceding consonant or consonants.

## ASSIMILATION OF CONSONANTS

If you pronounce the following pairs of consonants aloud you will realise that the former of each is 'voiceless' and the second 'voiced' : t—d; p—b; k—g; f—v. The following is a list of voiceless and corresponding voiced consonants :

| Voiceless : | č | ć | f | k | p | s | š | t |
|---|---|---|---|---|---|---|---|---|
| Voiced : | dž | đ | v | g | b | z | ž | d |

Consonant groups containing two or more of these consonants will nearly always consist of either all voiceless or all voiced consonants, unless one of the consonants is *f* or *v*. A voiceless consonant immediately preceding a voiced consonant becomes voiced, and a voiced consonant immediately preceding a voiceless consonant becomes voiceless; i.e. the first of a pair of two consonants must change, if necessary, in order that both shall be either voiced or voiceless. You will often notice this change in prepositional prefixes, e.g. *iz-* has become *is-* in *isterati* (to drive out), and *pod-* is *pot-* in *potpisati* (to sign). (The prefix *pred* is an exception, e.g. *predstaviti*— to introduce.)

The adjective *težak* therefore has fem. *teška*, neut. *teško ;* *sladak* has fem. *slatka*, neut. *slatko*; the noun *redak* (row, line) has gen. sing. *retka*, and the adjective *redak* (rare, sparse) has fem. *retka*. In these words the change has become necessary because a 'moveable *a*' has dropped.

Exercise : Give the feminine of nizak, gladak, and the genitive singular of vrabac (sparrow), Šabac (a town in Serbia). All these words have a 'moveable *a*' in their second syllable.

*D* and *t* usually disappear before *c*, *č*, and *dž* : the genitive singular of *otac* and *sudac* (judge), in each of which a ' moveable *a* ' will have dropped, are *oca* and *suca*.

When a ' moveable *a* ' drops from an adjective whose masc. sing. ends -*stan*, the *t* also drops : bolestan (ill), fem. bolesna.

Exercise : Give the nom. pl. of the following nouns, which have a ' moveable *a* ' in their last syllable : početak (beginning), ostatak (remainder) ; and the feminine of : radostan (joyful), žalostan (sad), koristan (useful).

## Disappearance of *l* at the End of Words, and More Notes on ' Moveable *a* '

In most words which originally ended -*l*, this consonant has become -*o*, as in *beo* (white), *ceo* (whole)—originally *bel*, *cel*.[1] This change has only taken place in those forms of the word which would otherwise end -*l*, i.e. in the masculine nominative singular, and in the masculine accusative singular of an adjective qualifying an ' inanimate ' noun ; thus the genitive singular of these adjectives is *belog(a)*, *celog(a)* ; fem. sing. *bela*, *cela*, etc.

Where this final -*l* was preceded by the vowel *o*, the *l* has only dropped, as in *sto* (table), declined : *sto, stola, stolu*, etc. ; plural *stolovi*.

As certain groups of consonants are not tolerated in Serbo-Croat at the end of words, in some words a ' moveable *a* ' separates a final -*l* from a consonant immediately preceding it ; this *a* remains even when the *l* has become *o*, as in *posao* (job, masc.), declined : *posao, posla, poslu*, etc. ; plural *poslovi*. The feminine noun *misao* (thought), which had similarly ended in the consonant -*l*, is declined like *stvar* : *misao, misli, misli, misao, misli, misli (mišlju), misli* ; plural *misli*, etc.

In adjectives such as *topao* (warm), again the final -*o*

[1] In the *ije*-dialect the nominative masculine singular of these and some similar words may end -*io* or -*ijel*, e.g. *bio, bijel*.

represents an earlier *-l*, and the *a* is ' moveable '. The genitive of the masculine singular is therefore *toplog(a)* ; nom. fem. sing. *topla*, etc.

It may now be understood why the active past participle, masculine singular, ends *-o*, instead of *-l* (masc. *imao*, fem. *imala*), and why the ' moveable *a* ' is sometimes inserted before this *o* (*mogao, mogla*, from *moči*).

In a few words the same change has taken place at the end of a syllable which is not the final syllable ; hence *čitalac* (reader) has genitive singular *čitaoca*, and nom. plural *čitaoci* ; but genitive plural *čitalaca* (see Lesson VI).

Exercise : Decline : veseo (like *beo*) ; vo (ox—like *sto*) ; prevodilac (translator—like *čitalac*).

Concerning the consonant groups which are not tolerated at the end of words it is hardly possible to give definite rules as to which these are, but a good dictionary gives where necessary the genitive singular as well as the nominative singular of masculine nouns, and the masculine and feminine nominative singular of adjectives, and thus shows whether an *a* in the final syllable of the nominative singular of these words is ' moveable ' or not, e.g. *vetar* (wind), gen. *vetra ; tužan* (sad), fem. *tužna*.

Notice the monosyllables such as *pas* (dog, plural *psi*) and *san* (sleep, dream, plural *snovi*), in which the *a* is ' moveable '. ' In a dream ' is *u snu*.

## VOCABULARY

biftek—steak

brinuti se, brinem se (ipf.)— to be anxious

činiti (ipf.)—to do

državni—concerned with the State

đak—schoolboy, pupil

francuski—French

kapak, gen. kapka—shutter

korak—step, stride

miting—meeting

odlazak, gen. odlaska—departure

odličan, fem. odlična—excellent

oštar, fem. oštra—sharp

pekmez—jam

prepoznati, prepoznam (pf.) —to recognise

prihvatiti—to accept

radost (f.)—joy, pleasure

razlog—reason

uspeh—success

vojska—army

Read and translate : 1. Njegovi razlozi su bili dobri, i radnici su ih prihvatili s radošću. 2. Zašto niste rekli majci da je njena sestra bolesna ? Bojala sam se da će se brinuti. 3. Vojnici su prešli preko mosta brzim koracima. 4. — Zbogom, oče — rekla je Marija i izišla žalosno iz sobe. 5. U kojoj knjizi ste videli retke slike iz Jugoslavije ? 6. Naši psi vole da se kupaju u reci samo kad je voda topla. 7. Pitam se da li je zadovoljna svojim najnovijim uspesima. 8. Da li će razgovarati o državnim poslovima na mitinzima ? 9. Prevodioci francuskih romana imaju dosta posla, jer ima (there are) mnogo čitalaca za takve knjige. 10. Vojniče, da li ste našli svoje ime u ovim člancima ? 11. Počeci svih zadataka su dosta teški. 12. Više volim da sečem hleb oštrijim nožem. 13. Kapci na ovim prozorima nisu dosta jaki ; već su slomljeni. 14. Šta će činiti ovi siromasi posle odlaska vašeg dobrog oca ? 15. Imamo dva stola, ali samo pet stolica : gde će svi đaci sedeti ?

Translate : 1. Your reasons aren't clear to me. 2. The steaks which we ate in that restaurant were excellent. 3. In that poem you read about a cottage with green shutters. 4. He always speaks at these meetings with the greatest courage. 5. Will you give something to these poor men ? They're ill. 6. ' Good morning, Colonel,' I said to him as soon as I saw him. 7. Is the wound on her arm or leg ? 8. You won't be able to recognise her in the picture in this book. 9. He came into the room with rapid strides. 10. The soldiers in their army are all very strong men. 11. There were [1] many readers in the library, and their books were lying on all the tables. 12. We live in Šabac now and rarely return to Belgrade. 13. 'Father,' he said, 'is this mother's ticket or yours?' 14. This jam is called *slatko* in Serbo-Croat because it is very sweet. 15. Do you think that these sentences have been very difficult?

1. There were—*bilo je.*

## LESSON XIX

## THE CONDITIONAL.  LETTER WRITING

Corresponding to both ' I should (*or* would) read' and
' I should (*or* would) have read', Serbo-Croat has only *ja bih
čitao*—composed of the aorist tense of *biti* [1] and the active
past participle of *čitati*. The full forms of the aorist of *biti*
are :

(ja) bih (literally ' I was ', ' I have been ')
(ti) bi
(on, ona, ono) bi
(mi) bismo
(vi) biste
(oni, one, ona) biše

Shorter forms of this tense are often used in forming the
conditional, just as shorter forms of auxiliary verbs are used
in forming the compound past tense and the future tense ;
though the restrictions applied to the use of the full forms of
these auxiliary verbs are not applied to the use of the full
forms of *bih*, etc. The short forms are alike for almost every
person : bih, bi, bi, bi, bi, bi.

The Conditional is, then, usually :

| | |
|---|---|
| ja bih čitao (čitala) | *or* čitao (čitala) bih |
| ti bi čitao (čitala) | čitao (čitala) bi |
| on bi čitao | čitao bi |
| ona bi čitala | čitala bi |
| ono bi čitalo | čitalo bi |

---

[1] Apart from this use of the aorist of *biti* you will not need to use
the aorist tense.

mi bismo (*or* bi) čitali (čitale)   čitali (čitale) bismo (*or* bi)
vi biste (*or* bi) čitali (čitale)   čitali (čitale) biste (*or* bi)
oni bi čitali                        čitali bi
one bi čitale                        čitale bi
ona bi čitala                        čitala bi

A question is usually introduced by *da li* if no other interrogative word introduces it : da li bih bio ?—should I be ? (*or* should I have been ?) ; da li bi (ona) čitala ?—would she read ? (*or* have read ?) ; koliko bi (*or* biste) platili ?—how much would you pay ? (*or* have paid ?) ; ko bi to verovao ?—who would have believed it ?

The negative is : ja ne bih čitao *or* ne bih čitao—I should not read (*or* I should not have read) ; oni ne bi bili *or* ne bi bili—they would not be (*or* they would not have been).

As shown before, questions in the negative form are often introduced by *zar* (instead of *da li*)—a conjunction which suggests a note of surprise : zar ne bi vaš sin prihvatio poziv ?—wouldn't your son really accept the invitation ? zar ne bi došao ?—do you mean to say he wouldn't come ?

The short forms of the aorist of *biti* are enclitic, and the rules of word order applying to other enclitic verbs apply here too : ja bih mu ga dala—I (f.) would give it to him ; ja mu ga ne bih dala—I wouldn't give it to him (although *ne* and *bih* are separate words the word order is the same as for sentences containing *nisam* and *neću*) ; on bi mi ga dao—he would give it to me ; on mi ga ne bi dao—he wouldn't give it to me.

The appropriate imperfective and perfective aspects of the verb are, of course, used in the conditional : on bi došao (pf.) možda jedanput, ali ne bi dolazio (ipf.) često—he would come perhaps once, but he wouldn't come often ; ona bi pročitala (pf.) kratku pripovetku, ali ne bi čitala (ipf.) romane—she would read a short story, but she wouldn't read novels.

The conditional may be used, as in English, to denote repeated or habitual action: on bi govorio celo vreme—he would talk the whole time.

The request: Would you...? is generally 'hoćete li...?' with an infinitive (or *da* and the present tense): would you pass me a roll?—hoćete li mi pružiti zemičku? But one may also use the conditional: da li biste zatvorili prozor?—would you close the window? *Da* followed by the conditional may mean 'in order that': došao je da bi razgovarao s njom—he came in order that he might talk with her.

### VOCABULARY

poznati, poznam (pf.)—to
   know, recognise
slagati se, slažem se (ipf.)—
   to agree

strašno—frightfully
više voleti, volim (ipf.)—to
   prefer
zauzet—occupied, busy

Translate: 1. Ja ne bih želeo da idem s njim. 2. Da li bismo videli more sa vašeg prozora? Bismo. 3. On bi bio veseliji u Parizu. 4. Da li bih mogla putovati brzim vozom? 5. Ja ga ne bih poznao. 6. Bilo bi bolje da ostanemo u ovom hotelu. 7. Zar ne bi pristao da čeka nekoliko minuta? 8. Znam da se ne bi slagala s ovim predlozima. 9. Da li biste vi verovali ono što mi je kazao? Bih. 10. Mogla bih da ga pozovem, ali da li bi došao? Ne bi.

1. You wouldn't be able to hear his voice. 2. They would like to stay there. 3. I know that she would not come. 4. He would learn more quickly, but he's very busy. 5 Would you prefer to write to me? 6. I'd never speak to him again. 7. I really couldn't carry that bag; it's frightfully heavy. 8. You wouldn't recognise her in her new coat. 9. I wouldn't agree with his suggestion. 10. Would you tell the doctor your name, please?

### CONDITIONAL CLAUSES

In order to decide what tense to use in a clause introduced
by 'if', it is necessary to distinguish between 'real' and
'unreal' conditions. A 'real' condition expresses something
which actually may happen, or may have happened : I'll see
him if he has come (it is implied that he may or may not have
come) ; I'd see him if he should come (he may or may not
come). An 'unreal' condition is purely hypothetical : I
should see him if he were here (implying that he isn't) ;
I should have seen him if he had come (implying that he had
not come).

The tense of the verb of the main clause, or first part, of
each of the above sentences will be the same as in English.

'If' when introducing a 'real' condition is *ako*, and the
tense of the verb in this clause will be the same as in English.

'If' when introducing an 'unreal' condition is *da*, and the
tense of the verb in this clause will be either the present tense
or the compound past tense, according to the sense.

The sentences given above are, then :

'Real' condition : Videću ga, ako je došao.

           Video bih ga, ako bi došao.

'Unreal' condition : Video bih ga, da je ovde.

           Video bih ga, da je došao.

'If' may be *kad* followed by the conditional in the 'if-
clause' of an 'unreal' condition with a present meaning :
pevao bih kad bih imao lep glas—I'd sing if I had [1] a nice
voice (*or* pevao bih, da imam lep glas).

When the present tense with a future meaning is used in
English in the 'if-clause' of a 'real' condition the future
perfect tense (see p. 134) is generally used in Serbo-Croat :
I'll see him if he comes : videću ga ako bude došao.

Notice that an 'unreal' condition may be negative : I'd be

---

[1] See footnote 1, p. 120.

happier if she weren't [1] here : bio bih srećniji da nije ona ovde.

When English ' if ' means ' whether ', *da li* must be used : do you know if he will come ? Znate li da li će doći ?

## VOCABULARY

društvo—society, company
poziv—invitation
poznanik—acquaintance
pozvati, pozovem (pf.)—to invite
preseliti se (pf.)—to move house

produžiti (pf.)—to go on, continue
rado—gladly
sneg—snow
šiti, šijem (ipf.)—to sew
zar ne ?—isn't it so ?

Read and translate : 1. Zar ne bi bilo bolje da pođemo na stanicu da je dočekamo ? 2. Vi biste želeli pivo, zar ne ? 3. Da ste došli na vreme, čuli biste početak predavanja. 4. Preselili smo se u Zagreb, da bismo bili sa svojim poznanicima tamo. 5. Ako se vaš otac slaže s ovim predlozima, onda je sve u redu. 6. Turisti su se popeli na vrh brda da bi videli more. 7. Dok je ona šila on bi joj čitao naglas. 8. Ako bi sutra pao sneg ostao bih kod kuće. 9. Da ne bi opet morao ručati blizu takvog društva, koje samo nedeljom dolazi, on je danas ostavio varoš.[2] 10. Da sam primio vaše pismo ne bih očekivao da ćete doći.

Translate : 1. If you come you'll certainly see him. 2. If he were here with us I know that he wouldn't want to return to London. 3. If the train is quicker why did you travel by car ? 4. She would certainly understand him better if she were to see him more often. 5. I'd like to listen (' I would gladly listen ') if his voice were more beautiful. 6. We should arrive at the river if we went on by this road. 7. Would you have

---

[1] These English verbs are only *apparently* past tenses : in fact they are subjunctives, and as they have a present meaning the Serbo-Croatian verb must be in the present tense.

[2] Quoted from the Serbian writer Ljubomir Nenadović.

accepted the invitation if you had believed that her son was ill ? 8. You would have been very tired if you had been with us. 9. If she comes please will you call me ? 10. If you knew what I read in the paper this morning !

## LETTER WRITING

A letter beginning in English ' Dear John ', ' Dear Father ', ' Dear Mr. Petrović ', ' Dear Mrs. Pavlović ', will begin similarly in Serbo-Croat: ' Dragi Jovane,' ' Dragi oče,' ' Dragi gospodine Petroviću,' ' Draga gospođo Pavlović.' (Remember to use the vocative case.) Concluding a letter, ' Voli te ' or ' Voli Vas ' (followed by your signature, which may be preceded by *Vaš* or *Vaša*) corresponds to ' Yours affectionately '. Slightly more formal is ' Srdačno Vas pozdravlja Vaš (*or* Vaša) ' or ' Mnogo srdačnih pozdrava ', followed by your signature. These mean ' Cordially greets you, Your . . . ' and ' Many cordial greetings '. Notice that in letters *Vi, Vas,* and *Vam(a)* are written with initial capital letters. Writing to someone whom you do not know very well, or to whom you would like to convey your special esteem, you will begin : ' Poštovani gospodine Petroviću,' ' Poštovana gospođo Pavlović.' In business letters the surname is omitted : ' Poštovani Gospodine,' ' Poštovana Gospođo.' Such letters may end : ' S poštovanjem '—' With respect.'

## VOCABULARY

okup—gathering (na okupu— assembled)

porodica—family

potvrditi (pf.)—to confirm

praznik—holiday

prihvatati (ipf.)—to accept

provesti, provedem, proveo (pf.)—to spend (time)

rezervacija—reservation

Uskrs—Easter

uz—up, along, along with, besides (with acc.)

večera—supper, dinner

zadovoljstvo—satisfaction, pleasure

zahvalan, zahvalna—grateful

zahvaljivati, zahvaljujem (ipf.)—to thank

Read and translate :

Dragi gospodine Petroviću,

Zahvaljujem Vam na pismu i pozivu da provedem sa Vama i Vašom porodicom nedelju dana o Uskrsu. Prihvatam poziv sa velikim zadovoljstvom. Poći ću u petak, u 3.30 posle podne. Biću kod Vas oko 6 sati. Bio bih Vam zahvalan ako biste poslali Jovana da me dočeka na stanici, jer ću imati mnogo prtljaga.

Nadam se da će cela porodica biti na okupu o praznicima.

Srdačno Vas pozdravlja,
Milan Popović.

Direktoru hotela ,, Dalmacija ",
Dubrovnik.

Poštovani Gospodine,

Molim Vas da rezervirate sobu sa dva kreveta u Vašem hotelu za moju ženu i mene. Ostaćemo u Dubrovniku od 2-og do 23-eg jula. Uz sobu želimo doručak i večeru, a nedeljom i ručak.

Biću Vam zahvalan ako potvrdite ovu rezervaciju što pre.

S poštovanjem,
Jovan Jovanović.

# LESSON XX

## THE IMPERATIVE AND PROHIBITIONS. FURTHER NOTES ON NOUN DECLENSIONS

IMPERATIVE

The imperative is formed by adding endings of the following two types to the stem of the present tense :

Type 1 : -j          Type 2 : -i     (2nd person singular)
         -jmo                 -imo    (1st person plural)
         -jte                 -ite    (2nd person plural)

Endings of Type 1 are taken by verbs with the vowel *a* in the endings of the present tense, and by verbs in which the stem of the present tense ends -*j* : i.e. these endings are taken by all verbs with the present tense ending (1st person singular) -*am*, -*jim*, or -*jem* :

pevam (I sing) :  pevaj !—sing (thou) !  pevajmo !—let's
                    sing !  pevajte !—sing !
pijem (I drink) :  pij !  pijmo !  pijte !
čujem (I hear) :  čuj !  čujmo !  čujte !

All other verbs take the endings of Type 2 :

govorim (I speak) :  govori !  govorimo !  govorite !
pišem (I write) :    piši !  pišimo !  pišite !

The *n* of the present ending -*nem* sometimes drops in the imperative, e.g. sednem (I sit down) : sedi !  sedimo !  sedite !
Note the following imperative forms, in which the consonant changes explained in Lesson XVIII have taken place :

reci ! (recimo, recite)—say !  vuci !—pull !  lezi !—lie down !
pomozi ! (from pomoći, pomognem, pomogao, pomogla)—help !

The imperative of *biti* (to be) is :  budi, budimo, budite.

Exercise: Give the imperative of: dati (pres. dam), uzeti (uzmem), voziti (vozim), verovati (verujem), kazati (kažem), čekati (čekam).

The 1st person sing. and pl. of the present tense preceded by the conjunction *da* may also have the sense of an imperative: da vidim!—let me see! da sednemo!—let's sit down!

The 3rd person singular or plural of the present tense preceded by *neka* also expresses an imperative: neka ostane ovde—he's to stay here, *or* let him stay here; neka čekaju— they're to wait, *or* let them wait.

The imperative of the verb *pustiti* may be used in similar sentences: pustite ga da govori—let him speak.

The appropriate aspect of the verb must be used in the imperative, e.g. 'skinite kapu' (pf.) means 'take off your cap' (once); 'skidajte kapu' (ipf.) means 'take off your cap' (generally, always, regularly).

Exercise: Translate: let's go; let them sing; let us hear; let me write; he's to sit down; let him wait.

As shown in the previous chapter, the 2nd person, singular or plural, of the present tense of the verb *hteti*, followed by the interrogative particle *li* and an infinitive, expresses a request: hoćeš li doći?—wilt thou come? hoćete li mi dati tu knjigu?—will you give me that book?

## PROHIBITIONS

There are two ways of expressing a prohibition.

The imperative may be preceded by *ne*: ne govori!—don't speak!

Or (a less abrupt prohibition) the verb *nemoj, nemojmo, nemojte*, corresponding to the English 'don't (thou), 'let's not', 'don't (you)', may be used, followed (as in English) by an infinitive: nemoj trčati!—don't run! nemojmo misliti o tome—let's not think about that ; nemojte gledati !—don't look !

The aspect of the verb in prohibitions is usually imperfective. Common exceptions are zaboraviti and dopustiti.

Exercise : Form brief prohibitions with the following verbs : ići, govoriti, učiti, zaboraviti, doći, svirati (to play an instrument).

## FURTHER NOTES ON NOUN DECLENSIONS

Nouns with the ending *-in*, denoting men of certain nationalities, professions, and other categories, drop this ending in the plural before adding the plural endings : građanin (citizen), pl. građani.

Exercise : Decline : Srbin (a Serb), Ciganin (a gypsy), Beograđanin (a native of Belgrade).

*Oko* (eye) and *uho* or *uvo* (ear) are neuter in the singular, and declined like *selo*, but their plurals, *oči* and *uši*, are feminine and declined as follows : oči, očiju, očima, oči, oči, očima, očima.

## VOCABULARY

ćutati, ćutim (ipf.)—to be silent

eto !—there ! (voila !)

grbača—spine

jastuk—cushion, pillow

k, ka—to, towards (with dat.)

kajati se, kajem se (ipf.)—to regret

koleno—knee

mir—peace

nazeb—cold in the head

nemoguće—impossible

nezavisan, nezavisna—independent

odjednom—suddenly

odsečno—abruptly, curtly

oglas—announcement, personal advertisement

paziti (ipf.)—to take care, pay attention

plemenit—noble

pogreška—mistake

pokloniti se (pf.)—to bow
pomalo—a little
poslušati (pf.)—to listen; obey
predlagati, predlažem (ipf.)—
  to suggest
predložiti (pf.)—to suggest
pričati (ipf.)—to tell, relate
razbijati, razbijam (ipf.)—to
  break, smash
razbiti, razbijem (pf.)—to
  break, smash
savet—advice
saviti, savijem (pf.)—to bend
skidati (ipf.), skinuti, skinem
  (pf.)—to take off, remove

smetati (ipf.)—to disturb
  (with dat.)
smeti, smem (ipf.)—to dare,
  be allowed
spreman, spremna—ready,
  prepared
stalno—constantly
tužiti se (ipf.)—to complain
vladalac (gen. vladaoca)—
  ruler
zaboleti, zaboli (pf.)—to hurt,
  begin to ache
zaseban, zasebna—separate
život—life

Read and translate :

1. Molim vas, hoćete li mi pružiti taj jastuk ? Hvala. Sada budite dobri pa sedite mirno i čitajte ; nemojte govoriti, jer sam vrlo zauzeta ; verujte mi, imam mnogo posla danas. Slušajte ! Mislim da je gospođica Ilić napolju. Otvorite vrata : neka uđe. Dobar dan, gospođice ! Dođite k meni. Hoćete li sesti ovde ? Pazite, to je moja knjiga. Sad ćutite dok ja pišem, a posle pričajte mi sve što ste činili danas.

2. Poslušajte me ! Budite miran građanin, skidajte kapu svakom koji je ma i malo [1] viši od vas ; naučite da se i dublje poklonite ; naučite se da pomalo i kolena savijete, pa kad vas grbača zaboli [2] nemojte se tužiti, već [3] kažite svakom da je to od nazeba. Velikim ljudima nemojte istinu u oči [4] govoriti, a najmanje smete tu pogrešku učiniti prema vladaocima i ženama. Budite uvek spremni da kažete vladaocu da je plemenit, i ženi da je lepa. U novinama čitajte samo oglase. Eto, to vam je moj savet, radite tako i vi se nećete kajati.

(Branislav Nušić.)

1. ma i malo—even only a little. 2. . . . kad vas grbača zaboli. *Boleti* (ipf.) and *zaboleti* (pf.) take the accusative case : boli me glava—my head aches ; boli me zub—I have toothache. 3. *već* or *nego* (' but ') are used when a strong contrast of ideas is presented, and usually follow a negative, e.g. neću biti u hotelu nego u svojoj kući. 4. . . . u oči—' to their face '.

Translate :

' Tell me,' I said to her. ' Is life more peaceful for you [1] now that you live with the colonel's wife ? '

' No,' she replied abruptly. ' Listen. Would you say that life was peaceful if you lived with a woman who is constantly telling you : do this ; don't do that ; bring me my book ; shut the door ; don't forget that the cat is in the garden ; let me see what you're reading ; don't forget to go to the post office [2] this afternoon ; pass me my cigarettes, please ; take care—don't smash that cup ? It's worst of all [3] when she suddenly says : " Talk to me ! " What would you do if you were in my place ? ' [2]

' I don't know. I'd probably say : " If you want me to stay in this house give me a separate room, where I can work in peace,[2] and please don't disturb me when I want to study." '

' But what shall I do if she answers : " All right, if you're not contented here, go ! " ? '

' Be independent. Look for a flat for yourself and leave her.'

' Don't suggest that. You know that it's impossible.'

1. For you : dative (without preposition). 2. The preposition *na* is used with *pošta*, *mesto*, and *mir*. 3. It's worst of all : najgore je.

# LESSON XXI

## PASSIVE PARTICIPLES AND VERBAL NOUNS

Passive participles are used less often than in English because the passive voice is less used. Where in English one might say : ' the man was bitten by the dog ' it would be more natural in Serbo-Croat to put it : ' the dog bit the man '—though the order of the nouns might be the same as in the English sentence : čoveka je ujeo pas. As *čoveka* has the accusative ending there can be no doubt as to which bit which. We have also noted (p. 79) that a verb may be used reflexively where the passive voice is used in English.

But passive participles do frequently occur, and many are in such common use that they may be regarded as adjectives. All are declined like adjectives, agreeing with the noun to which they refer ; and the past tense is often already implicit in the participle itself ; so that whereas in English one says : I *was* born, Serbo-Croat has : Ja *sam* rođen (m.) *or* rođena (f.).

Passive participles are formed from the infinitive stem of verbs of either aspect.

Most verbs with infinitive ending *-ati* have passive participle ending *-an* :

pisati : pisan, pisana, pisano—written.
zvati : zvan, zvana, zvano—called.
pozvati : pozvan, pozvana, pozvano—invited.
opravdati : opravdan, etc.—justified.

Most verbs with infinitive ending *-iti* and *-eti* have passive participle ending *-jen* ; the consonant *j* ' softens ' the final consonant of the stem :

učiniti : učinjen, učinjena, učinjeno—done.
slomiti : slomljen, etc.—broken.

hvaliti : hvaljen, etc.—praised.
kazniti : kažnjen, etc.—punished.
videti : viđen, etc.—seen.

Verbs with infinitive ending -*ti* preceded by a consonant
have passive participle ending -*en* :

krasti (from *krad-ti*) : kraden [1]—stolen.
peći (from *pek-ti*) : pečen [2]—baked.

Verbs with infinitive ending -*nuti* have passive participle
ending -*nut* :

podignuti : podignut, podignuta, podignuto—raised ;
prekinuti : prekinut—interrupted.

Verbs with infinitive ending -*eti* and present -*mem* or -*nem*
have passive participle ending -*et* :

preduzeti (to undertake ; pres. preduzmem) : preduzet,
etc.—undertaken.
prokleti (to curse ; pres. prokunem) : proklet, etc.—
accursed.

Give the passive participles of : kuvati (to cook), slikati (to
paint, take photo), brijati, prihvatiti, pustiti (see p. 110),
svršiti, voleti, plesti (to plait, knit, from *plet-ti* [1]), seći (from
*sek-ti*),[2] naviknuti (to accustom),[3] početi.

The five groups given above represent the commonest forms
of passive participle ; but some exceptions to these rules
should be noted. Verbs with infinitive ending like *prostreti*
(or *prostrti*)—to spread, usually have passive participle ending
-*t* : *prostrt, prostrta, prostrto*. Verbs whose infinitive consists
of two syllables, or of two syllables preceded by a prepositional

---

[1] The present tense (kradem, pletem) gives the clue to the consonant which formerly preceded the infinitive -*ti* ending.
[2] See p. 109 (Lesson XVIII).
[3] Followed by *na* and the accusative case : to accustom (somebody)
to . . .

prefix, vary; e.g. *čuti*—to hear—has *čuven* (which has acquired the meaning of 'famous'); *dati* has *dan*, but *prodati*—to sell—may have *prodat* or *prodan*, and *udati* (se)—to marry (of a woman)—has *udata* : ona je udata—she is married (c.f. ona se udala—she got married); *liti*—to pour—has *lit*, *lijen* or *liven*, and *viti*—to wind—has *vit* or *vijen* : *razviti*—to develop : *razvijen*. A good dictionary will give the passive participles which are in common use.

Verbal nouns are formed from passive participles by suffixing -*je* to the masculine form, when the usual 'softening' of the preceding consonant will take place : zvanje—calling, vocation ; opravdanje—justification ; do viđenja—au revoir ('until the seeing'); preduzeće—undertaking, enterprise. You will not often need to form verbal nouns yourself, as you will find them in the dictionary, but this will help you to recognise them.

## VOCABULARY

(Note : new words occurring in these and subsequent reading passages taken from Yugoslav authors which are not given in the individual vocabularies will be found in the General Vocabulary, p. 187.)

boja—colour
cipela—shoe
crven—red
divan—couch, divan
fini—fine
Francuskinja—Frenchwoman
kakav, kakva—some kind of (in questions : what kind of ?)

kao—as
končić (diminutive of *konac*) —little thread
kosa—(head of) hair
marama—scarf
nemati—not to have (negative of imati) [1]
ni—not even
obojiti (pf.)—to dye

[1] Used only in the infinitive and the present tense. In compound tenses *imati* with a negative auxiliary verb must be used.

obrve (f. pl.)—eyebrows
osim—except, besides (with gen.)
postaviti (pf.)—to put, place
prebaciti (pf.)—to throw across
predsednik—president
preko—across (with gen.)

sazidati (pf.)—to build
sem (see *osim*)
rukavica—glove
ukrasti, ukradem, ukrao, ukrala (pf.)—to steal
upravnik—director, manager
vešt—skilful
zidati (ipf.)—to build

Read and translate :

1. Hteo sam posetiti ministra pravde, ali on nije bio u zemlji. Otišao je u inostranstvo da proučava škole za gluvonemu decu.[1] Kako ta stvar, kao vrlo važna, nije mogla trpeti odlaganja, odmah su preduzeti najnužniji koraci. Sem toga što je poslat ministar pravde da proučava uređenje takvih škola, sa vrlo velikim dodatkom uz platu, odmah je postavljen upravnik škola a već je početo zidanje velike zgrade koja je namenjena za stan upravnikov.

Radoje Domanović (1873–1908).

[1] See p. 140.

2. U vrhu sale, na jednom uzvišenom divanu, između dva velika prozora, kao kakav predsednik, jedna mlada Francuskinja prebacila je nogu preko noge i sedi. Sve su[1] haljine na njoj crvene. Rukavice, marama, cipele : sve je od najcrvenije boje. Nakit na glavi, oko vrata, na rukama, samo su fini crveni korali. Nijednoga končića što se [2] na njoj vidi nema [3] od druge boje. Osim toga, njena lepa kosa i obrve obojene su najfinijom crvenkastom bojom tako vešto, da bi svaki rekao da je s takvom kosom rođena.

Ljubomir Nenadović (1826–95). Adapted.

1. The enclitic form of the present tense of ' to be ' is sometimes placed between an adjective and noun occurring at the beginning of a sentence. This need not be imitated. 2. See p. 79. 3. The genitive is generally used with *nema*— ' there isn't ', ' there aren't '.

Translate : 1. Were your gloves always (of) this colour ? No, they're dyed. 2. He was born on the 5th November, 1920. 3. I believe these things have been stolen. 4. Don't look at this picture : it isn't finished. 5. I found five broken cups in this cupboard ; do you know who broke them ? 6. He has been sent abroad to study the organisation of the best hotels. 7. Have the most necessary steps already been taken (say ' undertaken ') ? 8. The houses on the coast aren't built yet ; building hasn't even been begun. 9. Au revoir, Mr. Petrović ; we'll see each other tomorrow. 10. If they have been invited to lunch with your parents will you go too ?

# LESSON XXII

## OTHER TENSES. THE VERBS *TREBATI* AND *MORATI*. SOME IMPERSONAL EXPRESSIONS

The Aorist

This tense is seldom used in the spoken language, but writers often use it in narrative. It is a past tense denoting a completed action, and verbs in the aorist are therefore usually perfective. It is formed by adding the following endings to the infinitive stem:

|            | Singular | Plural |
|------------|----------|--------|
| 1st person | -h       | -smo   |
| 2nd ,,     | -        | -ste   |
| 3rd ,,     | -        | -še    |

The vowel preceding the -*ti* ending of the infinitive of the verb will take the place of the dashes, e.g. (from *pisati*) pisah (I wrote, I have written), pisa, pisa, pisasmo, pisaste, pisaše; (from *početi*) počeh, poče, poče, počesmo, počeste, počeše; (from *učiti*) učih, uči, uči, učismo, učiste, učiše; (from *čuti*) čuh, ču, ču, čusmo, čuste, čuše. When the -*ti* ending of the infinitive is preceded by a consonant, as in krasti (from *krad-ti*), plesti (from *plet-ti*), tresti, to shake (from *tres-ti*), seći (from *sek-ti*), moći (from *mog-ti*),[1] the vowel o is supplied before all the aorist endings, but the 2nd and 3rd person singular end -*e*: kradoh, krade, krade, kradosmo, kradoste, kradoše. The consonant changes k to č, g to ž, h to š explained

---

[1] The final consonant of the stem of infinitives ending -*sti* with present tense -*dem* or -*tem* (krasti, kradem; plesti, pletem) were originally *d* or *t* respectively; that of infinitives ending -*sti* with present tense -*sem* (tresti, tresem) was *s*. The consonant ending the stem of the 3rd person plural of the present tense of verbs with infinitive ending -*ći* was originally that of the infinitive: seći, pres. sečem, sečeš, seče, sečemo, sečete, *seku* (see p. 109).

on p. 109 will take place in the 2nd and 3rd person singular of the aorist of these verbs, i.e. before the vowel *e* : sekoh, seče, seče, sekosmo, sekoste, sekoše. Some verbs with infinitive ending *-ati*, e.g. *imati, znati, ostati, morati*, have alternative aorist forms : imadoh, imade ; znadoh, znade, etc. *Dati* has only *dadoh, dade*, etc., and *hteti* has only *htedoh, htede*, etc. *Ići* has aorist *idoh, ide*, etc., but forms of this verb with a prepositional prefix which ends in a vowel, e.g. *ući, naći*, have aorist endings of the type *uđoh, uđe ; nađoh, nađe*.

## THE IMPERFECT

This tense must be mentioned although it is very rarely used now, either in literature or in the spoken language. Verbs with infinitive ending *-ati* add the following personal endings to the infinitive stem : -ah, -aše, -aše, -asmo, -aste, -ahu, e.g. (from *pisati*) : pisah (I was writing), pisaše, etc. These are the endings for the imperfect tense of all verbs ; but where verbs have infinitive ending *-iti, -eti, -uti* the endings of the imperfect tense are preceded by *j*, which ' softens ' a preceding consonant, e.g. (from *nositi*) nošah, nošaše, etc. ; and verbs having the infinitive stem ending in a consonant have imperfect tense endings *ijah*, etc. ; e.g. (from *plesti*, originally *plet-ti*) : pletijah, pletijaše, etc. Here the consonant changes *k* to *c*, *g* to *z* and *h* to *s* take place before the vowel *i*, e.g. peći (*pek-ti*) has imperfect tense *pecijah, pecijaše*, etc. The imperfect of *biti* is : bejah or beh, beše, beše, besmo, beste, behu ; and of ići : iđah, iđaše, etc.

## THE FUTURE PERFECT

A compound tense formed from the perfective present tense of *biti* (to be) : budem, budeš, etc., and the active past participle is used to express an action preceding another which is in the future tense, e.g. kad bude došao u London on će vas videti : when he comes (will have come) to London he will see you.

### Morati and Trebati

*Morati* means 'to be obliged', 'to have (to)', and may be followed by *da* and the present tense, or by the infinitive : moram da se žurim—I must hurry ; moram priznati—I must admit ; morao sam da idem na poštu—I had to go to the post ; moraću ostati ovde—I'll have to stay here ; morao bih da predam prtljag—I'd have to register the luggage. The negative, *ne moram*, means 'I need not' : ne mora da mu kaže sve što je čuo—he needn't tell him everything he has heard.

*Trebati* means 'to be necessary', and is generally used as an impersonal verb, i.e. with the pronoun 'it' understood as its subject : treba da idem—it's necessary that I go (I must go) ; treba mi dve poštanske marke—I need two stamps. The negative, *ne treba*, usually means 'it's wrong to', e.g. ne treba krasti—one mustn't steal. (' It's not necessary ' is ' nije potrebno '.) The conditional, *trebalo bi*, usually means '. . . ought to . . .', e.g. sada bi trebalo da tražite nekoga koji bi razgovarao s vama na srpskohrvatskom—now you ought to look for someone who would talk with you in Serbo-Croat. The compound past tense, *trebalo je*, usually means '. . . ought to have . . .', e.g. trebalo je da mi pišu unapred—they ought to have written to me beforehand ; nije trebalo to da uradite—you ought not to have done that. The active past participle will of course always be neuter singular.

### Other Impersonal Expressions

*Valja,* another verb used impersonally, means 'it's worth while', or sometimes 'it's right' : valja učiti strane jezike—it's a good thing to study foreign languages. *Ne valja* has the same meaning as *ne treba* : ne valja to da kažete—you ought not to say that ; whereas *ne vredi* (also impersonal) means 'it's not worth while' : ne vredi da dođete—it's not worth while for you to come.

Other impersonal expressions are : žao mi je što—I'm sorry
that ; šteta je što—it's a pity that ; milo (or drago) mi je što—
I'm glad that. (The conjunction *što* is often used instead of *da*
after expressions of emotion : žalim što—I'm sorry that ;
radujem se što—I'm pleased that.) Moguće je da—it is
possible that ; verovatno je da—it is probable that ; sme se,
or slobodno je—one may. (*Smeti*, pres. *smem*—to dare, to be
allowed, is also used as a personal verb : da li smem ?—
may I ?)

' I am cold ' is ' zima mi je ' or ' hladno mi je ' (but ' I am
hungry ' is a personal expression : ' gladan sam ').

*Ima*—there is, there are, and *nema*—there isn't, there aren't,
may be used with the genitive singular or plural : ima li
hleba ?—is there any bread ? ; nema mesta—there's no room
(plaće) ; nema pisama—there are no letters. The nominative
singular may also be used after this impersonal *ima* : ima
jedna crkva u **o**vome selu—there's one church in this village ;
ima li stolica za mene ?—is there a chair for me ?

In the past and future tenses, and in the conditional, the
appropriate tenses of *biti* (to be) are generally used impersonally with the sense of ' there was ', ' there will be ', ' there
would be ' : nije bilo hleba, biće hleba, ne bi bilo hleba—
there wasn't any bread, there will be some bread, there
wouldn't be any bread.

## VOCABULARY

balkon—balcony

činovnik—official, clerk

hladan, hladna—cold

inače—otherwise

izgledati (ipf.)—to seem,
  appear

iznenaditi (pf.)—to sur-
  prise

krevet—bed

kucati (ipf.)—to knock, tap

led—ice

mrak—darkness

naglo—suddenly

naočari—spectacles

napred—forward ; come
  in !

neočekivan—unexpected

nos—nose

nositi (ipf.)—to carry, wear

oduševljen—enthusiastic

poručiti (pf.)—to order,
    send for

poseta—visit

stranac (gen. stranca)—
    foreigner

tek što—as soon as, the
    moment that

ugledan, ugledna—distin-
    guished, eminent

upitati (pf.)—to ask

upoznati (pf.)—to recognise

uraditi (pf.)—to do

usna—lip

uzviknuti, uzviknem (pf.)—to
    shout

zakucati (pf.)—to knock, tap

zbuniti (pf.)—to embarrass,
    confuse

zima—cold ; winter

Read and translate :

1. Tek što sam zatvorio vrata za sobom začuh kucanje na vratima.

— Napred ! — rekoh.

U sobu uđe gospodski obučen čovek, s naočarima na nosu. Pokloni se duboko (što i ja, razume se, uradim) i predstavi se kao viši činovnik iz ministarstva.

— Drago mi je ! — rekoh iznenađen ovom neočekivanom posetom.

— Vi ste prvi put sada u našoj zemlji, gospodine ? — upita me.

— Prvi put.

— Vi ste stranac ?.

— Stranac.

— Došli ste nam kao poručeni, verujte ! — uzviknu taj viši činovnik oduševljeno.

Mene to još više zbuni.

(Domanović.  Continued in Lesson XXIV.)

2. (This extract is in the *ije*-dialect.)

Nađoh staricu u velikoj starinskoj postelji.  Ležala je s glavom na jastuku.  Sve je na njoj bilo tužno i umorno, samo su joj se usne smiješile.[1] Kad je pozvah, ona me ne ču. Njena ruka mi se pričini studena kao led. Ja se nečega pobojah ; pomislih da će doskora biti mrak, i da ne mogu dugo uz nju ostati. I naglo se na nešto odlučih. Izađoh, jurnuh niz stube, potrčah kući. Rekoh roditeljima što se sad zbiva u kući s balkonom. Majka dade svakome od nas da nešto nosi. Pohitasmo svi skupa k starici.

                          Vladimir Nazor (1876–1949).

1. *e*-dialect : smešile.

Exercise : Re-write the above passages using the compound past tense where Domanović and Nazor have used the aorist.

Translate : 1. You ought to knock on the door before you go into the room. 2. I'm glad he called out ' come in ! ' otherwise I'd have gone away. 3. You must be well dressed and wear spectacles if you want to look like a distinguished old man. 4. Is this place free ? May I sit here ? 5. He says he is pleased that he'll be going (he'll go) abroad, although it's quite unexpected. 6. You needn't introduce her to me ; we've already met each other. 7. She'll have to bring a pillow if she wants to sleep on that bed. 8. I must admit that the view from your balcony is lovelier than from ours. 9. You mustn't stay here (any) longer. 10. I'll have to go in ; I'm cold ; my hands are (as) cold as ice.

# LESSON XXIII

## MORE NOTES ON NOUNS.   COLLECTIVE NUMERALS

### MASCULINE NOUNS

Instead of regular plural forms, *brat* and *gospodin* have feminine singular 'collective' forms : *braća* (brothers) and *gospoda* (gentlemen, Sirs), declined like *žena*. Although adjectives and participles agreeing with these nouns must be feminine singular, the verbs of which they are the subjects are plural : moja braća putuju—my brothers are travelling ; ova gospoda su bila u Engleskoj—these gentlemen have been in England. (The word *gospodin* is used more freely than the word ' gentleman ' is in English.)

Some masculine nouns have genitive plural ending *-i* instead of the usual *-a*. The commonest of these are *sat* (hour), *mesec* (moon, month), *ljudi* (men, people) : [1] pet sati—5 o'clock ; dvanaest meseci—12 months ; devet ljudi—9 men.

### FEMININE NOUNS

Some nouns are feminine in form though masculine in meaning, e.g. sluga (servant), vođa (leader), gazda (proprietor), pismonoša (postman). These are declined like *žena*. Adjectives qualifying them in the singular are masculine, but in the plural feminine : dobar sluga ; dobre sluge.

Besides *majka* (mother) and *kćerka* (daughter), which are declined regularly, the following forms are often used :

|      | Singular |       | Plural    |         |
|------|----------|-------|-----------|---------|
| Nom. | mati     | kći   | matere    | kćeri   |
| Gen. | matere   | kćeri | matera    | kćeri   |
| Dat. | materi   | kćeri | materama  | kćerima |
| Acc. | mater    | kćer  | matere    | kćeri   |

[1] See p. 88, footnote.

|       | Singular |              | Plural    |          |
|-------|----------|--------------|-----------|----------|
| Voc.  | mati     | kćeri        | matere    | kćeri    |
| Instr.| materom  | kćeri (kćerju)| materama | kćerima  |
| Loc.  | materi   | kćeri        | materama  | kćerima  |

*Noga* (foot, leg) and *ruka* (hand, arm) have genitive plural *nogu, ruku*.

A number of feminine nouns with nom. sing. ending *-a* have gen. pl. ending *-i* instead of the usual *-a*. These are nouns with a stem ending in two consonants but without a 'moveable *a*', e.g. bomba (bomb), gen. pl. bombi ; borba (struggle), funta (pound), pomorandža (orange), radnja (shop), senka (shade), tajna (secret), and nouns ending *-anka*, such as *Muslimanka* (Moslem woman). (Cf. *pesma*, gen. pl. *pesama*.[1])

*Grudi* and *prsi* (chest, breast) are always plural ; they are feminine, and are declined like the plural of *stvar*, but *prsi* has gen pl. *prsiju*.

NEUTER NOUNS

*Dete* (child), which is declined in the singular like *dugme* (see p. 20), has no regular plural form, but a feminine singular 'collective' form : *deca*. Like *braća* and *gospoda* this takes a plural verb, but fem. sing. adjective or participle : mala deca su pevala—the little children were singing.

Some neuter nouns denoting young creatures have as their plural a feminine singular 'collective' form ending *-ad*, declined like *stvar*, e.g. jagnje (lamb)—jagnjad (lambs), unuče (little grandson)—unučad. Again, these fem. sing. collectives take a plural verb but a fem. sing. adjective or participle. Many of them have alternative, more regular, plural forms.

The neuter singular collective noun *lišće* corresponds to English 'foliage', though it is more frequently used than 'foliage' is, as the plural of 'leaf'. *Lišće* takes a singular

[1] See p. 29.

verb, with neuter singular adjective or participle, e.g. lišće je
zeleno—the foliage is green. *List* also has a regular plural
*listovi*, used when the leaves are considered as individual
objects rather than as a mass. Other similar neuter singular
collective nouns are: *cveće* (from *cvet*—flower); *granje*
(*grana*—branch); *drveće* (*drvo*—tree); *kamenje* (*kamen*—
a stone, rock).

*Kola, vrata, leđa*—cart or car, door, back (of a body), are
neuter plural nouns with singular meaning: vrata su
otvorena—the door is open.

The declension of *oko* (eye) and *uho* (ear) was given in
Lesson XX. *Pleće* (shoulder) may take regular neuter plural
endings or the plural endings of feminine nouns like *stvar*, i.e.
*pleći*, etc.

*Podne* (noon) and *doba* (time, period) are neuter singular
indeclinable nouns.

*Veče* (evening), which also has a form *večer* which may be
either masculine or feminine, is declined: veče, večera,
večeru, veče, veče, večerom, večeru. The feminine form
*večer* is declined like *stvar*, and either form has only one
plural: *večeri*, fem., like *stvari*.

## COLLECTIVE NUMERALS

Serbo-Croat has three types of 'collective' numerals.

1. Corresponding roughly to the English nouns 'pair' (or
'couple'), 'trio', etc., referring to people or other living
creatures, are the neuter forms: dvoje, troje, četvoro, petoro,
šestoro, sedmoro, osmoro, devetoro, desetoro, jedanaestoro,
etc. These 'neuter singular collective numerals' are generally
used instead of the cardinal numerals given in Lesson XIV
when referring to people or other living creatures if both male
and female are represented; they take a singular verb, and
the pronoun or noun which they qualify is always in the
genitive plural: troje nas (gen. pl.) je čekalo u gostionici,

dok je petoro pošlo da traži gazdu—three of us (men and women) waited in the inn, while five went off to look for the proprietor. ' We two ' (m. and f.) is *nas dvoje* (again *nas* is genitive plural). These neuter singular collective numerals are often used with *deca*, e.g. troje dece—three children ; sed-moro dece—seven children ; and although *braća*—' brothers ' are all boys or men, these collective numerals whose corre-sponding cardinal numerals take the genitive plural may be used with this noun : osmoro braće, *but* dva brata. As *ljudi* may mean ' people ' or ' men ', *šestoro ljudi* means ' 6 people ' (both sexes), and *šest ljudi* means ' 6 men '.

The neuter singular collective numerals are not declined in the modern language : sa šestoro dece—with 6 children.

2. Very similar to these in form are collective numerals which have adjectival form, and agree, as adjectives, with the nouns which they qualify : dvoji, dvoje, dvoja ; troji, troje, troja ; četvori, četvoro, četvora ; petori, etc., šestori, sed-mori, osmori, devetori, desetori, etc. These must be used with those nouns which have only plural forms in common use, e.g. troja vrata—three doors ; petore novine—five news-papers ; u dvojim novinama—in two newspapers. They may also be used with nouns denoting things which occur in pairs, e.g. troje čarape—three pairs of stockings (instead of *tri para čarapa*).

3. Collective numerals ending -*ica*, which may be regarded as feminine nouns : dvojica, trojica, četvorica, petorica, šestorica, etc., are used only to refer to men. Instead of *dva čoveka* one can simply say *dvojica*. The verb following these collective numerals is plural, but participles may be feminine singular or masculine plural : dvojica su došla *or* došli. They are generally used when the men to whom they refer have already been mentioned : opazio sam pet vojnika ; dvojica su dolazili prema meni, ali trojica su pobegli u šumu—I noticed 5 soldiers ; two were coming towards me, but 3 ran away

into the forest. They may all be followed by a masculine noun in the genitive plural, e.g. petorica Engleza su putovali sa mnom—5 Englishmen travelled with me.

All three types of collective numerals have equivalents of English 'both': Type 1 has *oboje*, Type 2 *obadvoji*, *obadvoje*, *obadvoja*, etc., and Type 3 *obojica*.

Notice that it is only cardinal numerals (Lesson XIV) which must necessarily be followed by either the genitive singular or genitive plural according to whether they are 2 to 4, 5 to 20, etc.

## VOCABULARY

bol (pl. bolovi)—pain  
izgoreti, izgorim (pf.)—to  
  burn out, be burned down  
koncerat *or* koncert—concert  
mnogi—many (with pl.);  
  many a (with sing.)  

neprijatelj—enemy  
slikati (ipf.)—to paint, to  
  photograph  
živ—alive; lively  

Read and translate : 1. U ovoj sobi ima dvoja vrata : jedna vode u kupatilo, a druga u hodnik. 2. Ko su ona gospoda ? Video sam ih juče s vašom braćom. 3. Uzmite šest pomorandži i dajte ih onoj deci. 4. Je li istina da imate sedmoro braće ? 5. Jest. Trojica su lekari, kao i moj otac, a četvorica su činovnici. 6. U pozorištu ih je bilo šestoro : dve glumice i četiri glumca. 7. Nas dvojica smo ostali do kraja koncerta. 8. Svake nedelje kupuju četvore novine; mislite li da ih čitaju ? 9. Pitajte onu četvoricu studenata kako se zovu. 10. Neprijatelj je bacio deset bombi, od kojih je izgorelo nekoliko velikih radnji.

Translate : 1. Did you say I'd need five hours, five days, five weeks or five months to learn all these new words ? 2. 'Gentlemen,' he said, 'may I introduce my brothers to you ?' 3. She could paint the flowers, leaves and branches on the trees if she were here now. 4. Do you feel the pain in your chest or in your back ? 5. They would have 8 children—5 sons and 3 daughters—if their eldest son were alive. 6. There were (*bilo je*) at least ten men in the cart ; two were singing but many were silent. 7. I've seen this advertisement in 3 newspapers. 8. We four will wait here while you two go and (to) look for him. 9. Don't stand at (*na*) the door ; you'll be cold. 10. I hoped to talk (that I shall talk) Serbo-Croat with the two Yugoslavs in our compartment, but they both knew English much better than I knew their language.

## LESSON XXIV

### GERUNDIVES. *KOGOD, KO GOD*, ETC.

The present gerundive—the verbal adjective which in
English has the ending *-ing*—can be formed only from imperfective verbs, and has the form of the third person plural
of the present tense with *-ći* suffixed, e.g. *gledati* has *gledajući*,
*govoriti* has *govoreći*, *seći* (pres. *sečem*, 3rd pers. pl. *seku*)—
*sekući*. A few of these present gerundives are commonly used
as adjectives, e.g. *idući* (from *ići*), which literally means
'going' has also acquired the meaning of 'next': *iduće
godine*—next year; *tekući* (from *teći*—to flow), literally
'flowing', also means 'current'.

The past gerundive (e.g. English 'having sent') is little
used in speech. It is formed from verbs of either aspect. The
*-ti* of the infinitive ending is dropped and *-vši* (occasionally
only *v*) added; verbs whose infinitive ending *-ti* is preceded
by a consonant take *-avši*: primiti—primivši; gledati—
gledavši; videti—videvši; metnuti—metnuvši; tresti—
tresavši; peći (pek-ti)—pekavši. The past gerundive of *ići*
is *išavši*; that of its compounds is similar, e.g. *doći—došavši.*
*Bivši*, from *biti*, is in common use, meaning 'the former',
e.g. bivši predsednik—the former president.

With the exception of the few gerundives, present and past,
which are in common use and which may be declined as
adjectives (definite, with 'soft' stems), as in the phrase 'iduće
godine' above, or 'video sam bivšeg predsednika', the
gerundives may only be used to refer to a noun in the nominative case, and they do not change if this noun is feminine or
neuter or plural: the actress came down the stairs singing
loudly—glumica je sišla niz stepenice, pevajući glasno. Here
*pevajući* refers to *glumica*, but retains its *i* ending. Again:
having put the books on the table she sat down and began to

read—metnuvši knjige na sto, sela je i počela da čita. (In English there is a preference for the present gerundive, and this sentence might be : putting the books, etc. But Serbo-Croat is more precise in this respect.)

As these gerundives can only refer to nouns in the nominative case they cannot be used in sentences such as ' I heard the actress singing ', where ' singing ' refers to ' the actress ' (accusative case). This sentence must be ' čuo sam glumicu kako peva '—' I heard the actress how (or as) she sings '. *Gde* may be used instead of *kako*: we saw him coming—videli smo ga gde dolazi. Notice that the verb after *kako* or *gde* is always imperfective in such sentences.

### *Kogod, ko god, etc.*

The pronouns *ko* and *što* with *-god* suffixed have the meaning of ' someone ' and ' something ' when ' some ' is slightly emphasised in English : kogod će sigurno doći—someone will surely come ; dajte mu štogod—give him something.

When *ko*, *što* and certain other words are followed by *god* as a separate word they have the meaning of ' whoever ', ' whatever ', etc.: ko god je to rekao, ja to ne verujem—whoever said that, I don't believe it ; činiću što god je moguće—I'll do whatever is possible. (Notice that the stress accents in *kogod* and *ko gód* happen to coincide with those of their English equivalents : *some*one and who*ever*.) *Koliko god* means ' however much '—uzmite koliko god hoćete—take as much as you like. *Kakav god*—whatever kind of ; *gde god*—wherever. These words have a similar meaning when they are preceded by *ma* instead of being followed by *god : ma ko*—whoever ; *ma šta* (not *što* !)—whatever ; *ma gde*—wherever.

The prefix *i-* corresponds to an emphasised ' any ' : da li će iko doći ?—will *any*one come ?

## Vocabulary

izlog—display, e.g. in shop window

kelner—waiter

ličnost—person, personage

odelo—suit, clothing

odjednom—suddenly

posmatrati (ipf.)—to watch, observe

požuriti (pf.)—to hurry

rad—work

uskočiti u (pf.)—to jump in

tramvaj—tramcar

zaustavljati (ipf.)—to stop, bring to a halt

žurno—hastily

Read and translate :

1.—Imamo još jedno prazno mesto za konzula. Tu biste imali dobru platu i dobre dodatke, što biste vi, razume se, trošili na svoje lične stvari. Vi ste star, iskusan čovek, a dužnost vam je laka. Već više od mesec dana mučimo se tražeći pogodnu ličnost za taj važan položaj. Koje ste vi narodnosti, ako smem pitati ?

— Pa ja, upravo, kako da vam kažem, i sam još ne znam — rekoh zastiđen, ali me je on prekinuo pljesnuvši oduševljeno dlanom o dlan.

— Prekrasno, prekrasno ! Nikad bolje ! Vi ćete tek moći savesno vršiti ovako važan zadatak. Odmah idem ministru, a za nekoliko dana možete poći na put ! — izgovori viši činovnik, i odjuri da saopšti svome ministru važno otkriće.

(Domanović, continued.)

2. Tek što smo seli, kelner odmah pritrča, donese nam jelovnik na francuskom jeziku, i upita : Šta želite jesti ? Moj drug i ne uzimajući kartu u ruke reče : » Supu i tako dalje «. Kelner ga pogleda, kao da bi hteo znati šta on razume pod time ,, i tako dalje ''. Ali ne dobivši nikakva objašnjenja, okrenuo se k meni sa istim pitanjem. Ja mu odgovorih : » Donesite i meni isto «. Kelner ode. U dnu bašte, odakle se jelo donosi, razgovarao se malo s gazdaricom ; po svoj

prilici savetuje se šta će nam posle supe doneti. Oni su bili radoznali šta smo mi pod tim ,, i tako dalje " razumevali ; a mi smo radoznali kako će oni to razumeti, i šta će nam doneti.

Dobro smo učinili što smo tako kelneru kazali, jer on nam je izabrao mnogo bolji ručak nego da smo mi birali. Prekrasno svojstvo moga druga da za ručkom [1] ništa ne govori, bilo mi je već poznato. Ručali smo brzo i slatko. Kelner donese nam račun ćuteći ; mi mu platismo ćuteći.

(Nenadović.)

3. Marko [2] dođe u Beograd. Kola, tramvaji, ljudi, sve to juri, žuri ; činovnici žure u kancelariju, radnici za svojim radom.

Sretne jednog uglednog, lepo obučenog gospodina. Priđe mu Marko i pozdravi ga. Onaj je bio malo zbunjen ; bi ga stid od Markova loša odela.

— Ja sam Marko Kraljević. Došao sam amo da pomognem svojoj braći — reče Marko i ispriča sve : kako je došao, zašto je došao, šta je sve bilo s njim, i šta misli dalje raditi.

— Ta-ako. Milo mi je što sam vas upoznao, g. Kraljeviću ! Baš mi je milo, verujte ; ali izvinite me, žurim u kance-lariju ! — reče onaj i ode žurno.

Marko sretne drugog, trećeg. Koga god sretne, tako se mahom svrši razgovor sa onim : Žurim u kancelariju ! Marko ide ulicama i ćuti ; ne zaustavlja nikog, ne pita nikog ništa. A i kog će više pitati ? Koga god vidi, žuri u kancelariju.

(Domanović.)

[1] za ručkom : at luncheon.
[2] Marko Kraljević. The satirical short story from which this extract is taken describes how this semi-legendary hero returns to Belgrade. Notice that Domanović uses sometimes the ' historic ' present and sometimes a past tense.

Translate : 1. Hastily greeting (having greeted) him, I jumped into the tram. 2. She went slowly along the street, stopping in front of every shop window. 3. Having finished his work in the office he hurried home. 4. Watching him writing I suddenly remembered where I had seen him earlier. 5. Whoever you met, I can't believe she is an important person. 6. Wherever you are you must not wear such old clothes. 7. I'm glad they told us that we could take as much as we liked, for I'm hungry. 8. Look at him running along the street ! He's probably hurrying home. 9. Having read the menu we called the waiter. 10. I stood in the street watching the people coming and going.

## LESSON XXV

## A SUMMARY OF THE USES OF THE CASES

Only uses of the cases without prepositions are discussed here ; the Locative Case, which is used only after prepositions, is therefore omitted.

*Nominative.*

The case of the subject of the sentence, and of nouns, pronouns, and adjectives after the verb ' to be ' : *njegov sin* je bio *najmlađi advokat* u Beogradu. For the use of the nominative singular after the impersonal ' ima '—' there is ', see p. 136.

*Genitive.*

1. Of possession : književnost *naše zemlje*—the literature of our country ; život *seljaka*—the life of the peasants.

2. Of description : karta *prve klase*—a first class ticket (a ticket of the first class) ; čovek *visokog rasta*—a man of tall stature. The genitive of description is used much more freely than in English, e.g. ležim *otvorenih očiju*—I'm lying with open eyes.

3. Partitive Genitive : komad *sira*—a piece of cheese ; hoćete li *mleka* ?—would you like some milk ? on nema *nikakvih knjiga*—he has no books. For the use of the genitive after *ima* and *nema* used impersonally see p. 136. The genitive is used for the contents of a vessel, etc., when the vessel and its contents are commonly associated with each other : čaša *piva*—a glass of beer ; šolja *čaja*—a cup of tea. (Otherwise *sa* is used with the instrumental case : kutija sa igračkama— a box of toys.) The genitive is also used after adverbs such as *mnogo* (much, many), *malo* (a little, few), *nekoliko* (some, several) : mnogo *umornih putnika*—many weary travellers.

4. In time expressions, usually denoting ' time when ' : *prošloga meseca*—last month ; *jednog dana*—one day.

5. As object of a verbal noun : *čitanje knjiga*—the reading of books.

6. Denoting origin : *engleskog porekla*—of English origin.

7. Material : venac *ruža*—a wreath of roses.

8. After *evo* (here is, here are), *eto* (there is, there are—of objects fairly near the speaker) and *eno* (there is, there are— farther away) : evo *ga* !—here he is !

9. The genitive is used after many reflexive verbs, e.g. sećam se *vaših roditelja*—I remember your parents. (A list is given in the Appendix.)

10. Sometimes (but very rarely now) the object of a negative verb is in the genitive instead of the accusative.

### Dative.

1. The case of the indirect object : dajte ovo pismo *svome ocu*—give this letter to your father.[1]

2. The dative is occasionally used to denote direction : ići *kući*—to go home.

3. Indicating possession when the thing possessed, e.g. a relative or a part of the body, is closely associated with the possessor : majka *mu* je inteligentna žena—his mother is an intelligent woman. Notice its use in the poem on p. 9 : zeleni *im* kapci. This use of the dative is very similar to the ' dative of advantage or disadvantage ' : vetar je *seljacima* oborio šupe—the wind overthrew the peasants' huts.

4. In the expressions : zima *mi* je, hladno *mi* je—I am cold ; vrućina *mi* je—I'm hot.

5. The Ethic Dative. The dative of the personal pronoun inserted in certain statements or questions implies a personal interest in the answer : kako si *mi* ?—how are you (to me) ?

---

[1] Notice that the reflexive-possessive adjective ' svoj ' is used, because the subject (understood) of the imperative verb is ' you '.

6. The dative is used after certain verbs which you might expect to take the accusative : *pretio mi* je—he threatened me. (A list is given in the Appendix.)

*Accusative.*

1. The direct object : pišem *pismo*—I'm writing a letter. Note that the verb ' boleti '—to hurt, ache, takes an accusative : boli *me* glava—my head aches (the head hurts me) ; boli *me* zub (tooth), etc. Verbs taking two accusatives are rare : u**č**itelj *nas* je u**č**io *pesmu*—the teacher taught us a song ; upitao *ga* je samo *jednu reč*—he asked him only one word.

2. Expressions denoting duration of time,[1] extent of space, weight, and value : *celu noć*—the whole night ; sto je visok *jedan metar*—the table is 1 metre high ; ovo je teško *jedan kilogram*—this weighs one kilogram.

3. In the expressions : strah *me* je—I'm afraid ; stid *me* je, sramota *me* je—I'm ashamed.

*Vocative.*

Is only used in addressing people, whether you are writing or talking : *dragi gospodine Pavloviću*—dear Mr. Pavlović ; *draga gospođo Pavlović*—dear Mrs. Pavlović ; Gospodo !— Gentlemen ! [2]

*Instrumental.*

1. Denoting the instrument used : šijem vrlo *malom iglom*— I'm sewing with a very small needle ; ova slika je naslikana *rukom*—this picture is painted by hand.[3] The use of the instrumental denoting way or direction (after verbs of motion) and manner is very similar to this : idem *ulicom*—I'm going

[1] See p. 104.
[2] See p. 139.
[3] But *N.B.* ' naslikana od moga oca '—' painted by my father ' ; though it is better to say ' ovu sliku je naslikao moj otac ' (see Lesson XXI).

along the street; išli su *redom*—they went in turn; govorite
*šapatom* !—speak in a whisper !

2. In expressions of time. See p. 105.

3. In the following expressions: detetom—as (i.e. when)
a child; stotinama—by the hundred; *tokom* rata—in the
course of the war; putem—on the way; delom—partly (from
*deo*—'part'); većinom—for the most part (from *većina*—
'majority').

4. To denote origin: on je *rodom* (ili *poreklom*) Srbin—he
is by birth (or origin) a Serb.

5. After the following verbs which take a direct object, and
others with similar meanings: smatrati—to consider: smatram ga *poštenim čovekom*—I consider him an honest man;
nazvati—to call: nazvali su ga *Vukom*—they called him
Vuk; učiniti, načiniti, napraviti—to make: njegov rad ga je
načinio *velikim čovekom*—his work made him a great man.
imenovati—to nominate: imenovali smo ga *predsednikom*—
we nominated him president; osećati—to feel, when used
reflexively: osećao sam se *mirnim*—I felt calm; osećao se
junakom—he felt a hero.

6. After certain verbs where a direct object might be
expected. (A list of these is given in the Appendix).

## VOCABULARY

ikad(a)—ever
ispratiti (pf.)—to accompany,
  see off
kašičica (diminutive of *kašika*
  —spoon)—tea-spoon
mašina—machine; type-
  writer
milja—mile
običaj—custom

ogroman, ogromna—enor-
  mous
pokazati, pokažem—to show
ponosan, ponosna—proud
poslednji—the last
poslužavnik—tray
pošto—after; as, since,
  because

poznavanje—knowledge, acquaintance

pravi—real, authentic

pravilno—correctly, regularly.

priča—story

privlačan, privlačna—attractive

priznati—to admit, confess

svuda—everywhere

šoljica (diminutive of *šolja*)— small cup

tada—then

tanjirić (diminutive of *tanjir* —plate, dish)—little dish

tečno—fluently

trenutak (gen. trenutka)— moment, second

turski—Turkish

udobno—comfortably

Read and translate : 1. Više bih volela da mi piše rukom, ali sva njegova pisma su pisana mašinom. 2. Beograđanin koji je stigao prošle nedelje bio je čovek dugačkog nosa, širokih leđa i crne kose. 3. Molim vas dajte mi jedan kilogram hleba i sto grama sira. 4. Svakog dana viđam istu staricu u varoši. Eno je, i sada ide ulicom. 5. Zima joj je ; ruke su joj hladne kao led. 6. Zapitao sam ga kad će doći, a on mi je odgovorio da će stići do pet sati. 7. Put pored mora je bio dugačak samo jednu milju, ali nije mogao dalje ići jer su ga bolele noge. 8. Već godinama živi u Jugoslaviji i naravno govori srpskohrvatski kao pravi Jugosloven. 9. Žao mi je, draga gospođo, što neću moći da vas posetim, ali subotom i nedeljom uvek posećujem svoju decu. 10. Rekao je da najzad govorim dosta tečno i pravilno ; iako mu nisam verovao, njegove reči su me učinile vrlo srećnim.

Translate : Mr. Simić, in whose house I spent the last 5 days in Belgrade, told me that he usually visited his sister on Sundays ; but as he wanted to take me with him we went to see her on Friday (for I had to return to England, of course, last Saturday). We bought first class tickets and travelled comfortably by train. We were pleasantly surprised when we saw that Miss Simić was waiting for us at the station. I must tell you that she's an extremely attractive woman with

enormous dark eyes like her brother's,[1] and I believe that
everybody considers her very intelligent. We went on foot,
by way of narrow paths, and arrived in front of the smallest
and prettiest cottage that I have ever seen. After we had sat
and talked for an hour she left us for a few moments, and came
back into the room carrying a tray on which were a little cup
of the sweet black Turkish coffee which is drunk everywhere
in Yugoslavia, a tumbler of water, a little dish of *slatko* and
a tea-spoon. ' Would you like me to teach you this custom
of ours ? ' she asked me, smiling. But I already knew what
I had to do. I took a spoonful of the *slatko* (only one—
remembering a terrible story of an Englishman who ate it all) ;
holding the spoon in my hand, I took the tumbler with my
other hand and drank a little water. Then I placed the spoon
in the tumbler, which I then put on the tray, and finally drank
the cup of coffee. My knowledge of this little custom (on
account of which, I must admit, I was rather proud) surprised
them both, and still more my knowledge of their language.
' You must come again next year,' they said, ' and stay with
us longer. Then nobody will think that you're not a real
Yugoslav.' Miss Simić accompanied us to the station half an
hour later, and whenever I remember that day I see her
standing on the platform and hear her saying to me : ' Come
again next year ! Happy journey ! Goodbye ! '

[1] Use *kao u* with the genitive of ' her brother '.

## APPENDIX

## 1. KEY TO SENTENCES AND PASSAGES FOR TRANSLATION INTO SERBO-CROAT [1]

Page 12.

1. Putujemo brzo. 2. Čitam kad jedem. 3. Učimo polako i pažljivo. 4. Peva glasno i veselo kad radi. 5. Ne stanujete ovde. 6. On ne razume kad govorim. 7. Rade ovde ali spavaju kod kuće. 8. Govorimo polako. 9. Dobro čitate. 10. Pevamo kad radimo, ali ne pevamo suviše glasno. 11. On uvek govori. 12. Zimi sedimo kod kuće. 13. Oni obično putuju leti. 14. Ne pušim. 15. On često ustaje rano. 16. Obično sede ovde. 17. Govorite suviše brzo. 18. Ne pišete. 19. On radi a oni gledaju. 20. Ustajem.

Page 18.

1. Dobro jutro, gospodine Petroviću! 2. Pišemo lekaru. 3. Gospodin Pavlović je lekar. 4. On piše romane. 5. Studenti sede na podu i puše. 6. Šećer je u čaju. 7. On ne voli gradove. 8. On ne ide u Beograd bez pasoša. 9. Gde je Jovan? 10. Sedi blizu prozora i čita. 11. Pijemo čaj bez šećera. 12. Putujem u Zagreb sa gospodinom Petrovićem. 13. Putujemo vozom. 14. Gledaju konja. 15. On daje pasoš gospodinu Pavloviću. 16. Zašto ne sedite? 17. On uvek putuje brodom. 18. Zbogom, Jovane. 19. Gde je grad? 20. Ne razumem jezik. 21. Oni ne puše u bioskopu. 22. Nemam šećera. 23. Bregovi su blizu grada. 24. Ne vidim Jovana na brodu. 25. Studenti ne slušaju: oni spavaju.

[1] Your word order in the early sentences and passages may differ from that given here, without being incorrect. The rules for word order which must be observed are given in those Lessons where it becomes necessary to apply them.

Page 22.

1. Tražimo restoran. 2. Gde je profesor ? 3. On peva u kupatilu. 4. Ne mogu da razumem kad govorite. 5. Vino je sa pivom u ormaru. 6. Obično provodim proleće i leto blizu jezera. 7. Gledaju konje u poljima. 8. Tražim ogledalo. 9. Ne mogu da pišu bez pera. 10. Idemo u pozorište. 11. Oni žele da putuju automobilom na more. 12. Jovan želi da dobro govori jezik. 13. Moram da idem u polja. 14. Ne mogu da radim kad pevate. 15. On je često u pozorištu : voli pozorišta u Londonu. 16. Oni žive u stanu u predgrađu Zagreba. 17. Radimo u selima blizu mora. 18. Mogu da vidim jezera. 19. Dajem detetu komad mesa. 20. On jede komad hleba sa mesom.

Page 25.

1. Ko je Milan ? 2. On je Jugosloven. 3. Da li su u Beogradu ? 4. Ne, nisu ; u Sarajevu su. 5. On nije u automobilu ; ovde je. 6. Ne znamo gde je brod. 7. Ne putujem kad je Jovan u Londonu. 8. On nije lekar. 9. Jesmo li u selu ? 10. Da li su studenti ovde ? 11. Da, ovde su ; oni su sa gospodinom Petrovićem. 12. Da li ste Jugosloven ? Ne, nisam. 13. Vi niste Hrvati. 14. Znam da su ovde. 15. Da li je Jovan sa lekarom ? Jest.

Page 27.

### Razgovor u vozu

— Nemate dosta mesta.

— Ne, nemamo. Imamo suviše prtljaga.

— Možete metnuti kofer tamo gore.

— Dobro. Sada je u redu.

— Vrlo dobro govorite. Jeste li Jugosloveni ?

— Ne, nismo. Mi smo Englezi, ali ovde provodimo mnogo

vremena. Dolazimo iz Dubrovnika i putujemo u Sarajevo, zatim u Beograd.

— Dobro. Možemo putovati zajedno do Sarajeva.

— Da li znate da li možemo da ručamo u vozu ?

— Naravno. U vagon-restoranu.

— Da li znate gde je vagon-restoran ?

— Mislim da je sasvim blizu.

— Sada idem na ručak. A vi ?

— Da. Hajdemo.

Page 31.

1. Čita li on roman ? Ne, čita vesti. 2. Da li gledate slike ? Da ; one su u knjizi. 3. Da li on dobro spava ? Ne, noću uči. 4. Gde su knjige ? Nisu ovde. 5. Da li su na policama ? Ne znam. 6. Mislim da gospođa Petrović zna gde su, te sada tražim godpođu Petrović. 7. Da li razumete kad ja govorim ? Obično razumem kad ne govorite suviše brzo, ali ne razumem gospodina Petrovića. 8. Da li je on Jugosloven ? Da, jest. 9. Da li je gospođa Petrović Engleskinja ? Ne, nije. 10. Gde je ona ? Ona je sa gospodinom Petrovićem. 11. Gde su oni ? Jesu li u kući ili u vrtu ? 12. Mislim da su u vrtu pred kućom. 13. Da li slušate ritam pesme ? Da ; ja volim muziku. 14. Znam da je žena Engleskinja. 15. Da, a muž je, mislim, Jugosloven.

Page 32.

— Gospođo Petrović, gde ste ? Jeste li u kuhinji ?

— Ne, nisam. Ovde sam.

— Gde ? Da li ste u salonu ?

— Da, jesam. Tražim knjigu o Jugoslaviji — knjigu sa slikama. Da li znate gde je ? Stalno gubim stvari.

— Znam da je sa kartama ; mislim da su u fijoci. Imate li ključ, molim ? Hvala. Ne, nisu ovde.

— Gde je Jovan ? Možda on zna gde je.

— Mislim da nije u kući. On obično provodi dan u biblioteci. Zašto gledate kroz prozor ?

— Tražim Jovana. Možda je u vrtu. Da, tamo je. Sedi na travi sa knjigom u ruci.

Page 39.

1. Na žalost, nisam čitao kad sam video profesora u biblioteci. 2. Da li je rekao da radite suviše mnogo ? 3. Ne, naprotiv ; rekao je da moram da radim više. 4. Kafana je bila pred hotelom. 5. Ne mogu da platim za taksi. 6. Kazala je da je Engleskinja. 7. On nije uvek ustajao rano. 8. Niste primetili izgled sa prozora. 9. On je već zaboravio adresu. 10. Nisam razumeo (razumela). 11. Nisam mogao (mogla) da razumem kad su oni govorili. 12. Mi smo već ručali u vozu. 13. Da li ste zaboravili pasoše ? 14. Stigla je avionom. 15. Putnici su gledali bregove i jezera. 16. Crkva je bila blizu hotela. 17. Video (videla) sam hotel kad smo bili u vozu. 18. Jesu li sedeli na stolicama ili na podu ? 19. Oni su samo razgovarali i pušili. 20. Rekao je da voli ritam pesama.

Page 40.

— Šta ste radili kad ste stigli na stanicu ?

— Uzeli smo taksi. Mislili smo da znamo jezik vrlo dobro, ali šofer nije razumeo kad smo govorili. Srećom, razumeo je adresu hotela ; nije bio daleko od stanice. Pružio sam šoferu nešto novca, ali ne znam koliko je uzeo.

— Teško meni ! Vidite da je bolje znati jezik dobro pre nego što putujete po inostranstvu.

— Znam. Ali mislim da nije uzeo suviše, jer je vrlo pažljivo izbrojio novac.

— Dakle, stigli ste u hotel.

— Da, — hotel sa kafanom i parkom. Naravno, nismo mogli da vidimo park noću. Rezervirali smo sobe unapred. Već smo večerali u vozu i samo smo želeli da spavamo, te smo odmah legli, i dugo smo spavali.

Page 47.

1. On ide u pozorište sa mojom sestrom. 2. Ne možete razgovarati sa onim gluvim starim gospodinom. 3. Da li ste primili dobre vesti od svog sina ? 4. Jovanova majka je kupila ovu novu kuću. 5. Obično radimo u svojim sobama. 6. Moram čitati vašu novu knjigu ; čuo (čula) sam da je vrlo zanimljiva. 7. Ona voli da ruča u dobrom hotelu. 8. Kupio je jednu marku za svoje preporučeno pismo. 9. Ove mlade Engleskinje uče naš jezik. 10. Možete videti njihovo selo sa vrha onog visokog brda. 11. To je žena u zelenom kaputu. 12. Ovo je važno pismo. 13. Vi ste zaista vrlo ljubazni, draga gospođo Petrović ! 14. Putovali smo brzim vozom i uskoro stigli na veliku stanicu. 15. Ne volim da živim u velikim gradovima. 16. Poslao (poslala) sam vašu dopisnicu avionskom poštom. 17. Zaista morate videti njegov novi automobil i šofera ! 18. On razgovara sa ljubaznom i učtivom mladom gospođicom. 19. Primili su preporučena pisma od svojih prijatelja u inostranstvu. 20. Da li ste znali da naš stari lekar sada živi u ovom selu ?

Page 49.

Idem na poštu ; mogu uzeti vaše dopisnice, ako hoćete. Šta mislite, da li je bolje da pošaljem svoja pisma avionskom poštom, preporučena ? Naročito su važna i želim da stignu što brže. Zar ne mislite da je ona mlada gospođica u pošti vrlo ljubazna i učtiva ? Ona mi je rekla na srpskohrvatskom, vrlo strpljivo, koliko dana putuju pisma do Engleske običnom poštom i avionskom poštom, kad sam juče tamo kupio ove marke. Ona govori vrlo jasno, i lako sam razumeo kad je rekla koliko moje marke koštaju. Zaboga ! Zaboravio sam da treba da pišem svome advokatu. Molim vas, dajte mi moje pero i list hartije i jedan koverat.

Page 54.

1. On obično stavlja svoje stvari na pod, ali ova važna pisma stavio je u fijoku. 2. Učim pažljivo ali ne mogu reći da sam naučio jezik. 3. Pitam vas da li znate gde su moja pisma. 4. Zapitao (žapitala) sam devojku da li zna gde živi lekar. 5. Zamolila je svoju prijateljicu da da šoferu nešto novca. 6. Jedem hleb. 7. Nije mnogo pojeo. 8. Rekla je : molim vas, dajte mi svoj šešir. 9. Ostavljam ove stvari u kući svoje majke. 10. Vaš sin je ostavio svoje knjige u našoj biblioteci. 11. Zar ste zaista bacili onaj lepi šešir u reku ? 12. On uvek baca svoje stare stvari. 13. Vaše dete spava u mojoj sobi. 14. Bili smo umorni i uskoro smo zaspali. 15. Obično ne pijem, ali pre ručka sam popio (popila) jednu čašu vina. 16. Kupio (kupila) sam koverte a sada kupujem marke. 17. Zamolili su gospodina Nikolića da napiše knjigu o svojim putovanjima. 18. Zar ne dajete mleka detetu ? 19. Moja žena je otišla u radnju da kupi nov kaput. 20. Pišete li pisma ?

Page 60.

Razgovarao sam s drugim putnicima, ali sam bio vrlo umoran jer sam već dugo putovao, i kad su oni izišli iz voza i ja sam bio sam u kupeu, legao sam i zaspao. Spavao sam dok je voz prolazio kroz Austriju, ali kad smo stigli na jugoslovensku granicu kondukter je došao u moj kupe. » Carinik i drugi činovnici dolaze «, rekao je. » Hvala «, odgovorio sam pospano i počeo da otvaram svoje kofere. Međutim, ovo nije bilo potrebno. Kad je carinik došao, samo je pogledao na moj prtljag, rekao : » U redu «, i izišao, iako sam već hteo da kažem : » Imam ovu veliku kutiju cigareta «. Došao je drugi Jugosloven i zatražio moj pasoš. Progovorio je nekoliko reči na srpskohrvatskom i ja sam sve razumeo. I carinik i drugi činovnik bili su vrlo ljubazni i učtivi. Iako je bila noć i bio sam tako umoran, mislio sam da je moje putovanje po Jugoslaviji počelo vrlo prijatno.

Page 67.

1. Kad ćemo stići u Zagreb ? 2. Neću pročitati svoja pisma pre doručka. 3. On će sedeti pod velikom jabukom u našoj bašti posle podne. 4. Metnućemo ovaj telefonski imenik pod ove druge velike knjige. 5. Molim vas, hoćete li poslati ovaj mali paket kad odete na poštu ? 6. Kad će izići iz bioskopa ? Da li obično izlaze kasno ? 7. On će pojesti taj sladoled. 8. Da li će putnici videti ona lepa jezera i planine kad prolaze kroz Sloveniju, ili putuju noću ? 9. Hoće li ovo biti dobra knjiga za njihovog sina ? 10. Ovaj voz će uskoro poći ; obično polazi na vreme. 11. Zar vojnici neće moći da spavaju ovde ? 12. Hoćete li, molim vas, dati ove stvari svojoj sestri ? 13. Nećemo izići iz voza : jugoslovenski činovnici će doći u naš kupe. 14. Zar vaši studenti neće ići na to predavanje ? 15. Da li će profesor napisati članak o knjizi koju je čitao ?

Page 68.

Da li ste gladni ? Ući ćemo u ovaj mali restoran. Moj muž je rekao da će biti ovde ; možda će doći docnije. Gde ćemo sesti ? Hoćete li vi sesti na ovu stolicu ? Staviću ovu veliku torbu pod svoju stolicu : da li je to u redu ? Evo jelovnika ; šta ćete vi izabrati ? Sigurna sam da ćete moći da pojedete dosta mesa i povrća posle svog dugog puta ; ali prvo ćemo uzeti supu. Posle ćemo misliti na voće i sir : sir je ovde verovatno dobar. Imamo dosta vremena. Posle nećemo ići peške ; uzećemo taksi i otići u pozorište.

Page 74.

1. Otišao sam da ga tražim ali ga nisam našao. 2. Pevala je divnu pesmu ; da li ste je čuli ? 3. Rekao mi je da neće doći. 4. Zahvalili smo im kad su nas pozvali na ručak, ali smo im rekli da nećemo biti slobodni. 5. Daću mu njenu adresu ; ona je rekla da će mi je dati. 6. On joj je ponudio cigaretu

ali je nije uzela. 7. Gledao sam njegove džepove ; u njima
ima mnogo stvari. 8. Eno vašeg kaputa : metnuo sam ga na
stolicu. 9. Obećali su nam kod » Putnika « da će nam dati
karte sutra. 10. Moj pas neće da ide s njim, ali će možda ići
s vama. 11. Ona hoće da nas povede sa sobom. 12. Nisam
ga razumeo kad je s njima govorio. 13. Zar vi zaista dajete
ovo meni ? 14. Meni nije jasno zašto mu nisu pisali. 15. Rekli
su da će nas dočekati na stanici, ali ja ih ne vidim.

Page 75.

Galama na ulici nas je rano probudila i odmah smo ustali.
» Ja ću spremiti kafu « — rekao mi je Jovan. — » Gde ste je
metnuli ? « » Mislim da sam.metnuo sve potrebne stvari u
vaš kofer. Zar ih niste videli kad ste ga otvorili sinoć ? Evo
ih ! Dok je spremate, odlučićemo kuda ćemo ići danas.
Imate li vodić ? Molim vas, dajte mi ga. Hvala. Evo slike
one lepe crkve ; juče smo je videli, znate, kad smo tamo
prolazili. Možda ćemo moći danas da uđemo u nju. Moramo
otići i u ovaj muzej.« Čitao sam o njemu naglas dok je Jovan
spremao kafu. » Moramo ga posetiti posle podne,« rekao sam
mu. On mi je pružio šolju. » Ah, ovo je vrlo prijatno ! Sunce
sija i kafa je dobra. Popićemo je i izići ćemo da vidimo grad.«

Page 81.

1. Mila se izgubila. 2. Ne znam da li će se vratiti. 3. Nadam
se da će me povesti sa sobom. 4. Zašto ste se smejali ?
5. Nisam se smejao ; samo sam se smešio. 6. Ona se, naravno,
boji njega, zbog njegovog strogog lica. 7. » Vina, Milo ! «
vikali su kad je Mila služila u kafani. 8. Da li se sećate one
noći kad smo se izgubili u onoj tamnoj šumi ? 9. Kupila sam
ovu sliku za sebe, zato što sam joj se toliko divila. 10. Srećom,
to se ne događa često. 11. Čim je pročitala njegova pisma,
ona ih je vratila meni. 12. To se desilo kad smo bili kod vas.

13. Komedija od Marina Držića se daje u pozorištu ; moramo je videti. 14. Šta se govori o ovoj knjizi ? 15. Nisu se često viđali, iako su se mnogo voleli. 16. Automobil se zaustavio pred jednom velikom zgradom i šofer je izišao. 17. On se popeo uz zid, skočio na zemlju i potrčao stazom. 18. Naše malo selo se nalazi na obali. 19. Kako se zovete ? 20. Obradovao sam se kad sam primio dobre vesti o vama.

Page 88.

1. Povešću tri mlade devojke (pet mladih devojaka) sa sobom. 2. Vratio se sa četiri teška paketa (šest teških paketa). 3. Mislim da ste pročitali ova dva važna članka (ovih pet važnih članaka) ; hoćete li mu ih vratiti ? 4. Ona je primila pedeset i jednu čestitku (pedeset i sedam čestitaka) o Božiću ; uvek prima mnogo. 5. Imamo dosta hrane za trideset siromašnih žena (trideset i dve siromašne žene). 6. Kaže da je pročitao sve tri stranice (svih osam stranica) ovog pisma za četiri minuta (četrnaest minuta). 7. Jedan vodič je otišao u muzej sa jedanaest umornih turista. (Dva vodiča su otišli (or otišla) u muzej sa dvadeset i dva umorna turista.) 8. Kupaju se u mirnoj vodi ovog jezera triput dnevno (pet puta dnevno). 9. Učim ove reči ; već sam naučio sto novih reči (sto dve nove reči) danas. 10. Da li ste primetili ona dva čoveka (onih šest ljudi) ? Svaki od njih putuje sa tri različita pasoša (pet različitih pasoša) !

Page 92.

1. Desilo se prvog decembra. 2. Koji je (datum) danas ? Mislim da je trideset prvi novembar. 3. Ne može biti ; novembar ima samo trideset dana. 4. Otvorio sam prvih deset koverata ; peti i sedmi su bili prazni. 5. Mnogi srpski junaci su poginuli na Kosovu hiljadu tri stotine osamdeset devete godine. 6. Koliko je sati ? Mislim da je pet i trideset (or pet i po ; or pola šest). 7. Večerali su u četvrt do osam. 8. Naći

ćete knjigu na trećoj polici; dajte mi je, molim vas. 9. Slušaćemo vesti na radiju u šest sati. 10. Zar nije čudno, ovaj sat uvek stane u ponoć, ili možda u podne; u svakom slučaju u dvanaest sati. 11. Otišao je od kuće u četiri i deset, devetog avgusta, i nije se vratio. 12. Da li ona nosi prsten na trećem prstu leve ili desne ruke? 13. Vi ste prvi na spisku, ja sam drugi, ona je treća a on je četvrti. 14. On se rodio trećeg aprila hiljadu devet stotina četrdeset pete godine. 15. Naša je četvrta kuća u drugoj ulici levo.

Page 99.

1. Pitam se da li je onaj hotel bolji od ovoga. 2. Lakše je čitati nego prevoditi. 3. U Beogradu ima sada većih i lepših zgrada nego pre rata. 4. Zašto ne dolazite češće? 5. Breskve i smokve su svakako ukusnije u vašoj zemlji nego u našoj. 6. On je, očigledno, hrabriji od mene. 7. Mislite li da je srpskohrvatski teži od engleskog? 8. Da li će vaše dve knjige biti skuplje od ovih? 9. Da li su rekli da je on njihov najbolji slikar? Video sam ovde bolje slike od njegovih. 10. Ovde će vam biti mirnije. 11. Med nije slađi od šećera ali je ukusniji. 12. Došli smo vrlo rano, ali oni su stigli još ranije. 13. Kad su je molili da prestane, ona je pevala sve glasnije. 14. Da li je voda dublja ovde nego na tom mestu? Mi više volimo da se kupamo u najdubljoj vodi. 15. Ovde ima najviše saobraćaja zato što je ovo najšira ulica. 16. Govorio je jasnije kad je primetio da sam Englez. 17. Da li su najjeftinije novine najzanimljivije u vašoj zemlji? 18. Ovo platno je grublje, ali, srećom, ja volim grubo platno. 19. Ona je najinteligentnija žena u ovoj kancelariji. 20. Riba u sledećoj narodnoj pesmi svakako je vrlo inteligentna.

Page 106.

1. Ne sećam se imena onoga čoveka koji mi je govorio o vama u utorak. Ko je on? 2. Nadao se da će sresti devojku

koju je video u vozu. 3. Kome ste dali pismo ? 4. Šta je to ? Je li to stranica iz knjige koju ste čitali ? 5. Koga ćemo videti večeras u pozorištu ? 6. Čime je pisao — perom ili olovkom ? 7. S čijim sinom ste razgovarali ? 8. Niko nikada ne živi dugo u ovim kućama. 9. Stidim se ove sobe ; u njoj nije nikada ništa u redu. 10. Čije su bile one stvari koje ste stavljali u fijoku kad sam ušao u sobu ? 11. Ovo je najduže pismo koje sam ikada primio. Neću nikada imati dosta vremena da ga pročitam. 12. Nismo nikoga videli, iako smo bili bliže od vas. 13. Ceo dan ste jeli i pili. 14. Dva mladića s kojima sam se sinoć vratila iz pozorišta, bili su Milan i njegov mlađi brat. 15. Ne možete verovati sve što on kaže ; ono što vam je jutros rekao nije istina. 16. Ko je čovek koga uvek posećujete sredom ? 17. Možete li doći na jedan sat ? Nadam se da ćete stići do četiri i trideset. 18. Nešto strašno se desilo. Izgubili smo novac koji ste nam dali. 19. Da li znate čiji je ovaj stan ? 20. Pitam se o čemu joj je pisao.

## Page 114.

1. Vaši razlozi mi nisu jasni. 2. Bifteci koje smo pojeli u tom restoranu bili su odlični. 3. U toj pesmi ste čitali o kućici sa zelenim kapcima. 4. On uvek govori na tim mitinzima sa najvećom hrabrošću. 5. Hoćete li dati nešto ovim siromasima ? Bolesni su. 6. » Dobro jutro, pukovniče «, — rekao sam mu čim sam ga video. 7. Da li je rana na njenoj ruci ili nozi ? 8. Nećete moći da je prepoznate na slici u ovoj knjizi. 9. Ušao je u sobu brzim koracima. 10. Vojnici u njihovoj vojsci su svi vrlo jaki ljudi. 11. Bilo je mnogo čitalaca u biblioteci, i njihove knjige su ležale na (po) svim stolovima. 12. Sada živimo u Šapcu i retko se vraćamo u Beograd. 13. » Oče «, — rekao je on » — da li je ovo majčina ili tvoja karta ? « 14. Ovaj pekmez se zove » slatko « na srpskohrvatskom, zato što je vrlo sladak. 15. Mislite li da su ove rečenice bile vrlo teške ?

Page 118.

1. Ne biste mogli da čujete njegov glas. 2. Voleli bi da ostanu tamo. 3. Znam da ne bi došla. 4. Učio bi brže ali je vrlo zauzet. 5. Da li biste više voleli da mi pišete ? 6. Nikad više ne bih govorio s njim. 7. Zaista, ne bih mogla nositi tu torbu ; strašno je teška. 8. Ne biste je prepoznali u novom kaputu. 9. Ne bih se složio sa njegovim predlogom. 10. Da li biste rekli lekaru svoje ime, molim ?

Page 120.

1. Ako dođete, sigurno ćete ga videti. 2. Da je on ovde s nama, znam da ne bi želeo da se vrati u London. 3. Ako je voz brži, zašto ste putovali kolima ? 4. Sigurno bi ga razumela bolje kad bi ga češće viđala. 5. Rado bih slušala da je njegov glas lepši. 6. Stigli bismo do reke ako bismo produžili ovim putem. 7. Da li biste prihvatili poziv da ste verovali da je njen sin bolestan ? 8. Bili biste vrlo umorni da ste bili sa nama. 9. Ako ona dođe, hoćete li me, molim vas, pozvati ? 10. Kad biste znali šta sam jutros pročitao u novinama !

Page 127.

— Kažite mi — rekla sam joj — da li vam je život mirniji sada kad živite kod pukovnikove žene ?

— Ne ; — odgovorila je odsečno — slušajte. Da li biste rekli da je život miran kad bi živeli sa ženom koja vam stalno govori : » Uradite ovo, nemojte raditi to ; donesite mi moju knjigu ; zatvorite vrata ; nemojte zaboraviti da je mačka u bašti ; da vidim šta čitate ; nemojte zaboraviti da odete na poštu danas posle podne; pružite mi, molim vas, cigarete; pazite, nemojte razbiti tu šolju ! « Najgore je kad odjednom kaže : » Razgovarajte sa mnom ! « Šta biste radili kad biste bili na mome mestu ?

— Ne znam. Verovatno bih rekla : » Ako hoćete da ja ostanem u ovoj kući, dajte mi zasebnu sobu, gde mogu raditi na miru, i molim vas nemojte mi smetati kad hoću da učim.«

— Ali šta ću raditi ako ona odgovori : » Dobro, ako niste zadovoljni ovde, idite ! « ?

— Budite nezavisni. Tražite stan za sebe i napustite je.

— Nemojte to predlagati. Znate da je to nemoguće !

## Page 132.

1. Da li su vaše rukavice bile uvek ove boje ? Ne, obojene su. 2. Rođen je petog novembra, hiljadu devet stotina dvadesete godine. 3. Verujem da su ove stvari ukradene. 4. Nemojte gledati ovu sliku : nije svršena. 5. Našao sam pet razbijenih šolja u ovom ormaru ; da li znate ko ih je razbio ? 6. Poslat je u inostranstvo da proučava uređenje najboljih hotela. 7. Da li su već preduzeti najpotrebniji koraci ? 8. Kuće na obali nisu još sazidane ; zidanje nije ni početo. 9. Do viđenja, gospodine Petroviću ; videćemo se sutra. 10. Ako su oni pozvani na ručak kod vaših roditelja, da li ćete i vi ići ?

## Page 138.

1. Trebalo bi da zakucate na vrata pre nego što uđete u sobu. 2. Radujem se što je rekao » napred «, inače bih otišao. 3. Morate biti lepo obučeni i nositi naočare ako hoćete da izgledate kao ugledan star čovek. 4. Da li je ovo mesto slobodno ? Mogu li sesti ovde ? 5. Kaže da se raduje što će ići u inostranstvo, iako je to sasvim neočekivano. 6. Ne morate da mi je predstavite, već smo se upoznali. 7. Ona će morati da donese jastuk, ako hoće da spava na tom krevetu. 8. Moram priznati da je izgled sa vašeg balkona lepši nego sa našeg. 9. Ne smete ostati ovde duže. 10. Moraću da uđem, hladno mi je ; ruke su mi hladne kao led.

## Page 143.

1. Da li ste rekli da će mi trebati pet sati, pet dana, pet nedelja ili pet meseci da naučim sve ove nove reči ?

2. » Gospodo «, rekao je on » mogu li vam predstaviti svoju braću ? « 3. Mogla bi da slika cveće, lišće i granje na drveću da je sada ovde. 4. Da li osećate bol u grudima ili u leđima ? 5. Imali bi osmoro dece — pet sinova i tri kćeri — da je njihov najstariji sin živ. 6. Bilo je najmanje deset ljudi u kolima ; dvojica su pevali, ali mnogi su ćutali. 7. Video sam ovaj oglas u trojim novinama. 8. Nas četvoro ćemo čekati ovde dok vas dvoje idete da ga tražite. 9. Nemojte stojati na vratima, biće vam hladno. 10. Nadao sam se da ću razgovarati srpskohrvatski sa dvojicom Jugoslovena u našem kupeu, ali obojica su znali engleski mnogo bolje nego što sam ja znao njihov jezik.

Page 149.

1. Pozdravivši ga žurno, uskočio sam u tramvaj. 2. Išla je polako ulicom, zaustavljajući se pred svakim izlogom. 3. Završivši rad u kancelariji, požurio je kući. 4. Posmatrajući ga kako piše, odjednom sam se setio gde sam ga ranije video. 5. Koga god ste sreli, ne mogu da verujem da je važna ličnost. 6. Ma gde da se nalazite ne treba da nosite tako staro odelo. 7. Radujem se što su nam rekli da možemo uzeti koliko god hoćemo, jer sam gladan. 8. Gledajte ga kako trči ulicom ! Verovatno žuri kući. 9. Pročitavši jelovnik, pozvali smo kelnera. 10. Stajao sam na ulici gledajući ljude kako (gde) dolaze i odlaze.

Page 154.

Gospodin Simić, u čijoj sam kući proveo poslednjih pet dana u Beogradu, rekao mi je da on obično posećuje svoju sestru nedeljom ; ali pošto je hteo mene da povede sa sobom, otišli smo da je posetimo u petak (jer, razume se, morao sam da se vratim u Englesku prošle subote). Kupili smo karte prve klase i putovali udobno vozom. Prijatno smo se iznenadili kad smo videli da nas gospođica Simić čeka na stanici. Moram vam reći da je ona vrlo privlačna žena, ogromnih crnih očiju, kao u njenog brata, i verujem da je svi smatraju vrlo inteligentnom. Pošli smo pešice, uskim stazama, i stigli pred najmanju i najlepšu kućicu koju sam ikada video. Pošto smo sedeli i razgovarali jedan sat, ona nas je ostavila na nekoliko trenutaka i vratila se u sobu noseći poslužavnik na kome su bili šoljica slatke, crne, turske kafe koja se svuda pije u Jugoslaviji, čaša vode, tanjirić slatka i jedna kašičica. » Da li biste hteli da vam pokažem ovaj naš običaj ? « upitala me je smešeći se. Ali ja sam već znao šta treba da radim. Uzeo sam kašičicu slatka (samo jednu — setivši se strašne priče o Englezu koji je pojeo sve) ; držeći kašičicu u ruci, uzeo sam drugom rukom čašu i popio malo vode. Tada sam stavio kašičicu u čašu, koju sam zatim stavio na poslužavnik, i, najzad, popio šoljicu kafe. Moje poznavanje ovog malog običaja (zbog čega sam, moram priznati, bio dosta ponosan) iznenadilo je oboje, a još više moje znanje njihovog jezika. » Morate opet doći iduće godine «, rekli su, » i ostati duže kod nas. Tada niko neće misliti da niste pravi Jugosloven «.

Pola sata docnije gospođica Simić nas je ispratila na stanicu, i kad god se setim tog dana, vidim je kako stoji na peronu, i čujem je kako mi kaže : » Dođite opet iduće godine ! Srećan put ! Zbogom ! «

## 2. KEY TO SENTENCES AND PASSAGES FOR TRANSLATION INTO ENGLISH

The translations are literal wherever possible. Words and phrases which in Serbo-Croat are omitted, but which are supplied here in the English, are indicated thus: ' You can start on [your] way '. Where it is necessary to translate freely, a literal translation follows thus: ' . . . clapping (' having clapped ') his hands '.

Page 12.

1. They sing merrily when they are travelling. 2. I'm sitting here (*or* I sit here). 3. We don't sleep well (*or* We aren't sleeping well). 4. He's constantly eating and drinking. 5. You don't read, you don't write, and you don't study. 6. They are watching carefully. 7. We live here. 8. I don't drink. 9. They always sing loudly. 10. They sit at home and read. 11. I don't travel in winter but I often travel in summer. 12. I read quickly but carefully. 13. I usually work at home. 14. He sometimes speaks too quickly. 15. In winter we don't get up early. 16. He's constantly working. 17. They smoke when they work. 18. I write carefully. 19. I sit at home and read. 20. They read too quickly.

Page 18.

1. The young man sits (*or* is sitting) in the (*or* a) train and reads (*or* is reading). 2. I have a piece of bread. 3. They drink tea without sugar. 4. We're sitting near the window. 5. We don't smoke in the cinema. 6. Mr. Petrović has a car and a horse. 7. Jovan is with Mr. Petrović. 8. The students aren't studying. 9. The professor has a passport in [his] pocket. (See p. 17, footnote 2.) 10. The young men have knives in [their] pockets. 11. I see Mr. Pavlović through the window. 12. We're giving the passports to Mr. Petrović. 13. We're going to Belgrade. 14. I have a son in Belgrade. 15. Goodbye, Mr. Pavlović! 16. The students don't listen to the professor when he speaks. 17. The professor doesn't go to the cinema with the students. 18. I don't read novels. 19. We aren't travelling by ship. 20. Why are you sitting on the floor? 21. They don't see Jovan. 22. I'm sitting on a (*or* the) hill and looking at the roofs. 23. We are talking with the young man. 24. I understand the language. 25. Thank you. Enough!

Page 22.

1. Jovan is sitting in the train and looking at the mountains and fields. 2. I like to go ('that I go') to the theatre. 3. I always write with a pen. 4. You cannot read ('that you read'). 5. We're sitting near the window to watch the sea. 6. They don't like beer, they prefer wine. 7. Jovan usually spends the spring and summer in a village near a lake. 8. We live in a flat in a suburb of London. 9. I want to see Dubrovnik. 10. You must read loudly. 11. He cannot understand. 12. The bathroom is here. 13. The looking-glass is in the bathroom. 14. I have a pen but I cannot write. 15. You don't speak clearly enough. 16. The professors live near the theatre, and often go to the theatre. 17. We sit here, we drink beer and smoke. 18. I often get up early and go to the village. 19. In winter I like cities; in summer I prefer the village (*or* the country). 20. They eat bread with cheese or meat.

Page 25.

1. Are you a doctor? No, I'm not; I'm a professor. 2. Are *you* a doctor? Yes, I am. 3. The students aren't in Belgrade, they're in the country (*or* the village). 4. Are they here? Yes, they are. 5. Is Mr. Pavlović in Dubrovnik? Yes, he is. 6. You are Yugoslavs; we aren't. 7. I don't know where the village is. 8. We know that Jovan and the professor are in London. 9. Where are the passports? They're here. 10. Who are you? 11. You're not Mr. Pavlović. 12. Are we in Belgrade? No, we're not. 13. Are they on the ship? Yes, they are. 14. Do you know where you are? 15. No, I don't know where I am.

**Page 26.**

## Conversation in a train

Have you enough room (' place ')?

I have, thank you. I can put the case up there.

You have a lot of luggage.

Yes, I have, for I'm travelling to Dubrovnik, where I usually spend spring and summer; I stay in an hotel near the sea.

You are a Yugoslav?

No, I'm not, I'm an Englishman.

You speak well.

I'm studying the language here and with a professor (*or* teacher) in London.

You're coming from London now?

Yes. I like travelling. I often travel by aeroplane but I prefer trains. And you, sir, you are from Belgrade?

No, I am from Zagreb. I am a Croat.

Do you go to London sometimes?

Often. I have a son there. He is a student. Oh, good! They're saying that we can now go to the restaurant car for luncheon. Let's go!

**Page 31.**

1. Are you reading the news? I'm not reading the news, I'm reading a novel. 2. Where are the books? They're in the room. 3. Are they on the shelves? No, they're not. The cups and tumblers are on the shelves. 4. Are they in the cupboard? Yes, they are. 5. Are you in the house? No, I'm not, I'm in the street. 6. Is the house near the street? Yes, it is. 7. Is Mr. Petrović in the town? No, he's not. I don't know where he is. 8. Do you see Mr. Petrović? Yes. He's in the garden with Mrs. Petrović. 9. Do you understand? No, I

don't understand. 10. Have we any bread? No, we haven't.
11. Where is the cheese? I know that the cheese is in a basket
on a shelf in the kitchen. 12. Have you the pictures of Yugoslavia? I have. They're in a book. 13. Have you the book
with the pictures? I have; it's here. 14. Are you looking
at the pictures? Yes. I'm looking at many pictures. 15. Are
you travelling to Yugoslavia? Yes. I often travel to Dubrovnik. 16. Do you usually listen to many songs in Dalmatia?
Yes. They sing a lot there. 17. You're writing a lot of letters.
18. Are the travellers in the church? No, they're not; they're
talking with the soldiers. 19. I think that you work by night.
No, I work by day and I sleep by night. 20. Do you understand now? Yes, now I understand well.


Page 32.

I cannot see Mrs. Petrović. Perhaps she's in the kitchen.
No, she's not. I think she's in the drawing-room. She's
looking for books about Dalmatia and pictures of Dubrovnik.
She doesn't know where they are—she's constantly losing
things. She says that she knows that the books are somewhere
with the maps and the pictures, and she thinks that they're in
a drawer, but now she doesn't know where the key of the
drawer is. She's looking for the key. She certainly thinks
that Milan knows where the key is, for she is now looking for
Milan; she's looking through the window; but he is probably reading in the library, where he usually spends the day.
No, he's sitting on a seat in the garden in front of the house;
the books about Dalmatia are lying on the grass.


Page 38.

1. We lived in Ljubljana for a long time. 2. When I (f.)
spoke he didn't understand. 3. Were you looking for Mrs.
Simić? 4. We haven't been here (*or* We weren't here).

5. We were in the garden when he arrived.   6. While you were sleeping he was working.   7. We often travelled when I (f.) was a child.   8. You weren't writing a letter.   9. Did you notice the view from the window?   10. Jovan went (*or* has gone) with the soldiers.   11. They sat in the café, talked, drank and sang.   12. Did you think that I (f.) had forgotten the books?   13. Didn't you really sleep after the journey?   14. We (f. pl.) have been in the town, and we have bought many things.   15. Fortunately I (f.) was reading attentively when I noticed that the professor was in the library.   16. You didn't understand because you were not listening.   17. We got up early when we were in the village (*or* the country).   18. The village was burning, but they only watched.   19. They have already lunched.   20. He couldn't eat, but he drank some milk.

## Page 39.

Mr. Nikolić had reserved the rooms in the hotel in advance. It was late when he arrived by train, with Mrs. Nikolić, at the station. They took a taxi, but unfortunately when they spoke with (to) the driver he said ' I don't understand '.   A pity, for they thought that they spoke very well.   However, they pronounced the address of the hotel clearly enough, and so they soon arrived at the hotel; it was near the station.   Mr. Nikolić did not know how much to pay (' that he pays ') for the taxi, so he drew out some money from (' out of ') his pocket, and passed [it] to the driver.   Probably the driver did not take too much, for he carefully counted out the money. They could see the park around the hotel, although it was night.   People were sitting, were drinking, and were talking outside in the café in front of the hotel.   Mr. and Mrs. Nikolić wished only to sleep (' that they sleep ');   they dined quickly in the hotel and immediately lay down (i.e. went to bed).

Page 47.

1. They were reading his new book in my room. 2. Have you seen her green dress and her black coat with the wide sleeves? 3. I always travel by a fast train. 4. Where is your house? Is it in this suburb? 5. His lecture was interesting. 6. Haven't you seen the new bridge across that river? 7. The young Serbian girls were singing their national songs. 8. Give this hat to that old lady. 9. That city is very beautiful. 10. Jovan's son lives in our flat in London. 11. [My] sister's house is not large, but it is in a lovely village. 12. Those books are now theirs. 13. Last night I was talking to (with) your sisters in the cinema. 14. Why are you writing these Serbo-Croatian sentences so quickly? 15. He's constantly smoking cheap cigarettes and drinking red wine. 16. This is our mother and that is my son. 17. They listened to the professor's lecture very carefully, because it was important. 18. Unfortunately that old professor's lectures are often too boring. 19. I've received this letter from my friend (m.) in England. He always writes to me in Serbo-Croat. 20. I can't write with this cheap pencil.

Page 48.

### In the Post Office

Please, Miss, give me one stamp for a letter and one for a postcard.
For abroad or inland?
This letter is for abroad, and (*or* but) the postcard is for inland [post].
Do you want to send your letter by ordinary [mail] or by air mail?
How many days do letters travel to England?
I don't know exactly, sir, but it is certainly quicker by air.
Well then, by air mail please, because it's urgent. What do

you think, is it necessary for me to ('that I') send the letter registered?

No, it's not necessary if it's not particularly important. Here are your stamps: this is the stamp for your letter, sir, and this is for your postcard.

Thank you. How much do they cost? Unfortunately I haven't change ('small money').

It doesn't matter. I have enough small change.

## Page 53.

1. Why are you drinking [your] tea so slowly? 2. The man quickly drank up [his] beer and asked for the bill. 3. When did you buy that hat? 4. Why do you always buy hats like that? 5. Have you learned the Serbo-Croatian words on this page? 6. Unfortunately our young students study slowly. 7. I gave her old dresses to this poor woman. 8. Their companions departed last night. 9. Why are you giving tea to your little child? 10. He ate a piece of bread and (with) cheese, and went off to the theatre. 11. When we went into his room he was looking through the window. 12. I asked (requested) him to come home early. 13. She asked the policeman where the post office was ('is'). 14. Did you fall asleep immediately? 15. I know that you have bought a new house. 16. My sons, my husband and I usually rise early, but today we got up late. 17. Have you read this book? No, I'm still reading it. 18. Do you often go to the theatre? 19. Jovan went off to school yesterday without his books. 20. I've written (or I wrote) a lot of letters.

## Page 60.

When our train was passing through Austria we were able to lie down. Immediately we fell asleep. We slept right until we arrived at the frontier. There we wanted to get out of the

train and drink a glass of beer in the buffet on the station
platform, but the guard said that we must sit in our compartment; he said that the customs officer and other officials
come into the train before the train crosses the frontier. So
we sat down and waited. Soon a Yugoslav official came and
asked for our passports. When he had gone my friend glanced
into the corridor and said: ' The customs officer is coming.
We must say that we have these boxes of English cigarettes.'
The customs officer—a very polite and agreeable man—came
into our compartment, glanced at our luggage, spoke a few
words in Serbo-Croat, and went out.

Page 66.

1. When will the train start for Belgrade? It will start
immediately. 2. Jovan promised that he would come home
after lunch. 3. Shall we have to spend the night in Ljubljana?
4. She will sit in their beautiful garden and read these books.
5. The child will drink a large cup of milk before it goes to
sleep. 6. This evening we shall not go to the theatre; we
shall be too tired. 7. Will you visit Mrs. Petrović before you
go to the cinema? 8. Tomorrow we shall telephone [to] the
old professor. 9. Will those students really not be at Mr.
Petrović's lecture? It will be very interesting. 10. I will read
these important letters before I go to bed (' lie down '). 
11. Will you really not go to the station to ask when the train
starts? 12. I shall not go to sleep until I finish this task.
13. I expected that the doctor would arrive in time, but he
didn't. 14. We shall travel by night and sleep by day. 15.
Where will you sit? Near the window or near the cupboard?
16. We shall pass by your house this afternoon (' after noon ');
will you be at the window? 17. We shall get out of the train
when we arrive at the station. 18. Will you write a postcard
to my son? 19. I shall put my things under yours. 20. It's
already late: when shall we dine?

Page 68.

When she came home Jeca went into her room, drew out a chest from under the bed and hastily crammed into the chest those few things which were hers. Everything that she had got from Mrs. Lucija she left in the cupboard. Then she went to the station to ask when the first train starts for Drniš. She would go home, she would go for certain. She would travel via Drniš. She would arrive in the evening at Drniš, where she would have to spend the night, for she would not be able to go on foot across the mountain, by unknown paths.

(*Note:* The future tense is used in Serbo-Croat for the thoughts which were in Jeca's mind. See p. 65, and p. 39, footnote 1.)

Page 74.

1. We shall not see her tomorrow. 2. We didn't hear him when he was entering the house. 3. I was looking at her but she did not notice me. 4. We found them in the park and asked (requested) them to come tomorrow. 5. Now I'll go to look for him. 6. Yesterday he told me that he would go to the theatre with me. 7. We shall not invite them to lunch. 8. Did she tell him that his friend invited (*or* had invited) her to supper? 9. We will wait for you (i.e. meet you, wait until you come) at the station. 10. He gave her his address. 11. She promised me that she would be obedient. 12. He brought chairs for them and for me. 13. Did they understand you when you spoke Serbo-Croat? 14. We shall give them these dictionaries when we see them. 15. They were not at my home when you were looking for them.

Page 76.

In the afternoon (' after noon '), a little [while] before the departure of the train, Jeca took the chest. She found Lucija on the ground floor and said to her:

' I am going home.'

' You've gone mad! And my child?'

' All the same (' All-one '). Mine too has been waiting for me a long time.'

' You dare (must) not go ', shouted Lucija. ' I will send the police after you. I don't let you go!'

But Jeca flew out of the house and ran towards the station.

As soon as she had sat down in the carriage the train started. With her were travelling other passengers, but she took no notice of them (' she did not care about them '). Only one thought and wish lived in her: to arrive as soon as possible there where her Jovo was.


Page 80.

1. They don't remember your parents. 2. The Englishmen were not laughing at this joke because they didn't understand it. 3. For himself he left a very large piece of meat. 4. I hope that old woman will not be angry with me. 5. Our friend Mr. Petrović did not buy the house for himself but for his sister. 6. I wonder whether I've made a mistake. 7. That didn't happen yesterday; it happened the day before yesterday. 8. Were you really not able to return in time? 9. Jovan was washing while his father was taking a bath. 10. The young men at last realised that they had lost themselves (that they were lost) in the forest. 11. They greeted each other when they met. 12. It's written here that it's not allowed to (one must not) enter this building. 13. It is said that the mother of that actor was a great actress too. 14. They were climbing up that wall when I saw them. 15. The

travellers took all their things with them.  16. I am glad that
you have come.  17. We stopped immediately.  18. What is
the name of that village which is situated near the forest?
19. My son was afraid of your big dog, sir.  20. I couldn't
remember his name.

Page 82.

> Wine, Mila! [it] resounded
> While Mila was here.
> Now Mila has disappeared—
> Another's hands bear the wine.
> Anna pours,
> Anna serves,
> But for Mila the heart grieves.

That night, in the café, Petronije slept very well and very
soundly.  And the next day he awoke before the café lads had
awoken and he could scarcely wait (' scarcely waited ') for the
door to be opened.  He then went to the barber's, had a
haircut, was shaved, put on a black coat and set off for
(' directed himself to ') Terazije, for the ministry.  When he
arrived at the ministry it seemed to him as though somebody
was pulling (' is pulling ') him back by the coat, so he turned
to see who it was (' is ').

Page 87.

1. He wrote 6 important letters in 50 minutes.  2. Why do
you have 4 telephone directories?  3. We have reserved 5
nice rooms, one for my husband and 4 for Jovan and his 7
young friends.  4. You will see 21 buildings: two big houses
and 19 little cottages.  5. Her 2 sons were preparing luncheon
while she was sitting in the garden with her 3 friends (f.).
6. His wife told me that he had been in England 5 weeks

and that he smoked 50 English cigarettes a day. 7. We've lost 1,000 dinars; now we have only 31 English pounds in our pockets ('in pocket'). 8. There isn't enough room for these 15 large parcels in one car. 9. There were 18 students but only 14 chairs, so 4 students were sitting on the floor. 10. She promised that she would sing 10 folk songs. I am glad, because I like Yugoslav folk songs ('... songs please me') very much.

Page 92.

1. He came at 5.30 and went at a quarter to 8. 2. I shall arrive by train at 5.20. 3. It happened on either the 15th or the 16th of April. 4. At what time does the first train for Belgrade start? At 2.35. 5. I've read his third novel and now I'm reading the fourth; I like them very much. 6. He was born on 30th November 1922; in any case he is at least 40. 7. Is today the 11th or 12th of February? 8. He didn't get up till ('he got up only at') 10 o'clock and left the house at a quarter to 11. 9. My parents live in the fifth house on the right. 10. We hope that you will come at 7.30, because we usually dine at 8.

Page 93.

He was just going to ('he was just wanting to') cross the threshold, but it occurred to him to wonder ('that he asks himself') what was ('is') the date today. Was ('is') it perhaps the 13th? It was the first of April, thank God. He went into the waiting-room. Already when he had gone to be shaved he had bought a few good cigarettes and put [them] in his pocket. First of all he offered a cigarette to the youth who was standing before the minister's door, let him light up and take ('draw') two [or] three puffs, and only then began:

'Has (Mr.) the minister come yet?'

The youth first took a long puff, let it out through [his] nostrils, and answered indifferently:

'He will not come to the office today.'

'Oh, I see! ('thus', 'so').

Petronije was actually glad that the minister would not come to the office today. He offered the youth another cigarette and went off in a very good mood.


Page 99.

1. The street along by the bridge is not longer than ours; I think that it is much shorter. 2. Did you say that London is the largest city in the world? 3. The most expensive things are not always the best too. 4. Please give me stronger tea. 5. On November 10th the fog in London was denser than usual. 6. Olga's voice is always much softer than Milan's. 7. Jovan thinks that English is the most difficult language in the world, but you certainly think that Serbo-Croat is much more difficult. 8. Is December 30th the shortest day in the year? I don't know, but I think that June 21st is the longest. 9. We drove along the most beautiful road although it was more dangerous. 10. They say that honey is sweeter than sugar, but it isn't. 11. She ran faster and faster, right until she could go no further ('not go further'). 12. Do you believe that the richer man is not more contented than the poorer? 13. I promise you that I will send you as much money as possible. 14. I hope that the sea will be calmer this afternoon ('after noon'); I prefer to bathe in calmer water. 15. What are you doing? I'm learning words, I'm reading Serbo-Croatian sentences, I'm translating English sentences, and so on.

Page 100.

### The Fish and the Maiden

A maiden sits beside the sea
And she herself speaks to herself:
'Oh God, kind and dear!
Is there anything wider than the sea?
Is there anything longer than the plain?
Is there anything swifter than a horse?
Is there anything sweeter than honey?
Is there anything dearer than a brother?'
A fish speaks from the water:
' Maiden, crazy fool,
Wider is the sky than the sea,
Longer is the sea than the plain,
Swifter are eyes than a horse,
Sweeter is sugar than honey,
Dearer is the beloved than a brother.'

Page 106.

1. Do you know what she was reading about (' about what she was reading ') in that book which you gave to her? 2. I wonder who will come to dinner. Whom did you invite? 3. On Saturdays I am never free; we will see each other on Thursday. 4. Who is that woman with whom you were talking when I saw you last Sunday in the museum? 5. He has already forgotten everything that he had learned. 6. We shall arrive at the beginning of April and we shall remain the whole spring in Split, at the home of those friends about whom I've often spoken to you. 7. Whose is this parcel? The address on it cannot be read (' cannot read itself '). 8. What shall I write with? I've lost both pen and pencil. 9. Nobody told him whose ticket this is, so he put it in his pocket. 10. What did you answer when he asked you whether you like his pictures?

**Page 107.**

The next day the minister was in the office, but he immediately departed. The day after that the minister was in the office, but he would not (' will not ') receive [anybody].

On the 4th day two other ministers are with the minister, and 'they are having some important conversation' (the young man told him this confidentially), so it's not known whether he will get to receiving [anybody].

On the 5th day the minister said that he would receive only those who had very important business, which could not be postponed until the next day.

On the 6th day Petronije had to be shaved again. But on that day again the minister was not coming to the office.

On the 7th day there was a ministerial meeting, so the minister could not receive anybody.

On the 8th day the minister would not be receiving.

On the 9th day the minister was in the office, but he departed immediately.

On the 10th day the minister received 7 people, and then the young man said: those who still remained, to come (' that they come ') tomorrow.

On the 13th day Petronije had to be shaved again, but when he crossed the threshold at the ministry he remembered that it was already the 13th of April.


**Page 114.**

1. His reasons were good, and the workmen agreed to them with pleasure. 2. Why didn't you tell mother that her sister is ill? I was afraid that she would be anxious. 3. The soldiers crossed over the bridge with rapid strides. 4. 'Goodbye, father,' said Marija, and went sadly out of the room. 5. In which book did you see the rare pictures from Yugoslavia? 6. Our dogs like to bathe in the river only when the water is

warm. 7. I wonder whether she is satisfied with her latest ('newest') successes. 8. Will they talk about affairs of state at the meetings? 9. The translators of French novels have plenty of work, for there are many readers for such books. 10. Soldier, did you find your name in these articles? 11. The beginnings of all tasks are rather difficult. 12. I prefer to cut bread with a sharper knife. 13. The shutters on these windows are not strong enough; they are already broken. 14. What will these poor men do after your good father's departure? We have 2 tables but only 5 chairs; where will all the school-boys sit?

## Page 118.

1. I should not wish to go with him. 2. Should we see the sea from your window? Yes, we should. 3. He would be more cheerful in Paris. 4. Should I (f.) be able to travel by a fast train? 5. I should not recognise him. 6. It would be better for us to remain ('that we remain') in this hotel. 7. Would he not consent to wait a few minutes? 8. I know that she would not agree to ('with') these suggestions. 9. Would *you* believe what ('that which') he told me? Yes, I should. 10. I (f.) could invite him, but would he come? He wouldn't.

## Page 120.

1. Wouldn't it be better to go ('that we go') to the station to meet ('wait for') her? 2. You would like beer, wouldn't you? 3. If you had come in time you would have heard the beginning of the lecture. 4. We moved to Zagreb in order to be with our acquaintances there. 5. If your father agrees to ('with') these suggestions then everything is all right

(' in order '). 6. The tourists climbed to the top of the mountain so that they would see the sea. 7. While she was sewing he would read aloud to her. 8. If snow should fall tomorrow I would stay at home. 9. In order that he should not have to lunch again near such company, that only comes on Sundays, he left the town today. 10. If I had received your letter I would not have expected that you would come.


Page 122.

Dear Mr. Petrović,

I thank you for [your] letter and invitation to spend a week (' a week of days ') at Easter with you and your family. I accept the invitation with great pleasure. I shall start on Friday at 3.30 p.m. I shall be at your home at about 6 o'clock. I should be grateful to you if you would send Jovan to meet me at the station, for I shall have a great deal of luggage.

I hope that the whole family will be together during the holidays.

> With warmest greetings (' Heartily greets you '),
> Milan Popović.


To the Director of Hotel Dalmatia,
Dubrovnik.
Dear Sir,

Please will you reserve (' I beg you to reserve ') a room with 2 beds in your hotel for my wife and myself. We shall stay in Dubrovnik from the 2nd to the 23rd July. In addition to the room we wish for breakfast and dinner, and on Sundays luncheon as well.

I shall be grateful if you confirm this reservation as soon as possible.

> Yours faithfully (' With respect '),
> Jovan Jovanović.

Page 126.

1. Please will you pass me that cushion? Thank you. Now be so kind as to sit ('be kind and sit') quietly and read; do not speak, for I am very busy; believe me, I have a lot of work today. Listen! I think that Miss Ilić is outside. Open the door; let her come in. Good day, gospodjica! Come to me. Will you sit here? Mind, that's my book. Now keep quiet while I am writing, and afterwards tell me everything that you have done today.

2. Listen to me! Be a peaceful citizen, take off your cap to everyone (each [one]) who is even only a little higher than you; teach yourself to bow even more deeply; teach yourself to bend your knees a little, too, and when your back hurts don't complain but tell everyone that it is from a cold. Do not speak the truth to great men to their face, and least of all may you (' dare you ') make that mistake to rulers and women. Always be prepared to tell a ruler that he is noble and a woman that she is beautiful. In the newspaper read only the advertisements. There, that is my advice to you, act thus and you will not regret [it].

Page 131.

1. I wanted to visit the minister of justice, but he was not in the country. He had gone abroad to study schools for deaf and dumb children. Since this matter, as [being] very important, could not be postponed (' suffer postponement '), the most necessary steps had been immediately undertaken. Besides the fact that the minister of justice had been sent to study the organisation of such schools, with a very large supplement along with [his] salary, a director of the schools had immediately been appointed, and already construction had been begun of a large building which was earmarked for the director's residence.

2. At the top of the hall, on a raised divan, between 2 large windows, like some president, a young Frenchwoman has crossed her legs ('flung leg across leg') and is sitting. All the garments on her are red. Gloves, scarf, shoes: everything is of the reddest colour. The trinkets on her head, around her neck, on her arms, are only fine red corals. There isn't a single little thread of another colour to be seen on her. Besides this, her beautiful hair and eyebrows are dyed with the finest reddish colour so skilfully that everyone would say that she had been born with such hair.


Page 137.

1. As soon as I had closed the door behind myself I heard a tapping on the door.

'Come in!' I said.

Into the room comes a man dressed in gentlemanly style, with spectacles on his nose. He bows deeply (which I too, of course, do) and presents himself as a senior official from the ministry.

'How do you do? ('I am pleased')' I said, surprised by this unexpected visit.

'You are the first time now in our country, sir?' he asked me.

'The first time.'

'You are a foreigner?'

'Yes, a foreigner.'

'You have come to us as if sent for, believe me!' cried the senior official enthusiastically.

This confused me still more.


2. I found the old woman in a large old-fashioned bed. She was lying with her head on the pillow. Everything about ('on') her was sad and tired, only her lips smiled. When I

called her she did not hear me. Her hand seemed to me cold
as ice. I was afraid of something; it occurred to me that it
would soon be dark and that I could not stay long beside her.
And suddenly I decided on something. I went out, rushed
down the steps, ran home. I told my parents what was now
happening in the house with the balcony. Mother gave to
each of us something to carry. All together we hurried to the
old woman.

## Page 143.

1. In this room are 2 doors; one leads to the bathroom,
and the other to the corridor. 2. Who are those gentlemen?
I saw them yesterday with your brothers. 3. Take 6 oranges
and give them to those children. 4. Is it true that you have
7 brothers? 5. Yes, it is. Three are doctors, like my father,
and four are office-workers. 6. There were 6 (of them) in
the theatre—two actresses and 4 actors. 7. We two stayed
to the end of the concert. 8. Every Sunday they buy four
newspapers: do you think that they read them? 9. Ask
those 4 students what their names are (' how they call themselves '). 10. The enemy threw 10 bombs, due to (' from ')
which several large shops were burned out.

## Page 147.

1. 'We have one more vacant place for a consul. Here
you would have a good salary and good supplements, which
you would, of course, spend on your personal things. You
are an old, experienced man, and your duties are (' duty is ')
easy. More than a month (' month of days ') already we have
been struggling (' tormenting ourselves ') looking for a suitable
person for this important position. Of which nationality are
you, if I may ask? '

'Well, I—really—how can I tell you—don't even know,
myself, yet,' I said, ashamed, but he interrupted me, clapping

('having clapped') his hands ('with palm against palm') enthusiastically.

'Excellent, excellent! Never better! You will be able just to carry out such an important task conscientiously. I'm going to the minister immediately, and in a few days you can start on [your] way!' the senior official pronounced, and hurried off to report to his minister the important discovery.

2. As soon as we had sat down, a waiter immediately ran up, brought us the menu in French and asked: 'What do you wish to eat?' My companion, not even taking the card into his hands, said 'Soup etc.' The waiter glanced at him as if he would like to know what he meant ('understood') by ('under') that 'etc.'. But not having got any explanation he turned to me with the same question. I answered him: 'Bring me the same.' The waiter went away. At the bottom of the garden from where the food is brought, he talked a little with the proprietress; evidently he was taking advice [as to] what he would bring us after the soup. They were curious [to know] what we had meant by that 'etc.', and we were curious [to know] how they would understand it, and what they would bring us.

We had done well to have ('that we had') spoken to the waiter in such a way, for he chose us a much better luncheon than if we had chosen. My companion's excellent characteristic, that he doesn't talk at all ('speaks nothing') at luncheon, was already known to me. We ate quickly and with relish. The waiter brought us the bill in silence ('keeping silent'); we paid him in silence.

3. Marko comes to Belgrade. Cars, trams, people, all rush, hurry; clerks hurry to the office, workmen to their work.

He meets a distinguished, well-dressed gentleman. Marko goes up to him and greets him. The latter was a little embarrassed; he was ashamed [because] of Marko's poor clothes.

'I am Marko Kraljević. I have come here to help my brothers,' said Marko, and related everything: how he had come, why he had come, everything that had happened to him ('been with him'), and what he thought of doing further.

'So-o. I am pleased to have made your acquaintance, Mr. Kraljević! I really am pleased, believe me; but excuse me, I am hurrying to the office!' said he ('that one'), and hastily went off.

Marko meets a second, a third. Whoever he meets, so, instantly, the conversation ends with that 'I'm hurrying to the office'. Marko goes along the streets and is silent; he stops nobody, he asks nobody anything. But whom shall he ask any more? Whoever he sees is hurrying to the office.

## Page 154.

1. I would prefer that he wrote ('writes') to me by hand, but all his letters are written by typewriter. 2. The citizen of Belgrade who arrived last Sunday was a man with a long nose, a broad back, and black hair. 3. Please give me one kilogramme of bread and a hundred grammes of cheese. 4. Every day I see the same old woman in the town. There she is; now, too, she's going along the street. 5. She's cold, her hands are [as] cold as ice. 6. I asked him when he would come, and he answered (to me) that he would arrive by 5 o'clock. 7. The road alongside the sea was only a mile long, but he couldn't go further because his legs ached. 8. He has been living in Yugoslavia for years already, and of course he speaks Serbo-Croat like a real Yugoslav. 9. I am sorry, dear madam, that I shall not be able to visit you, but on Saturdays and Sundays I always visit my children. 10. He said that at last I speak fairly fluently and correctly; although I didn't believe him his words made me very happy.

## 2. VERB LISTS

The following is a list of the commonest of the verbs whose present tense cannot be deduced from their infinitive. It does not, therefore, include verbs with infinitive ending *-iti* (which always have present tense ending *-im*), unless the *i* preceding *-ti* is part of the stem of the verb, e.g. piti, pijem ; nor verbs with infinitive ending *-nuti* (present tense always *-nem*), nor those verbs with infinitive ending *-ovati*, *-ivati* which have present tense ending *-ujem*. Verbs with infinitive ending *-ati* and present tense *-am* are not given. The list consists principally of simple verbs, as their forms with prepositional prefixes have the same endings in the present tense, e.g. *piti, pijem ; popiti, popijem*. For most verbs it has only been necessary to give one aspect, e.g. *kretati, krećem* (ipf.) is given, but not its perfective counterpart *krenuti* (present tense obviously *krenem*). Where necessary, the active past participle is also given (for certain verbs both masculine and feminine singular forms). Only the most usual meanings of the verbs have been given, and the list should be used in conjunction with a dictionary.

bdeti, bdim (ipf.)—to stay awake

bežati, bežim (ipf.)—to flee

biti (see p. 57)—to be

biti, bijem (ipf.)—to beat

bojati se, bojim se (ipf.)—to fear

boleti, boli (ipf.)—to be painful, to hurt

bosti, bodem, bo, bola (ipf.)—to pierce

brati, berem (ipf.)—to gather, pluck

brisati, brišem (ipf.)—to wipe

crpsti, crpem, crpao (ipf.)—to draw (from), derive

čuti, čujem (pf. and ipf.)—to hear

davati, dajem (ipf.)—to give

derati, derem (ipf.)—to tear

dići, dignem, digao (pf.)—to raise

disati, dišem (ipf.)—to breathe

dizati, dižem (ipf.)—to raise

dobiti, dobijem (pf.)—to get

dobivati, dobivam (ipf.)—to get

doći, dođem, došao (pf.)—to come

doneti, donesem (pf.)—to bring

drhtati, dršćem (ipf.)—to tremble

držati, držim (ipf.)—to hold

goreti, gorim (ipf.)—to be burning

grejati, grejem (ipf.)—to heat

grepsti, grebem, grebao (ipf.) —to scratch

gristi, grizem, grizao (ipf.)— to bite, munch

hrkati, hrčem (ipf.)—to snore

hteti (see p. 62)

hvalisati se, hvališem se (ipf.) —to boast

ići, idem, išao (ipf.)—to go

iskati, ištem (ipf.)—to demand

istaći, istaknem, istakao (ipf.) —to project

izabrati, izaberem (pf.)—to choose

iznemoći, iznemognem, iznemogao (pf.)—to become exhausted

jahati, jašem (ipf.)—to ride (e.g. on horseback)

kajati se, kajem se (ipf.)—to regret, repent

kašljati, kašljem (ipf.)—to cough

kazati, kažem (pf. and ipf.)— to say, tell

klati, koljem (ipf.)—to slaughter

klečati, klečim (ipf.)—to kneel

kleti, kunem (ipf.)—to curse

klicati, kličem (ipf.)—to applaud

kovati, kujem (ipf.)—to forge (metal)

krasti, kradem, krao (ipf.)— to steal

kretati, krećem (ipf.)—to move

kriti, krijem (ipf.)—to hide

lagati, lažem (ipf.)—to tell a lie

lajati, lajem (ipf.)—to bark

leći, legnem, legao (pf.)—to lie down

leteti, letim (ipf.)—to fly

ležati, ležim (ipf.)—to lie, recline

liti, lijem (ipf.)—to pour

maći (maknuti), maknem, maknuo (pf.)—to move

mesti, metem, meo (ipf.)— to sweep

metati, mećem (ipf.)—to put

micati, mičem (ipf.)—to move

mirisati, mirišem (ipf.)—to smell

miti, mijem (ipf.)—to wash

moći (see p. 21)

mrzeti, mrzim (ipf.)—to hate

musti, muzem, muzao (ipf.)—to milk

naći, nađem, našao (pf.)—to find

napeti, napnem (pf.)—to stretch, strain

nastojati, nastojim (ipf.)—to endeavour

nazirati, nazirem (ipf.)—to be of opinion

nedostajati, nedostajem (ipf.)—to be lacking

nestajati, nestajem (ipf.)—to disappear

nestati, nestanem (pf.)—to disappear

nicati, ničem (ipf.)—to germinate

nići, niknem, nikao (pf.)—to germinate

nizati, nižem (ipf.)—to put in a row, string up

njihati, njišem (ipf.)—to swing

obazirati se, obazirem se (ipf.)—to bear in mind

obući, obučem, obukao (pf.)—to put on (clothes)

odbiti, odbijem (pf.)—to reject

odlagati, odlažem (ipf.)—to postpone

odoleti, odolim (ipf.)—to overcome

odreći, odrečem, odrekao (pf.)—to renounce

odricati, odričem (ipf.)—to renounce

odupirati, odupirem (ipf.)—to resist

oduzeti, oduzmem (pf.)—to subtract, deduct

okretati, okrećem (ipf.)—to turn

orati, orem (ipf.)—to plough

osnovati, osnujem or osnivati, osnivam (ipf.)—to found, establish

ostajati, ostajem (ipf.)—to remain

ostati, ostanem (pf.)—to remain

oteći, otečem, otekao (pf.)—to swell

oteti, otmem (pf.)—to carry off, seize

otezati, otežem (ipf.)—to drag out, delay

oticati, otičem (ipf.)—to swell

otići, otidem or odem, otišao (pf.)—to go away

pasti, padnem, pao (pf.)—to fall

pasti, pasem, pasao (ipf.)—to graze, pasture

peći, pečem, pekao (ipf.)—to bake

penjati se *or* peti se, penjem se (ipf.)—to climb

pisati, pišem (ipf.)—to write

piti, pijem (ipf.)—to drink

plakati, plačem (ipf.)—to weep

plesti, pletem, pleo (ipf.)—to knit, interweave

pljuštati, pljušti (ipf.)—to rain heavily

pobeći, pobegnem, pobegao (pf.)—to flee

pobledeti, pobledim (pf.)—to turn pale

pocrveneti, pocrvenim (pf.)— to blush

početi, počnem (pf.)—to begin

počinjati, počinjem (ipf.)—to begin

poći, pođem, pošao (pf.)—to start off

podupirati, podupirem (ipf.) —to support

podupreti, poduprem (pf.)— to support

pokazati, pokažem (pf.)—to show

poludeti, poludim (pf.)—to go mad

pomagati, pomažem (ipf.)—to help

pominjati, pominjem (ipf.)— to mention

pomoći, pomognem, pomogao (pf.)—to help

poneti, ponesem (pf.)—to take, bring

popeti se, popnem se (pf.)— to climb

poreći, porečem, porekao (pf.)—to revoke ; deny

poslati, pošljem (pf.)—to send

postajati, postajem (ipf.)—to become

postati, postanem (pf.)—to become

postići, postignem, postigao (pf.)—to attain, achieve

postojati, postojim (ipf.)—to exist

povesti, povedem, poveo (pf.) —to take, lead (a person)

poznavati, poznajem (ipf.)— to know

pozvati, pozovem (pf.)—to invite, summon

prati, perem (ipf.)—to wash

preći, pređem, prešao (pf.)— to cross

predavati, predajem (ipf.)—to hand over ; teach

predlagati, predlažem (ipf.)—to suggest

preduzeti, preduzmem (pf.)—to undertake

preklinjati se, preklinjem se (ipf.)—to swear (e.g. by oath)

prestajati, prestajem (ipf.)—to cease

prestati, prestanem (pf.)—to cease

presti, predem, preo (ipf.)—to spin ; purr

preteći, pretečem, pretekao (pf.)—to overtake ; surpass

prevesti, prevedem, preveo (pf.)—to translate

prići, pridem, prišao (pf.)—to approach

pripisati, pripišem (pf.)—to attribute

proći, prodem, prošao (pf.)—to pass

prokleti, prokunem (pf.)—to curse

pronaći, pronadem, pronašao (pf.)—to discover

prostirati, prostirem (ipf.)—to spread

prostreti or prostrti, prostrem, prostřo, prostrla (pf.)—to spread

provesti, provedem, proveo (pf.)—to spend (time)

prožeti, prožmem (pf.)—to penetrate, permeate

psovati, psujem (ipf.)—to curse

pući, puknem, pukao (pf.)—to burst

raspolagati, raspolažem (ipf.)—to dispose of, have at one's disposal

rastajati se, rastajem se (ipf.)—to part

rastati se, rastanem se (pf.)—to part

rasti, rastem, rastao, rasla (ipf.)—to grow

rasuti, raspem (pf.)—to spill ; squander

razbiti, razbijem (pf.)—to smash

razviti, razvijem (pf.)—to develop

reći, reknem, rekao (pf.)—to say

rezati, režem (ipf.)—to cut, carve

roktati, rokćem (ipf.)—to grunt

rzati, ržem (ipf.)—to neigh

sadržati, sadržim (ipf.)—to contain

sakriti, sakrijem (pf.)—to hide

sastajati se, sastajem se (ipf.) —to meet

sastati se, sastanem se (pf.)— to meet

sastojati se, sastoji se (ipf.)— to consist (of)

sašiti, sašijem (pf.)—to sew together

satrti, satrem, satřo, satrla (pf.)—to crush, pulverise

saviti, savijem (pf.)—to bend, fold, roll

seći, sečem, sekao (pf.)—to cut

sedeti, sedim (ipf.)—to sit

sejati, sejem (ipf.)—to sow

sesti, sednem (pf.)—to sit down

sići, siđem, sišao (pf.)—to descend

skakati, skačem (ipf.)—to jump, caper

slagati, slažem (ipf.)—to assemble

slagati se, slažem se (ipf.)—to agree

slati, šaljem (ipf.)—to send

sleći (slegnuti), slegnem, slegao (pf.)—to shrug

slegati, sležem (ipf.)— to shrug

smejati se, smejem se (ipf.)— to laugh

snaći, snađem, snašao (pf.)— to befall

spasti, spasem, spasao (pf.)— to save

spominjati, spominjem (ipf.) —to mention

spotaći se, spotaknem se, spotakao (pf.)—to stumble (against)

sresti, sretnem, sreo (pf.)—to meet

srkati, srčem (ipf.)—to sip

stajati, stajem (ipf.)—to stand (on)

stati, stanem (pf.)—to come to a halt

steći, stečem, stekao (pf.)—to acquire

stezati, stežem (ipf.)—to tighten

stići, stignem, stigao (pf.)—to arrive

stideti se, stidim se (ipf.)—to be ashamed

stizati, stižem (ipf.)—to arrive

stojati, stojim (ipf.)—to be standing

strugati, stružem (ipf.)—to saw

svideti se, svidim se (ipf.)—to be pleasing

šaptati, šapćem, *or* šaputati, sapućem (ipf.)—to whisper

šiti, šijem (ipf.)—to sew

štedeti, štedim (ipf.)—to save, economise

šuteti, šutim (ipf.)—to keep silent

teći, tečem, tekao (ipf.)—to flow

ticati, tičem (ipf.)—to touch

tkati, tkam or tkem or čem (ipf.)—to weave

trajati, trajem (ipf.)—to last

trčati, trčim (ipf.)—to run

treptati, trepćem (ipf.)—to vibrate ; blink

tresti, tresem, tresao (ipf.)—to shake

trpeti, trpim (ipf.)—to endure, bear

trti, tarem or trem, tŕo, trla (ipf.)—to rub

trzati, trzam or tržem (ipf.)—to jerk, tug

tući, tučem, tukao (ipf.)—to hit

ubiti, ubijem (pf.)—to kill

ući, uđem, ušao (pf.)—to enter

umaći, umaknem, umakao (pf.)—to escape

umirati, umirem (ipf.)—to die

umreti, umrem, umŕo, umrla (pf.)—to die

upiti, upijem (pf.)—to absorb

upirati, upirem (ipf.)—to lean

upreti, uprem, upŕo, uprla (pf.)—to lean

uprezati, uprežem (ipf.)—to harness

uspeti, uspem (pf.)—to succeed

uspeti se, uspnem se (pf.)—to climb up

ustajati, ustajem (ipf.)—to get up

ustati, ustanem (pf.)—to get up

uteći, utečem, utekao (pf.)—to flee

uvesti, uvedem (pf.)—to lead in, introduce

uzeti, uzmem (pf.)—to take

užeći, užežem, užegao (pf.)—to ignite

vesti, vezem, vezao (ipf.)—to embroider

vezati, vežem (ipf.)—to bind

videti, vidim (pf. and ipf.)—to see

vikati, vičem (ipf.)—to shout

viti, vijem (ipf.)—to wind

voleti, volim (ipf.)—to love, like

vrteti, vrtim (ipf.)—to revolve

vući, vučem, vukao (ipf.)—to pull

zaspati, zaspim (pf.)—to fall asleep

zateći, zatečem, zatekao (pf.) —to come upon

zepsti, zebem, zebao (ipf.)—to feel cold

zvati, zovem (ipf.)—to call

zvečati, zvečim (ipf.)—to clank

zveketati, zvekećem (ipf.)—to rattle

želeti, želim (ipf.)—to wish

žeti, žanjem (ipf.)—to harvest

živeti, živim (ipf.)—to live

žudeti, žudim (ipf.)—to crave

# LIST OF COMMON VERBS TAKING THE GENITIVE, DATIVE, AND INSTRUMENTAL CASES

## 1. Verbs Taking the Genitive Case

bojati se—to be afraid of

čuvati se—to beware of

dočepati se [1]—to grab

držati se—to hold, adhere to

gnušati se—to loathe

kloniti se—to get out of the way of

latiti se—to take up (e.g. latiti se posla—to set to work)

lišiti—to deprive (someone, acc.) of

mašiti se—to touch, reach for

najesti se—to eat one's fill of

napiti se—to drink one's fill of

napuniti se—to fill oneself with

nasititi se—to become satiated with

nestati—to disappear (used impersonally, e.g. nestalo ga—he has disappeared)

osloboditi se—to free oneself from

otresti se—to get rid of, shake off

plašiti se—to be scared of

primiti se—to take upon oneself

setiti se—to recall

spasti se—to save oneself from

stideti se—to be ashamed of

ticati se—to concern (e.g. to se ne tiče mene)

## 2. Verbs Taking the Dative Case

Examples : pomoći (nekome)—to help (someone) ; diviti se (nečemu)—to admire (something).

čestitati (nekome)—to congratulate

čuditi se (nečemu)—to wonder at

diviti se (nečemu)—to admire

---

[1] Many transitive verbs may be used reflexively in this way with the object in the genitive case.

dogoditi se (nekome)—to happen to

đolikovati (nekome)—to befit

dopadati se (nekome)—to be pleasing to

dopustiti (nekome)—to permit

dosaditi (nekome)—to bore

dozvoliti (nekome)—to permit

klicati (nekome)—to applaud

koristiti (nekome)—to profit, be useful to

laknuti [1] (nekome)—to give relief to

laskati (nekome)—to flatter

nadati se (nečemu)—to hope for

narediti (nekome)—to order

obećati (nekome)—to promise

obradovati se (nečemu)—to be delighted at

odgovoriti (nekome)—to answer

odoleti (nekome, nečemu)—to resist

oprostiti (nekome)—to forgive

podviknuti (nekome)—to admonish

pokoriti se (nekome, nečemu)—to submit to

pomoći (nekome)—to help

posvetiti se (nečemu)—to devote oneself to

poveriti (nekome)—to confide

prebaciti (nekome)—to reproach

pretiti (nekome)—to threaten

približiti se (nečemu, nekome)—to approach

prići (nečemu, nekome)—to approach

prigovoriti (nekome)—to find fault with

prilagoditi se (nečemu)—to adapt oneself to

priličiti (nekome)—to beseem

primaći se (nečemu, nekome)—to approach

pripadati (nečemu, nekome)—to belong to

prisustvovati (nečemu)—to be present at

prkositi (nekome)—to spite, challenge

protiviti se (nečemu, nekome)—to oppose

protivrečiti (nekome)—to contradict

protusloviti (nekome)—to contradict

radovati se (nečemu)—to rejoice at

[1] e.g. used in the neuter, as impersonal verb : laknulo mi je— I felt relief.

rugati se (nekome)—to mock

smejati se (nečemu, nekome) —to laugh at

smetati (nečemu, nekome)— to hinder, disturb

suditi (nekome)—to judge

suprotstaviti se (nečemu, ne- kome)—to oppose

škoditi (nečemu, nekome)—to harm

učiti (nekoga nečemu)—to in- struct (someone) in

verovati [1] (nekome)—to be- lieve (someone)

zabraniti (nekome)—to forbid

zameriti (nekome)—to blame

zapovedati (nekome)—to order

zavideti (nekome)—to envy

## 3. Verbs Taking the Instrumental Case

Examples : vladati zemljom—to rule the country; pro- glasiti se predsednikom—to proclaim oneself president.

baviti se—to be occupied with, concerned with

hvalisati se—to boast of

imenovati—to nominate, ap- point (e.g. imenovati ne- koga predsednikom)

koristiti se—to make use of

maknuti (maći)—to make a movement with

mahnuti—to make a sign or motion with

nazvati—to name (e.g. nazvali su ga Vukom)

obilovati—to abound in

osećati se—to feel, e.g. osećati se umornim, osećati se junakom

oženiti se—to marry (of a man ; e.g. oženiti se Engleskinjom)

ponositi se—to pride oneself in

proglasiti—to proclaim (see imenovati)

raspolagati—to dispose of, have at one's disposal

rukovoditi—to direct, manage

smatrati—to regard, consider (e.g. smatram ga dobrim čovekom)

trgovati—to trade in

upravljati—to govern, direct

vladati—to govern, rule

zabavljati se—to amuse one- self with

---

[1] *But* verovati nešto—to believe something ; verovati u nešto—to believe in something.

Also :

klimnuti glavom—to nod.
mignuti okom—to wink.
odmahnuti rukom—to make a sign with the hand, indicating
' No '.
slegnuti ramenima—to shrug the shoulders.
živeti (e.g. mirnim životom)—to live (a peaceful life).
umreti (e.g. strašnom smrću)—to die (a terrible death).
spavati (e.g. dubokim snom)—to sleep (a deep sleep).

## 4. FEMININE NOUNS WITH CONSONANTAL ENDINGS

The following are the commonest of the nouns declined like
*stvar*. To the list must be added all collective nouns ending
*-ad* (e.g. momčad—crew) and all abstract nouns ending *-ost*
(e.g. milost—mercy).

blagodet—blessing
bojazan—fear
bolest—illness
buđ—mould, mildew
cev—tube, pipe
čađ—soot
čast—honour
ćud—temperament
dob—period, age
dobit—gain
draž—charm.
glad—hunger
grudi (pl.)—chest, breast
jesen—autumn
kap—drop, drip
kob—fate

kokoš—hen
korist—use, usefulness
kost—bone
krv—blood
laž—lie, untruth
ljubav—love
mast—grease
misao (gen. misli)—thought
mladež—youth
moć—power
narav—nature, disposition
noć—night
obitelj—family
oblast—province
oči (pl.)—eyes
pamet—mind, intellect

paprat—fern
peć—stove
pomoć—help
povest—history
pripovest—story
propast—ruin, destruction
prsi (pl.)—breast
ravan—plain
raž—rye
reč—word
rumen—rosy glow
savest—conscience
slast—sweetness ; enjoyment
smrt—death
so (gen. soli)—salt
srž—marrow, pith

studen—bitter cold
stvar—thing, matter, affair
svest—consciousness
trulež—decay
uši (pl.)—ears
varoš—town
vaš—louse
vest—item of news
vlast—power ; authorities
zapoved—command
zapovest—command
zavist—envy
zob—oats
zver—wild animal
žeđ—thirst

## 5. PREPOSITIONS

Note : Only the commonest meanings of the prepositions are given here ; other uses of them have already occurred in this book, and you will discover others in your reading.

Governing only the genitive case :

bez—without
blizu—near
do—to, as far as ; until ; beside
duž—alongside
iz—out of
kod—at the home of (French *chez*) ; close to
kraj—alongside, beside
mesto—instead of
niže—below

od—from ; of ; since
oko—around
osim—except ; besides
pored—alongside ; besides
posle—after
pre—before (in expressions of time)
preko—across
protiv—against
radi—for the sake of, because of

sem = osim

spram—opposite, in front of

sred—in the middle of

suprot—opposite

van—outside

više—above

vrh—above

zbog—because of

In addition to this list, compound prepositions, e.g. između—between; nasred—in (or into) the middle of; iza—behind, govern the genitive case.

Governing only the dative case:

ka, k—towards, to.

uprkos—despite.

Governing only the accusative case:

kroz—through.

niz—down.

uz—up; close to

Governing only the locative case:

pri—by, near.

Governing the dative or locative case:

prema (with dat.)—towards; (with loc.)—according to; opposite.

Governing the genitive or instrumental case:

sa, s (with gen.)—from off; (with instr.)—with.

Governing the genitive or accusative case:

mimo (with gen.)—in spite of, contrary to; (with acc.)—past.

Governing the accusative or instrumental case:

među (with acc.)—among, between (indicating *motion towards* among or between); (with instr.)—among.

nad (with acc.)—above (*motion towards* above); (with instr.)—above.

pod (with acc.)—under (*motion towards* under); (with instr.)—under.

pred (with acc.)—in front of (*motion towards* in front of); just before (in expressions of time); (with instr.)—in front of.

Governing the accusative or locative case:

na [1] (with acc.)—on to; (with loc.)—on, at.

o (with acc.)—on to, against (when motion is indicated); (with loc.)—on, against; concerning, about.

po (with acc.)—for [2]; during [3]; (with loc.)—about [4], on; after.

Governing the genitive, accusative or instrumental case:

za (with gen.)—during the time of [5]; (with acc.)—for; behind (*motion towards* behind); within, in (in expressions of time); (with instr.)—behind, following along behind.

Governing the genitive, accusative or locative case:

u (with gen.)—in, in the case of [6]; (with acc.)—to, into; at, on (in certain expressions of time); (with loc.)—in.

1. A list of uses of this preposition follows this section. 2. In the sense of 'to fetch', e.g. ići po lekara. 3. e.g. po ceo dan— the whole day long. 4. e.g. šetati se po varoši. 5. e.g. za moga života—during my lifetime. 6. In such sentences as 'kosa kao u njegove majke'—'hair like his mother's'.

## USES OF THE PREPOSITION *na*

Although the usual meanings of *na* are 'on' or 'at' (with the locative case) and 'on to' (with the accusative), this preposition is used with many nouns and in many phrases where English has some other preposition. The following list includes the commonest of these. The locative case has been given in this list, but the accusative case must of course be substituted when *motion towards* is understood, e.g. biti na letovanju ; ići na letovanje.

na Balkanu—in the Balkans
na Bledu [1]—at Bled
na Cetinju—in Cetinje
na domaku—within reach
na doručku—at breakfast
na igranci—at a dance
na ispitu—at an examination
na istoku—in the east
na jezeru—on *or* by a lake
na jugu—in the south
na koncertu [2]—at a concert
na kraju—at the end
na letovanju—on (summer) holiday
na mesečini—in the moonlight
na mestu—at a place ; on the spot, at once
na miru—in peace
na moru—on the sea ; at the seaside
na nebu—in the sky
na odmoru—on holiday
na odsustvu—on leave
na početku—at the beginning
na poslu—at work
na pošti—at the post, post-office
na povratku—on the way back
na predavanju—at a lecture
na predstavi—at a performance
na radu—at work
na rastanku—at parting
na reci—on *or* by a river
na ručku—at luncheon
na sastanku—at meeting
na sednici—at a meeting
na selu—in the country (as opposed to town)
na severu—in the north
na stanici—at the station
na sudu (suđenju)—at a trial (legal)
na suncu—in the sunshine
na svadbi—at a wedding
na svetu—in the world
na uglu—at the corner
na ulici—in the street
na univerzitetu—at the university
na utakmici—in a competition

---

[1] *Na* is used with many names of places associated with lakes, rivers, etc.
[2] But ' u pozorištu '—' at the theatre '.

na večeri—at supper, dinner    na vratima—in the doorway
na venčanju—at a wedding    na zabavi—at a party
na vlasti—in authority    na zapadu—in the west

Phrases : Biti nekome na pomoći—to be of help to someone ; hvala na (with loc.)—thank you for ; ići na rad—to go
to work ; imati (držati) nekoga na oku—to keep one's eye on
someone ; misliti na nekoga—to think of someone ; odgovoriti na pitanje—to answer a question ; pasti na um—to occur
to one's mind ; raditi na nečemu—to be working on something ; zakasniti na (with acc.)—to be late for, to miss.

na nedelju (mesec, godinu, etc.) dana—for a week (month,
year, etc.) [1] ; na njegovo iznenađenje—to his surprise ; na
pamet—by heart ; na poklon—as a gift ; na primer—for
example ; na prvi pogled—at first glance ; na sav glas—at the
top of one's voice ; na silu—by force ; na taj način—in that
manner ; na to—thereupon ; na veru—on parole ; na
vreme—in time, punctually ; na moju veliku žalost—to my
great sorrow.

Note also that the adverb *napolju* means ' outside ' (position
outside), e.g. biti napolju, but the form *napolje* must be used
after a verb indicating motion towards outside, e.g. ici napolje.

[1] See p. 105.

# 6. GENERAL VOCABULARY

of Serbo-Croatian words occurring in the Lessons
and in the Sentences and Passages for Translation [1]

Note : This Vocabulary contains some words which have
two or more meanings. Only those meanings necessary to the
comprehension of the Serbo-Croatian sentences and passages
in this book are given here. Numerals have not been included
in this Vocabulary, as they may be found immediately by
reference to Lessons XIV, XV, and XXIII. Where there is
no ' moveable *a* ' the gen. sing. of nouns and the fem. sing.
of adjectives have not been given.

## A

a—and, but
adresa—address
advokat—lawyer
Ah !—Oh !
ako—if
ali—but
amo—hither
april—April
automobil—motor car
avgust—August
avion—aeroplane

## B

baba—old woman, granny
bacati (-am ; ipf.)—to throw,
throw away
baciti (-im ; pf.)—to throw,
throw away

balkon—balcony
baš—just, exactly
bašta—garden
beleg (*ije* : biljeg)—mark, sign
beo, bela (*ije* : bijel, bijela)—
white
Beograd—Belgrade
Beograđanin—native of Belgrade
berberin—barber
b(ij)esan, b(ij)esna—furious
bez—without
biblioteka—library
bife (m.)—buffet
biftek—steak
bioskop—cinema
birati (-am ; ipf.)—to choose
biti—to be
bivši—former, past

---

[1] See Introduction p. xii.

blag—mild, gentle
bl(ij)ed—pale
blizak, bliska—near, close
blizu—near
Bog—God
bogat, bogata—rich
boja—colour
bojati se (-im; ipf.)—to fear
bol—pain
bolestan, bolesna—ill
bol(j)eti (-i; ipf.)—to hurt, ache
bolji—better
bomba—bomb
borba—struggle, fight
Božić—Christmas
brat—brother
brdo—high hill
br(ij)eg—hill
breskva—peach
brijati (-em; ipf.)—to shave
brinuti se (-em; ipf.)—to be anxious
brod—ship
brz—quick
brzo—quickly
brže—more quickly
brži—quicker
bubreg—kidney
budala—fool

## C

carinik—customs officer

ceo, cela (*ije*: cijel *or* cio, cijela)—whole
Ciganin—gipsy
cigareta—cigarette
cipela—shoe
crkva—church
crn—black
crven—red
crvenkast—reddish
cv(ij)et—flower

## Č

čaj—tea
čarapa—stocking
čas—moment; hour; lesson
čaša—glass, tumbler
Čeh—a Czech
ček—cheque
čekaonica—waiting-room
čekati (-am; ipf.)—to wait
čekić—hammer
čest—dense, frequent
čestitka—greetings card
često—often
četvrt—quarter
četvrtak (gen. četvrtka)—Thursday
čiji, čija—whose
čim—as soon as
činiti (-im; ipf.)—to do
činovnik—official, clerk
čitalac (gen. čitaoca)—reader
čitati (-am; ipf.)—to read
članak (gen. članka)—article

čov(j)ek—man
čudan, čudna—strange
čuditi se (-im; ipf.)—to be surprised
čuti (-jem; pf., ipf.)—to hear
čvrst—firm, hard

## Ć

ćutati (-im; ipf.)—to be silent

## D

da—yes
da—that
dakle—so, well then
dalek—distant
daleko—far away
da li—whether
dalje—farther
Dalmacija—Dalmatia
dan—day
danas—today
danju—by day
dati (dam; pf.)—to give
datum—date
davati (dajem; ipf.)—to give
debeo, debela—thick, fat
decembar (gen. decembra)—December
deo (gen. dela; ije: dio)—part
desni—right-hand
d(ij)ete (gen. d(j)eteta)—child

d(j)evojka—girl
dignuti (-em; pf.)—to raise
dinar—Yugoslav coin
divan, divna—lovely
divan—divan, couch
diviti se (-im; ipf.)—to admire, wonder at
dizati (dižem; ipf.)—to raise
dlan—palm of hand
dnevno—daily
dno—bottom, end
do—to, as far as; until; beside
doba—time, period
dobar, dobra—good
dobiti (dobijem; pf.)—to get
dobro—well
dockan—late
docnije—later
dočekati (-am; pf.)—to wait for
doći (dođem; došao, došla; pf.)—to come
dodatak (gen. dodatka)—supplement
događati se (-a; ipf.)—to happen
dogoditi se (-i; pf.)—to happen
dok—while
dok ne—until
dolaziti (-im; ipf.)—to come
don(ij)eti (donesem; pf.)—to bring

donositi (-im ; ipf.)—to bring

dopadati se (-am ; ipf.)—to be pleasing

dopasti se (dopadnem ; pf.)—to be pleasing

dopisnica (dopisna karta)—postcard

dopuštati (-am ; ipf.)—to allow

dopustiti (-im ; pf.)—to allow

doručak (gen. doručka)—breakfast

dosadan, dosadna—boring

doskora—soon

dosta—enough, fairly

do viđenja—au revoir

dovoljno—enough

drag—dear

drug, drugarica—companion

drugi—other, another, second

društvo—company, society

drvo (gen. drveta)—tree

državni—belonging to the state

dubok—deep

dućan (gen. dućana)—shop

dug—long

dugačak, dugačka—long

dugme—button

dugo—for a long time

duh—spirit

dužnost—duty

dvoje—a couple

dvojica—a couple (of men)

## DŽ

džep—pocket

## Đ

đak—schoolboy, student

## E

Engleska—England

engleski—English

Engleskinja—Englishwoman

Englez—Englishman

eno—there is, are

eto—there (here) is, are

evo—here is, are

## F

februar—February

fijoka—drawer

fini—fine, splendid

francuski—French

Francuskinja—Frenchwoman

Fráncuz—Frenchman

funta—pound

## G

galama—noise, din

gazda—proprietor

gazdarica—proprietress

gd(j)e—where

gladak, glatka—smooth
gladan, gladna—hungry
glas—voice
glasno—loudly
glava—head
gledati (-am; ipf.)—to watch, look at
glumac (gen. glumca)—actor
glumica—actress
gluv—deaf
gluvonem—deaf and dumb
godina—year
gori—worse
gore—above
gor(j)eti (-im; ipf.)—to be burning
gospodin—Mr., gentleman
gospodski—in a gentlemanly fashion
gospođa—Mrs., lady
gospođica—Miss, young woman
gost—guest
gostionica—inn
gotov—ready, finished
govoriti (-im; ipf.)—to speak
grad—city
građanin—citizen
grana—branch
granica—frontier
grbača—spine
grub—coarse, rough
grudi (f. pl.)—chest, breast
gust—thick, dense

# H

hajdemo !—let's go !
haljina—dress, garment
hartija—paper
hitan, hitna—urgent
hladan, hladna—cold
hl(j)eb—bread
hodnik—corridor
hotel—hotel
hrabar, hrabra—brave
hrabrost (f.)—courage
hrana—food
Hrvat—Croat
Hrvatska—Croatia
hrvatski—Croatian
hrvatskosrpski—Serbo-Croatian
ht(j)eti (hoću, hoćeš, etc., ipf.)—to wish, want
hvala—thanks
hvaliti (-im; ipf.)—to praise

# I

i—and, too
i . . . i—both . . . and
iako—although
ići (idem; išao, išla; ipf.)—to go
idući—the next, the coming
igla—needle
igračka—toy
ikad(a)—ever
ili—or

ili . . . ili—either . . . or
ima—he (she, it) has; there
is, there are
imati (-am; ipf.)—to have
ime—name
imenik—directory
imenovati (imenujem; pf.
and ipf.)—to elect
inače—otherwise
inostranstvo—abroad
inteligentan, inteligentna—
intelligent
iskusan, iskusna—ex-
perienced
ispod—under, from under
ispratiti (-im; pf.)—to accompany, see off
ispričati (-am; pf.)—to
relate
ist(j)erati (-am; pf.)—to
drive out
isti—the same
istina—truth
iz—out of
izabrati (izaberem; pf.)—to
choose
izaći (see izići)
izbrojati (-im; pf.)—to count
out
izgled—appearance
izgledati (-am; ipf.)—to appear, seem
izgor(j)eti (-im; pf.)—to burn
out

izgovoriti (-im; pf.)—to pronounce
izgubiti (-im; pf.)—to lose
izići (iziđem; izišao, izišla;
pf.)—to go out
izlaziti (-im; ipf.)—to go out
izlet(j)eti (-im; pf.)—to fly
out
izlog—display (e.g. in shop
window)
između—between
iznenaditi (-im; pf.)—to surprise
izvaditi (-im; pf.)—to draw
out
izviniti (-im; pf.)—to excuse
izvući (izvučem; pf.)—to
pull out, draw out

## J

ja—I
jabuka—apple; apple tree
jagnje (gen. jagnjeta)—lamb
jak—strong
januar—January
jasan, jasna—clear
jasno—clearly
jastuk—cushion, pillow
jedan, jedna—one
jedva—scarcely
jeftin—cheap
jelo—food
jelovnik—menu

jer—because
jesti (jedem; ipf.)—to eat
jezero—lake
jezik—language, tongue
još—still, yet
još jedan—one more
Jovan—John
juče—yesterday
Jugosloven, Jugoslaven—a
  Yugoslav
jugoslovenski, jugoslavenski
  —Yugoslav
Jugoslavija—Yugoslavia
jul—July
jun—June
junak—hero
juriti (-im; ipf.)—to hasten
jurnuti (-em; pf.)—to dash
jutros—this morning

## K

k, ka—towards
kad, kada—when
kafa—coffee
kafana—café
kafanski—belonging to a café
kajati se (-em; ipf.) to repent,
  regret
kakav, kakva—what kind of;
  what a . . .
kako—how
kamen—stone, rock
kancelarija—office

kao—as
kao da—as if
kapak (gen. kapka)—shutter
kaput—coat
karta—card; ticket; map
kasno—late
kašika—spoon
kašičica—teaspoon
kazati (kažem; ipf.)—to say,
  tell
kazniti (-im; pf.)—to punish
kćerka—daughter
kći (gen. kćeri)—daughter,
kelner—waiter
kilogram—kilogram
klasa—class
klima—climate
klupa—bench, seat
ključ—key
knez—prince
knjiga—book
književnost—literature
ko—who
kod—at the home of; close to
kod kuće—at home
kofer—suitcase
kogod—someone
koji—who; which
kola (n. pl.)—car, cart
kol(j)eno—knee
koliko—how much, how
  many
kolovoz—August
komad—piece

komedija—comedy

konac (gen. konca)—thread

končić—little thread

koncerat (*or* koncert)—concert

kondukter—guard, conductor

konzul—consul

konj—horse

koral—coral

koristan, korisna—useful

kosa—hair

kost (f.)—bone

koštati (-am; ipf.)—to cost

kovčeg—box, chest

koverat (gen. koverta)—envelope

kraj (prepn.)—near, beside

kraj—end, extremity

kralj—king

krasti (kradem; ipf.)—to steal

kratak, kratka—short

krenuti (-em; pf.)—to start off

krevet—bed

kriv—crooked; guilty

krov—roof

kroz—through

krut—stiff, rigid

kucati (-am; ipf.)—to knock, tap

kuća—house

kućica—cottage

kuda—whither

kuhinja—kitchen

kupati (se) (-am; ipf.)—to bathe

kupatilo—bathroom

kupe (m.)—compartment in train

kupiti (-im; pf.)—to buy

kupovati (-ujem; ipf.)—to buy

kutija—box

kuvati (-am; ipf.)—to cook

## L

lak—easy, light

leći (legnem; pf.)—to lie down

led—ice

leđa (neut. pl.)—back (of one's body)

legati (ležem; ipf.)—to be in the act of lying down; to lie down (repeatedly)

l(j)ekar—doctor

l(ij)ep—beautiful, nice

l(j)eti—in summer

l(j)eto—summer

l(ij)evi—left-hand

ležati (-im; ipf.)—to lie, to be in a lying position

lice—face

ličan, lična—personal

ličnost—personality; personage

lipanj—June
list—leaf; sheet of paper; newspaper
listopad—October
litar (gen. litra)—litre
liti (lijem; ipf.)—to pour
loš—bad
lud—mad

## Lj

ljubav (f.)—love
ljubazan, ljubazna—amiable
ljudi—people; men
ljut—keen, hot; angry

## M

mačka—cat
magla—fog
mahom—instantly
maj—May
majka—mother
malen—small
mali—small
malo—a little
manje—less
manji—smaller
marama—scarf
marka—(postage) stamp
mariti za (-im; ipf.)—to care about
mart—March
mašina—machine, typewriter
mati—mother
mazga—mule

med—honey
među—among
međutim—meanwhile; however
mek—soft
m(j)esec—month, moon
meso—meat
m(j)esto—place
metar (gen. metra)—metre
metati (mećem; ipf.)—to put
metnuti (-em; pf.)—to put
mi—we
milicajac (gen. milicajca)—policeman
milo mu je—he is glad
milja—mile
ministar (gen. ministra)—minister
ministarstvo—ministry
mio, mila—dear
mir—peace
miran, mirna—peaceful, calm
misao (f., gen. misli)—thought
misliti (-im; ipf.)—to think
mlad—young
mnogi—many, many a
mnogo—much, many
moći (mogu, možeš, etc.; ipf.)—to be able
moguće—possible
moj—my, mine
molim—please
momak (gen. momka)—young man

morati (-am; ipf.)—to be obliged to, to have to

more—sea

most—bridge

možda—perhaps

mračan, mračna—dark

mrak—darkness

mučiti (-im; ipf.)—to torment

Muslimanka—Moslem woman

muzej—museum

muzika—music

muž—husband

## N

na—on, on to; at

načiniti (-im; pf.)—to make

naći (nađem; pf.)—to find

nad—over, above

naglas—aloud

naglo—suddenly

najmanje—least, at least

najzad—last, lastly

nakit—ornament

nalaziti (-im; ipf.)—to find

naljutiti se (-im; pf.)—to become angry

nam(j)eniti (-im; pf.)—to assign

naočari—spectacles

napisati (napišem; pf.)—to write

napolju—outside

napraviti (-im; pf.)—to make

napred—forward; come in!

naprotiv—on the contrary

napustiti (-im; pf.)—to abandon, leave

naravno—naturally, of course

naročito—specially

narodan, narodna—national

narodnost—nationality

naslikati (-am; pf.)—to paint; take photo

naslov—title, heading

naš—our, ours

natrag—back (e.g. ići natrag: to go back)

naučiti (-im; pf.)—to learn; teach

naveče—in the evening

na vreme—in time, punctually

naviknuti (-em; pf.)—to accustom

nazeb—cold, chill

nazvati (nazovem; pf.)—to call, name

na žalost—unfortunately

ne—no, not

nebo (pl. nebesa)—sky

ned(j)elja—week; Sunday

negd(j)e—somewhere

nego—than; but (on the contrary)

neko—somebody

neki—some, some sort of
nekoliko—some, several
nema—there is not, there are not
nemati (-am; ipf.)—not to have
N(j)emačka—Germany
nemoguće—impossible
neočekivan, neočekivana—unexpected
nepoznat, nepoznata—unknown
neprijatelj—enemy
nešto—something
ni—not even
ni . . . ni—neither . . . nor
ničiji—nobody's
nigd(j)e—nowhere
nijedan, nijedna—not one, not a single
nikad(a)—never
nikakav, nikakva—no kind of
niko—nobody
ništa—nothing
ništa ne mari—it doesn't matter
niz—down (prepn.)
nizak, niska—low
noć (f.)—night
noću—by night
noga—leg; foot
nos—nose
nositi (-im; ipf.)—to carry, wear

nov—new
novac (gen. novca)—money
novembar (gen. novembra)—November
novine (f. pl.)—newspaper
nozdrva—nostril
nož—knife
nužan, nužna—necessary

## Nj

njegov—his; its
njen, njezin—her, hers; its
njihov—their, theirs

## O

o—on, about; concerning; against
obala—coast, shore
obećati (-am; pf.)—to promise
obećavati (-am; ipf.)—to promise
običaj—custom
obično—usually
objasniti (-im; pf.)—to explain
objašnjenje—explanation
oboje—both
obojica—both (men)
obojiti (-im; pf.)—to dye
oboriti (-im; pf.)—to overthrow

obradovati se (obradujem se ;
pf.)—to be glad

obrijati (-em ; pf.)—to shave

obrva—eyebrow

obući (obučem ; obukao,
obukla ; pf.)—to put on
(clothes)

očekivati (očekujem ; ipf.)—
to expect

očigledno—obviously

od—from ; of ; since

odakle—whence

odavna—for a long time
past

od(ij)elo—suit, clothing

odgovarati (-am ; ipf.)—to
answer

odgovoriti (-im ; pf.)—to
answer

odjednom—suddenly

odjuriti (-im ; pf.)—to hurry
off

odlaganje—postponement

odlazak (gen. odlaska)—departure

odlaziti (-im ; ipf.)—to depart

odličan, odlična—excellent

odložiti (-im ; pf.)—to postpone

odlučiti (-im ; pf.)—to re-
solve, decide

odmah—immediately

ods(j)ečno—abruptly

oduševljen—enthusiastic

oglas—small advertisement,
announcement

ogledalo—looking-glass

ograda—fence, wall

ogroman, ogromna—enorm-
ous

oko—around (prepn.)

oko (pl. oči)—eye

okrenuti (-em ; pf.)—to turn

oktobar (gen. oktobra)—October

okup—gathering, assembly

olovka—pencil

on, ona, ono—he, she, it

onaj (ona, ono)—that

onakav, onakva—of that kind

onda—then

oni (masc.), one (fem.), ona
(neut.)—they

opasan, opasna—dangerous

opasnost (f.)—danger

opaziti (-im ; pf.)—to notice

opet—again

opravdanje—justification

opravdati (-am ; pf.)—to
justify

orah—walnut

oriti se (-i ; ipf.)—to resound

ormar—cupboard

osećati (-am ; ipf.)—to feel

osim—except

osm(j)ehivati se (osm(j)ehu-
jem se ; ipf.) —to smile

ostajati (-em; ipf.)—to remain

ostatak (gen. ostatka)—remainder

ostati (ostanem; pf.)—to remain

ostaviti (-im; pf.)—to leave, abandon

ošišati (-am; pf.)—to cut (hair)

oštar, oštra—sharp

otac (gen. oca)—father

otići (otidem, odem; otišao, otišla; pf.)—to go away

otkriće—discovery

otputovati (otputujem; pf.)—to start on a journey

otvarati (-am; ipf.)—to open

otvoriti (-im; pf.)—to open

ovaj (ova, ovo)—this

ovakav, ovakva—such, like this

ovako—thus, so

ovd(j)e—here

ožujak (gen. ožujka)—March


## P

pa—and, and so

padati (-am; ipf.)—to fall

paket—packet, parcel

pamet (f.)—mind, intelligence

par—pair

parče (gen. parčeta)—piece

park—park

pas (gen. psa)—dog

pasoš—passport

pasti (padnem, pao; pf.)—to fall

paziti (-im; ipf.)—to pay attention

pažljiv—careful

peći (pečem; pekao, pekla; ipf.)—to bake, roast

pekmez—jam

penjati se (penjem se; ipf.)—to climb

pero—pen; feather

peron—station platform

p(j)esma—poem, ballad, song

p(j)ešice—on foot

p(j)eške—on foot

petak (gen. petka)—Friday

p(j)evati (-am; ipf.)—to sing

pisati (pišem; ipf.)—to write

pismo—letter

pismonoša—postman

pitanje—question

pitati (-am; ipf.)—to ask

piti (pijem; ipf.)—to drink

pivo—beer

plakati (plačem; ipf.)—to cry, weep

planina—mountain

plata—salary, wages

platiti (-im; pf.)—to pay

platno—linen

pleće—shoulder

pleme—tribe

plemenit—noble.
plesti (pletem ; ipf.)—to knit
plitak, plitka—shallow
pljesnuti (-em ; pf.)—to applaud
po (prepn.)—by, on, about
po—half
pob(j)eći (pob(j)egnem ; pob(j)egao, pob(j)egla ; pf.)—to flee
pobojati se (pobojim se ; pf.)—to become afraid
početak (gen. početka)—beginning
početi (počnem ; pf.)—to begin
poći (pođem ; pošao, pošla ; pf.)—to start off
pod (prepn.)—under
pod—floor
podignuti (-em ; pf.)—to lift, pick up
podne—noon
poginuti (-em ; pf.)—to perish, be killed
pogledati (-am ; pf.)—to glance
pogodan,pogodna—favourable
pogreška—mistake
pohitati (-am ; pf.)—to hurry off
pojesti (pojedem ; pojeo ;·pf.)—to eat up

pokazati (pokažem ; pf.)—to show
pokloniti se (-im ; pf.)—to bow
pola—half
polako—slowly, gently
polazak (gen. polaska)—departure
polaziti (-im ; ipf.)—to depart
polica—shelf
policija—police
položaj (gen. položaja)—position
polud(j)eti (-im ; pf.)—to go mad
polje—field, plain
pomagati (pomažem ; ipf.)—to help
pomalo—a little
pomisliti (-im ; pf.)—to imagine, have an idea
pomoć (f.)—help
pomoći (pomognem ; pomogao, pomogla ; pf.)—to help
pomorandža—orange.
ponedeljak (gen. ponedeljka)—Monday
ponekad—sometimes
pon(ij)eti (ponesem ; pf.)—to bring, take
ponuditi (-im ; pf.)—to offer

popeti se (popnem se ; pf.)—to climb

popiti (popijem ; pf.)—to drink up

pored—alongside

por(ij)eklo—origin

porodica—family

poručiti (-im ; pf.)—to order, give order for

posao (gen. posla ; pl. poslovi)—job, work

pos(j)ećivati (pos(j)ećujem ; ipf.)—to visit

pos(j)eta—visit

pos(j)etiti (-im ; pf.)—to visit

poslati (pošljem ; pf.)—to send

posl(ij)e (prepn.)—after

posl(ij)e (adverb)—afterwards

posl(j)ednji—the last

poslušan, poslušna—obedient

poslušati (-am ; pf.)—to listen, obey

poslužavnik—tray

posmatrati (-am ; ipf.)—to observe

pospan—sleepy

postaviti (-im ; ipf.)—to put, place

postelja—bed

po svoj prilici—apparently, evidently

pošta—post, post office

poštanski—postal, postage

pošten—honourable, honest

pošto—after, since

poštovan—respected

poštovanje—respect

potpisati (potpišem ; pf.)—to sign

potpisivati (potpisujem ; ipf.)—to sign

potrčati (-im ; pf.)—to run off

potreban, potrebna—necessary

potvrditi (-im ; pf.)—to confirm

pov(j)erljiv—confidential

povesti (povedem ; poveo ; pf.)—to take, lead

povrće—vegetables

povući (povučem ; povukao, povukla ; pf.)—to pull, draw

pozajmiti (-im ; pf.)—to lend ; borrow

pozdrav—greeting

pozdraviti (-im; pf.)—to greet

pozdravljati (-am ; ipf.)—to greet

poziv—invitation

poznanik—acquaintance

poznati (-am ; pf.)—to get to know

poznavanje—knowledge, acquaintance

pozorište—theatre

**pozvati** (pozovem; pf.)—to invite, summon

**prag**—threshold

**pratiti** (-im; ipf.)—to accompany

**pravda**—justice

**pravi**—real, authentic

**pravilno**—regularly, correctly

**prazan, prazna**—empty

**praznik**—holiday

**pr(ij)e**—before

**prebaciti** (-im; pf.)—to throw across

**preći** (pređem; prešao, prešla; pf.)—to cross

**pred**—in front of; just before

**predati** (-am; pf.)—to hand over; register (luggage)

**predavanje**—lecture

**predgrađe**—suburb

**predlagati** (predlažem; ipf.)—to suggest

**predlog**—suggestion

**predložiti** (-im; pf.)—to suggest

**preds(j)ednik**—president

**predstaviti** (-im; pf.)—to introduce, present

**predstavljati** (-am; ipf.)—to introduce, present

**preduzeće**—undertaking

**preduzeti** (preduzmem; pf.)—to undertake

**predvid(j)eti** (-im; pf.)—to foresee

**predviđati** (-am; ipf.)—to foresee

**prekinuti** (-em; pf.)—to interrupt

**prekjuče**—the day before yesterday

**preko**—across

**prek(o)sutra**—the day after tomorrow

**prekrasan, prekrasna**—very beautiful, excellent

**prelaziti** (-im; ipf.)—to cross

**prema**—towards; opposite

**pre nego što**—before

**prenoćiti** (-im; pf.)—to pass the night

**preporučen**—registered

**prepoznati** (-am; pf.)—to recognise

**preseliti se** (-im; pf.)—to move house

**prestati** (prestanem; pf.)—to cease

**pr(ij)etiti** (-im; ipf.)—to threaten

**prevariti** (-im; pf.)—to deceive

**prevariti se** (-im; pf.)—to make a mistake

**prevodilac** (gen. prevodioca)—translator

prevoditi (-im ; ipf.)—to translate

priča—tale

pričati (-am ; ipf.)—to relate

pričiniti se (-im ; pf.)—to seem

prići (priđem ; prišao, prišla ; pf.)—to approach

prihvatati (-am ; ipf.)—to accept

prihvatiti (-im ; pf.)—to accept

prijatan, prijatna—pleasant

prijatelj—friend (m.)

prijateljica—friend (f.)

prijateljski—friendly

prilaziti (-im ; ipf.)—to approach

prilika—opportunity

primati (-am ; ipf.)—to receive

prim(ij)etiti (-im ; pf.)—to notice

primiti (-im ; pf.)—to receive

pripaliti (-im ; pf.)—to light, ignite

pripov(ij)etka—short story

pristati (pristanem ; pf.)—to consent

pritrčati (-im ; pf.)—to run up to

privlačan, privlačna—attractive

prizemlje—ground floor

priznati (-am ; pf.)—to admit, confess

probuditi (-im ; pf.)—to awaken

pročitati (-am ; pf.)—to read through

proći (prođem ; prošao, prošla ; pf.)—to pass

prodati (-am ; pf.)—to sell

prodavati (prodajem ; ipf.)—to sell

produžiti (-im ; pf.)—to continue

profesor—professor, teacher

progovoriti (-im ; pf.)—to utter

prokleti (prokunem ; pf.)—to curse

prolaziti (-im ; ipf.)—to pass

prol(j)eće—Spring

prosinac (gen. prosinca)—December

prostr(ij)eti (-em ; pf.)—to spread

prošao, prošla—past, last

protiv—against

proučavati (-am ; ipf.)—to study

provesti (provedem ; proveo ; pf.)—to pass (time)

provoditi (-im ; ipf.)—to pass (time)

prozor—window

prsi (f. pl.)—chest, breast

prst—finger
prsten—ring (on finger)
prtljag (gen. prtljaga)—
    luggage
pružiti (-im; pf.)—to pass,
    offer
prvi—first
prvo—firstly
pukovnik—colonel
pustiti (-im; pf.)—to let, let
    go
pušiti (-im; ipf.)—to smoke
puštati (-am; ipf.)—to let,
    let go
put—road; journey
put—time
putnik—traveller
putovanje—journey, travell-
    ing
putovati (putujem; ipf.)—to
    travel

## R

račun—bill
rad—work
radio (gen. radija)—wireless
raditi (-im; ipf.)—to work
radnik—worker
radnja—shop
rado—gladly
radost—joy
radostan, radosna—joyful
radovati se (radujem se; ipf.)
    —to be glad

radoznao, radoznala—inquisi-
    tive
rana—wound
rano—early
raspoložen—disposed; in a
    good mood
rast—growth
rasti (rastem; rastao, rasla;
    ipf.)—to grow
rat—war
ravnodušno—with equanimity
razbijati (-am; ipf.)—to
    smash
razbiti (-ijem; pf.)—to smash
razgovarati (-am; ipf.)—to
    talk, converse
razgovor—conversation
različit—different, various
razlog—reason
razumeti (-em; ipf.)—to
    understand
razumevati (-am; ipf.)—to
    understand
razviti (-ijem; pf.)—to de-
    velop
r(ij)eč (f.)—word
rečenica—sentence
r(j)ečnik—dictionary
reći (reknem; rekao, rekla;
    pf.)—to say
red—row, order
redak (gen. retka)—line
r(ij)edak, r(ij)etka—rare,
    sparse, infrequent

r(ij)eka—river
restoran—restaurant
rezervacija—reservation
rezervirati (-am; pf. and ipf.)—to reserve
riba—fish
ritam (gen. ritma)—rhythm
rod—birth, origin
roditi (-im; pf.)—to bear (children)
roditelj—parent
roman—novel
ručak (gen. ručka)—luncheon
ručati (-am; pf.)—to lunch
rujan (gen. rujna)—September
ruka—hand, arm
rukav—sleeve
rukavica—glove

## S

s, sa—with; from
sad, sada—now
sala—hall, room.
salon—drawing room
sam, sama—alone; oneself
samo—only
san (gen. sna)—dream, sleep
saobraćaj—traffic
saopštiti (-im; pf.)—to communicate, report
sastati se (sastanem; pf.)—to meet
sasvim—quite, completely

sat—hour.
sav (sva, sve)—all, the whole
sav(j)estan, sav(j)esna—conscientious
sav(j)et—advice
sav(j)etovati (sav(j)etujem; ipf.)—to advise
saviti (savijem; pf.)—to bend, twist
sazidati (-am; pf.)—to build
s(j)ećati se (-am; ipf.)—to remember
s(j)eći (s(j)ečem; s(j)ekao, s(j)ekla; ipf.)—to cut
s(j)edati (-am; ipf.)—to sit down, keep sitting down
s(j)edeti (-im; ipf.)—to sit, be sitting
s(j)ednica—meeting, assembly
selo—village
seljak (gen. seljaka)—peasant
sem (see osim)
s(j)eme—seed
s(j)enka—shadow
septembar (gen. septembra)—September
s(j)esti (s(j)ednem; s(j)eo, s(j)ela; pf.)—to sit down
sestra—sister
s(j)etiti se (-im; pf.)—to remember
sići (siđem; sišao, sišla; pf.)—to descend

siguran, sigurna—sure, certain

sigurno—certainly

sijati (-am ; ipf.)—to shine

siječanj (gen. siječnja)—January

silaziti (-im ; ipf.)—to descend

sin—son

sinoć—last night

sir—cheese

siromah—poor man

siromašan, siromašna—poor

sitan, sitna—tiny

sitnina—trifle, small change

skidati (-am; ipf.)—to take off

skinuti (-em ; pf.)—to take off

skočiti (-im ; pf.)—to jump

skup—expensive

skupa—together

sladak, slatka—sweet

sladoled—ice cream

slagati se (slažem ; ipf.)—to agree

slatko—sweetly ; with relish

slatko—a syrupy jam

sl(ij)editi (-im ; ipf.)—to follow

sl(ij)edeći—following, next

slika—picture

slikar—painter

slikati (-am ; ipf.)—to paint, draw ; take photograph

slobodan, slobodna—free

slomiti (-im ; pf.)—to break

slučaj—chance, event

sluga—servant (m.)

slušati (-am ; ipf.)—to listen

služiti (-im ; ipf.)—to serve

smatrati (-am ; ipf.)—to consider

smejati se (-em ; ipf.)—to laugh

sm(ij)ešiti se (-im ; ipf.)—to smile

smetati (-am ; ipf.)—to hinder, disturb

smeti (-em ; ipf.)—to dare, be allowed

smokva—fig

snaha—daughter-in-law

sn(ij)eg—snow

soba—room

spavati (-am ; ipf.)—to sleep

spisak (gen. spiska)—list

spreman, spremna—ready, prepared

spremati (-am ; ipf.)—to prepare

spremiti (-im ; pf.)—to prepare

sramota—shame

Srbin—Serb

srce—heart

srdačno—cordially

sreća—fortune, happiness

srećan, srećna—happy

srećom—fortunately

sr(ij)eda—Wednesday

sresti (sretnem ; sreo, srela ; pf.)—to meet

srpanj (gen. srpnja)—July

Srpkinja—Serbian woman

srpski—Serbian

srpskohrvatski—Serbo-Croatian

stajati (-em ; ipf.)—to stand

stalno—constantly

stan—flat, apartment

stanica—station

stanični—of the station

stanovati (stanujem ; ipf.)—to reside

stanovnik—inhabitant

star—old

starac (gen. starca)—old man

starica—old woman

starinski—old-fashioned, antique

stati (stanem ; pf.)—to stop, come to a halt

staviti (-im ; pf.)—to put, place

stavljati (-am ; ipf.)—to put, place

staza—path

stepenice (f. pl.)—stairs, steps

stići (stignem ; stigao, stigla ; pf.)—to arrive

stid—shame

stideti se (-im ; ipf.)—to be ashamed

stizati (stižem ; ipf.)—to arrive

sto (gen. stola ; pl. stolovi)—table

sto—a hundred

stojati (-im ; ipf.)—to stand

stolica—chair

strah—fear

stranac (gen. stranca)—foreigner

strani—foreign

stranica—page

strašan, strašna—frightful

stric—uncle

strpati (-am ; pf.)—to cram

strpljiv—patient

stube (f. pl.)—steps, stairs

studen (f.)—bitter cold

student—student (m.)

studentkinja—student (f.)

stvar (f.)—thing, matter

subota—Saturday

sudac (gen. suca)—judge

suh—dry

sunce—sun

supa—soup

sutra—tomorrow

sutradan—the next day

suv—dry

suviše—too, too much

svakako—certainly ; anyway

svaki—each

sve—everything

svejedno—it doesn't matter

sv(ij)et—world ; people

svi—everybody

svibanj (gen. svibnja)—May

svirati (-am ; ipf.)—to play
(instrument)

svoj—one's

svojstvo—characteristic,
--peculiarity

svršavati (-am ; ipf.)—to
finish

svršiti (-im ; pf.)—to finish

svuda—everywhere


## Š

šala—jest

šapat—whisper

šećer—sugar

šešir—hat

širok—broad

šiti (šijem ; ipf.)—to sew

škola—school

šofer—driver

šolja—cup

šoljica—small cup

šta—what

šteta—a pity

štogod—whatever

šuma—forest, wood

šupa—hut


## T

tada—then

tačno—exactly, punctually

taj (ta, to)—that

tajna—secret

takav, takva—such a

tako—thus

taksi—taxi

taman, tamna—dark

taman—just, exactly

tamo—there

tanak, tanka—slender

tanjir—plate

tanjirić—small plate

te—and so

tečno—fluently

tek—just, exactly

tek što—just when, just after

tekući—current

telefonirati (-am ; ipf. and
pf.)—to telephone

telefonski—of the telephone

teško meni !—dear me !

ti—thou, you

t(ij)esan, t(ij)esna—tight

tetka—aunt

težak, teška—heavy, difficult

tih—quiet

tko (*ije*-dialect)—who

točiti (-im ; ipf.)—to pour
out (wine, etc.)

tok—course (e.g. of river)

toliko—so much, so many

topao, topla—warm

torba—bag

tramvaj—tramcar

trava—grass

travanj (gen. travnja)—April

tražiti (-im; ipf.)—to seek, ask for

trčati (-im; ipf.)—to run

trebati (-am; ipf.)—to need, be necessary

trenutak (gen. trenutka)—moment, second

tresti (tresem; tresao, tresla; ipf.)—to shake

trošiti (-im; ipf.)—to spend, waste

trpeti (-im; ipf.)—to endure

tu—there

tuđ—foreign; someone else's

tup—blunt

turist—tourist

turski—Turkish

tužan, tužna—sad

tužiti se (-im; ipf.)—to complain

tvoj—thy, thine

tvrd—hard, firm

# U

u—in, into

ubiti (ubijem : pf.)—to kill

učiniti (-im; pf.)—to do

učiniti se (-im; pf.)—to seem

učitelj—teacher

učiti (-im; ipf.)—to teach, learn

učtiv—polite

ući (uđem; ušao, ušla; pf.) —to enter

udati se (-am; pf.)—to get married (of a woman)

udobno—comfortably

ugledan, ugledna—distinguished, eminent

uho—ear

ujesti (ujedem; ujeo, ujela; pf.)—to bite

ujutru—in the morning

ukrasti (ukradem; ukrao, ukrala; pf.)—to steal

ukusan, ukusna—delicious

ulaziti (-im; ipf.)—to enter

ulica—street

um(j)eti (um(ij)em; ipf.)— to be able, know how

umivati se (-am; ipf.)—to wash oneself

umoran, umorna—tired

umr(ij)eti (-em; umřo, umrla)—to die

unapr(ij)ed—beforehand

unuče—grandson

unutra—inside

unutrašnjost—interior

univerzitet—university

upitati (-am; pf.)—to ask

upiti (upijem; pf.)—to drink in, absorb

upoznati (-am; pf.)—to become acquainted with

upravnik—manager, director

upravo—just, exactly

uputiti (-im; pf.)—to direct

uraditi (-im; pf.)—to do

ur(ij)eđenje—arrangement, organisation

uskočiti (-im; pf.)—to jump in

uskoro—soon

Uskrs—Easter

usna—lip

usp(j)eh—success

ustajati (-em; ipf.)—to get up

ustati (ustanem; pf.)—to get up

utorak (gen. utorka)—Tuesday

uveče—in the evening

uv(ij)ek—always

uvid(j)eti (-im; pf.)—to realise

uvo—ear

uz—up, along

uzak, uska—narrow

uzeti (uzmem; pf.)—to take

uzimati (-am; ipf.)—to take

uzvišen—exalted, raised

## V

vagon-restoran—restaurant car

valjati (-am; ipf.)—to be valid, worth

varoš (f.)—town

vaš—your, yours

važan, važna—important

veče—evening

večera—dinner, supper

večeras—this evening

večeravati (-am; ipf.)—to dine

večerati (-am; pf. and ipf.)—to dine

već—already

već—but, on the contrary

veći—larger

većina—majority

veliki—large

veljača—February

v(ij)enac (gen. v(ij)enca)—garland

v(j)erovati (v(j)erujem; ipf.)—to believe

v(j)erovatno—probably

veseo, vesela—merry

v(ij)est (f.)—item of news

v(j)ešt—skilful

v(j)etar (gen. v(j)etra)—wind

vi—you

vid(j)eti (-im; pf. and ipf.)—to see

viđati (-am; ipf.)—to see often, regularly

vikati (vičem; ipf.)—to shout

vino—wine

visok—high, tall

više—more

viti (vijem ; ipf.)—to wind, twine

vladalac (gen. vladaoca)—ruler

vo (gen. vola ; pl. volovi)—ox

voće—fruit

voda—water

vodič—guide, leader

vodić—guide book

voditi (-im ; ipf.)—to lead, take (a person)

vođa—leader

vojnik—soldier

vojska—army

voleti (-im ; ipf.)—to like, love

voz—train

voziti (-im ; ipf.)—to drive

vrabac (gen. vrapca)—sparrow

vrag—devil

vrata (neut. pl.)—door

vratiti (se) (-im ; pf.)—to return

vr(ij)editi (-im ; ipf.)—to be worth

vr(ij)eme (gen. vremena)—time, weather

vrh—peak, top

vrlo—very

vršiti (-im ; ipf.)—to carry out, perform

vrt—garden

vruć—hot

vrućina—heat

vući (vučem ; vukao, vukla ; ipf.)—to pull, draw

## Z

za—for ; after

zaboga !—good heavens !

zaboleti (-i ; pf.)—to begin to hurt

zaboraviti (-im ; pf.)—to forget

začuti (začujem ; pf.)—to hear, catch a sound

zadatak (gen. zadatka)—task

zadovoljan, zadovoljna—contented, satisfied

zadovoljstvo—satisfaction

zahvalan, zahvalna—grateful

zahvaliti (-im ; pf.)—to thank

zahvaljivati (zahvaljujem ; ipf.)—to thank

zaista—really, indeed

zajedno—together

zakucati (-am ; pf.)—to tap, knock

zamoliti (-im ; pf.)—to pray, request

zanimljiv—interesting

zap(j)evati (-am ; pf.)—to begin to sing

zapitati (-am ; pf.)—to ask

zaplakati (zaplačem ; pf.)—to burst into tears

zar ne ?—isn't it so ?

zaseban, zasebna—individual, for oneself

zaspati (zaspim ; pf.)—to fall asleep

zastiđen—ashamed

zašto—why

zatim—then, after that

zato što—because

zatražiti (-im ; pf.)—to seek, ask for

zatvoriti (-im ; pf.)—to close

zaustaviti (-im ; pf.)—to stop, bring to a halt

zaustavljati (-am ; ipf.)—to stop, bring to a halt

zauzet—busy, occupied

završiti (-im ; pf.)—to finish

zbivati se (-a ; ipf.)—to happen

zbog—because of

zbogom—goodbye

zbuniti (-im ; ipf.)—to confuse, embarrass

zelen—green

zemička—roll (of bread)

zemlja—country, earth

zgrada—building

zid—wall

zidati (-am ; ipf.)—to build

zima—winter ; cold

zimi—in the winter

znati (-am ; ipf.)—to know

zub—tooth

zvanje—calling, vocation

zvati (zovem ; ipf.)—to call

## Ž

žaliti (-im ; ipf.)—to regret

žalostan, žalosna—sad

žao mi je—I am sorry

žel(j)eti (-im ; ipf.)—to wish

želja—wish

žena—woman

žestok—violent, fiery

živ—alive ; lively

živ(j)eti (-im ; ipf.)—to live

život—life

žuriti (se) (-im ; ipf.)—to hurry

# 7. DICTIONARIES RECOMMENDED

(This list is in chronological order, according to the dates of the most recent editions.)

1. F. A. Bogadek, *English-Croatian Croatian-English Dictionary*, 1 volume, 497 pp. Pittsburgh, 1947.

2. R. Filipović and others, *English-Croatian Dictionary*, 1 volume, 1430 pp. Zagreb, 1955.

3. S. Ristić, Ž. Simić and V. Popović, *English-Serbo-Croat Dictionary*, 2 volumes. An 'encyclopaedic' dictionary, containing the Serbo-Croatian equivalents of about 100,000 English words and phrases. Belgrade, 1956.

4. S. Ristić and Ž. Simić, *Englesko-srpskohrvatski rečnik*, 1 volume, 867 pp. Belgrade, 1959.

5. M. Drvodelić, *Croato-Serbian-English Dictionary*, 1 volume, 912 pp. Zagreb, 1961.

6. B. Grujić, *Englesko-srpskohrvatski školski rečnik*, 1 volume, 599 pp. Titograd, 1966.

7. M. Drvodelić, *English-Croato-Serbian Dictionary*, 1 volume, 1163 pp. Zagreb, 1970.

8. *Srpsko-hrratsko Engleski Rečnik*, Prosveta-Beograd,1971.

In the dictionaries numbered 1, 3, 4 and 5, two or more aspects of verbs are given. To check whether a dictionary supplies both perfective and imperfective aspects see (for example) whether the two forms *primiti* and *primati* are given for the verb 'receive'.

Numbers 5 and 7 are particularly recommended for students' use.

# THE BRITISH-YUGOSLAV SOCIETY
*President:* Sir Fitzroy Maclean, Bart., C.B.E.

The objects of the British-Yugoslav Society are to further friendship and mutual understanding between the peoples of Great Britain and Yugoslavia, to provide information about Yugoslavia and to promote every form of contact between the British and Yugoslav peoples that will further friendship between them. The Society was founded in 1947 and it is entirely non-political, and its members include people in all the main political parties as well as a large number whose interests are more academic or cultural. The Society enjoys the support and co-operation of the British Government and the Yugoslav Embassy.

The Society's activities include the publication of the Journal three times a year, which is sent free to all members, an annual reception at the House of Commons, an annual party to celebrate the Yugoslav National Day, and meetings addressed by speakers with specialised knowledge on various aspects of Yugoslavia, as well as film shows, folk dance performances, etc.

Anyone who agrees with the objects of the Society is invited to write for further information and details of subscriptions.

*Hon. Secretary:* 5 Court House, Basil Street, London SW3 1AJ

## TEACH YOURSELF BOOKS

# SERBO-CROATIAN PHRASE BOOK

## Viola Ellis

When in Yugoslavia, it helps if you can speak the principal language, Serbo-Croatian.

Included in this book are all the words and phrases so necessary to anyone visiting Yugoslavia. For instance, you will be able to:

PASS THE CUSTOMS—BOOK A HOTEL—ASK THE WAY—COUNT YOUR CHANGE—ORDER FOOD—TALK TO THE LOCALS.

And then there is a section on pronunciation, together with a brief outline of the grammar, making this a book that no prospective traveller should be without.

# TEACH YOURSELF BOOKS

## SAMOAN

### C. C. Marsack

This book is an introductory course to the Polynesian language of the Samoan Islands. Having carefully worked his way through it, the student should emerge with a sound working knowledge of Samoan, both spoken and written.

Following an account of the Samoan alphabet and pronunciation, the book is divided into a series of twenty graded lessons. Each lesson covers a definite aspect of the language such as personal pronouns, prepositions or idioms. Also included is a lesson on the important Language of Courtesy, while at the end of the book the student will find a two-way vocabulary. Exercises are used throughout the text, and the student will also find a number of translations designed to encourage fluency.

A practical working course in Samoan, expertly written both for the beginner and for the student of Polynesian languages.

# TEACH YOURSELF BOOKS

# RUSSIAN

## Michael Frewin

Russian is always thought to be a very difficult language but, in fact, it is not so much difficult as different. Only half the population of the Soviet Union speaks Russian as their mother tongue—the other hundred million learn it as a foreign language and accept this as natural.

This book aims to give a good working knowledge of the language. It consists of twenty lessons, each containing a reading passage, a section to explain new grammatical points, and exercises which practise the new material in many different ways. A key to the exercises is included and, as well as the grammar notes in each lesson, a summary of all the main forms is given in the appendix.

At the end of the book, a selection of reading passages is provided which are all derived from contemporary Soviet sources and are completely unabridged. They are thus a real guide to the progress the student is making and hence a particularly valuable feature of the book.

# TEACH YOURSELF BOOKS

- ☐ 05818 8 **Serbo-Croatian Phrase Book**    40p
  V. Ellis
- ☐ 21281 0 **Russian**    £1.95
  Michael Frewin
- ☐ 05816 1 **Samoan**    95p
  C. C. Marsack
- ☐ 05823 4 **Swahili**    75p
  D. V. Perrot
- ☐ 05824 2 **Swahili Dictionary**    50p
  D. V. Perrot
- ☐ 05995 8 **Yoruba**    £1.25
  E. C. Rowlands

*All these books are available at your local bookshop or newsagent, or can be ordered direct from the publisher. Just tick the titles you want and fill in the form below.*

Prices and availability subject to change without notice.

------------------------------------------------------------

TEACH YOURSELF BOOKS, P.O. Box 11, Falmouth, Cornwall.

Please send cheque or postal order, and allow the following for postage and packing:

U.K.—One book 22p plus 10p per copy for each additional book ordered, up to a maximum of 82p.

B.F.P.O. and EIRE—22p for the first book plus 10p per copy for the next 6 books, thereafter 4p per book.

OTHER OVERSEAS CUSTOMERS—30p for the first book and 10p per copy for each additional book.

Name .............................................................................

Address .........................................................................

.......................................................................................